REALISING THE CITY

MANCHESTER
1824

Manchester University Press

REALISING THE CITY

Urban ethnography in Manchester

edited by

Jessica Symons and Camilla Lewis

With contributions from Michael Atkins, Hannah Knox, Luciana Lang,
Camilla Lewis, Damian O'Doherty, Elisa Pieri, George Poulton,
Katherine Smith and Jessica Symons

and

Foreword by Kevin Ward

Manchester University Press

Published by Manchester University Press
Altrincham Street, Manchester M1 7JA
www.manchesteruniversitypress.co.uk

British Library Cataloguing-in-Publication Data
A catalogue record for this book is available from the British Library

ISBN 978 1 5261 0073 3 hardback
ISBN 978 1 5261 5169 8 paperback

First published 2018

Typeset by
Servis Filmsetting Ltd, Stockport, Cheshire

With thanks to the people of Manchester
For sharing their lives and insights with us.

CONTENTS

Part III: Realising urban communities

LIST OF FIGURES

Notes on contributors

About the editors

Camilla Lewis is Research Associate in Sociology at the University of Manchester, working on a project about place and belonging. Her research focuses on urban regeneration, community, social change and class. In 2014 she completed a PhD in Social Anthropology at the University of Manchester, in which she conducted an ethnographic study in East Manchester. Since then she has worked as a Research Associate in CRESC (Centre for Research on Socio-Cultural Change) carrying out research on Big Data and Urban Waste Management and on the Step Change project looking at travel, transport and mobility.

Jessica Symons is an urban anthropologist and Research Grant Writer at the University of Manchester. Her research explores culture, creativity, digital and the urban. She is currently focused on the processes through which imagined worlds are materialised and these effects on urban settings. As Research Fellow in the UPRISE Research Centre at the University of Salford, she worked on an AHRC Connected Community Project, *Cultural Intermediation*, focused on cultural activities in Ordsall, Salford. Her doctoral research followed the making of a civic parade in Manchester. Jessica also worked in the private sector for 20 years as IT consultant, business analyst and community project manager.

About the authors

Michael Atkins is an anthropologist and artist based in Manchester. His work involves using combinations of writing, drawing and performance as forms of storytelling, documentary and expression.

Hannah Knox is Senior Lecturer in Digital Anthropology and Material Culture at University College London. Her work explores the relationship between technology and the imagination, cultural creativity and material contingency, the politics of transformation and the challenge of rupture, crisis and the new. She has explored these issues through ethnographic research in the UK, Peru and Europe and has written about how culture permeates, shapes and is transformed by information systems, digital models, roads, energy infrastructure, carbon, and climate change. Recent publications include *Roads: An Anthropology of Infrastructure and Expertise* (Cornell University Press, 2015) and *Ethnography for a Data Saturated World* (forthcoming).

Luciana Lang is a researcher working in the broad area of socio-ecological anthropology in urban contexts. Her doctoral research explored the relationship between an urban fishing community and a mangrove swamp in Rio de Janeiro, Brazil. This dialogue between urban communities, the environment and policies continues to shape her research. Luciana is particularly interested in human-disturbed environments, in homespun alternatives to cope with socio-economic effects of increasingly precarious scenarios, and in the use and management of the commons.

Damian O'Doherty is Senior Lecturer in Organisation Analysis at the Alliance Manchester Business School. He has recently published his ethnography of the Manchester Airport Group, *Reconstructing Organisation: The Loungification of Society* (Palgrave Macmillan, 2017).

Elisa Pieri is Research Fellow at the University of Manchester. Her work explores securitisation and its impact on urban stakeholders. Her current research (Simon Fellowship, 2016–2019) investigates how Western cities securitise against the risk of global pandemics and the social implications that arise from pandemic preparedness protocols, technologies and practices. Elisa has worked on several interdisciplinary research projects, investigating controversial issues in policy, science and technology debates. She has published on security, urban sociology, Science and Technology Studies (STS), and on ethical, legal and social aspects of new technologies such as genomics and biometrics.

George Poulton is Senior Research Officer at the Department for Education. In 2013 he completed a PhD in Social Anthropology at the University of Manchester. His research was an ethnographic study of FC United of Manchester and explored the themes of community and politics as they played out amongst football supporters.

Katherine Smith is Lecturer in Social Anthropology at the University of Manchester. She has carried out ethnographic fieldwork in the North of England exploring issues of fairness and (in)equalities, social class, nationalisms, political correctness, political participation, race and ethnicity, belonging and humorous banter. She is author of *Fairness, Class and Belonging in Contemporary England* (Palgrave Macmillan, 2012) and co-editor of *Extraordinary Encounters: Authenticity and the Interview* (Berghahn Books, 2015).

Kevin Ward is a Professor of Human Geography and Director of the Manchester Urban Institute at the University of Manchester and a Visiting Professor at The City Institute, York University. His current work involves rethinking what is meant by 'the urban' in urban politics, as elements of different places are assembled and reassembled to constitute particular 'urban' political realms. Kevin has published over 100 journal articles and book chapters, and his books include the co-authored volumes *Urban Sociology, Modernity and Capitalism* (Macmillan, 2002) and *Spaces of Work: Global Capitalism and the Geographies of Labour* (Sage, 2004). Kevin is also editor of *Researching the City: a Guide for Students* (Sage, 2013) and co-editor of *City of Revolution: Restructuring Manchester* (Manchester University Press, 2002), *Neoliberalization: States, Networks, Peoples* (Blackwell, 2007), and *Mobile Urbanism: Cities and Policymaking in the Global Age* (Minnesota University Press, 2011). He currently edits *Urban Geography*.

FOREWORD

Kevin Ward

Introduction

The field of urban studies is as restless as the cities it would seek to describe and represent. While it might be argued that it has ever been thus, the 2010s would appear to have witnessed a particularly vibrant set of debates, sparked by questions around how best to theorise the urban condition when it is simultaneously the planetary condition. What does it mean to write about the urban as opposed to the non-urban? Does the notion of 'the city' still have meaning in an era when the whole planet is urbanising? Does the vocabulary currently exist to theorise the cities of the future? What methods are best to understand the process of global urbanisation? These questions – and others – have been given an added intellectual jolt, asked as they have been in the context of many of the largest cities of the future lying outside of the traditional theoretical homeland of North America and Western Europe. Urban theory generated out of the likes of Chicago, London, New York and Paris, which has disciplined cities elsewhere, worlding them as 'backward', 'deviant' or 'failing', has begun to be questioned.

While cities of the global South have often been represented through empirical description, through ethnography, through idiosyncratic knowledge, accounts of cities of the global North, also provincial of course, travel as Theory. Note the deliberate capitalisation of Theory, as that which masquerades as a universal, as that which claims global purchase, as that which can be capitalised. While Theory is assumed to have universal applicability, ethnography is seen to be homebound, unique, lacking the reach of generalisation. This is not just about differences between the global North and global South, although these are important. What is at stake is what kind of urban theory for what kind of future. What sorts of theories are to be generated out of the rapidly urbanising cities of the global South? What might a Southern turn in urban theory means for theorising cities of the global North, such as Manchester, for example? Might this mean not a renewal of Theory with a capital T but rather the emergence of a theory that is less quick to claim generalisation, to represent itself as universal?

In this intellectual context, in which the field of urban studies seems to be undergoing a period of intellectual rejuvenation and renewal, an edited book based upon a series of ethnographies seems particularly timely.

Summer in the city

It is the summer of 2016 and, once again, the city of Manchester is enjoying its political moment in the sun, if not much actual sun. It was not long ago – the 1990s and early 2000s – that the city was being widely lauded for the way it had apparently effected a transition to a post-industrial economy consisting of cultural industries, financial services and high-tech start-ups. When compared to other UK cities, it was argued to have been the most successful at playing the regeneration game. A gentrifying centre, a redeveloping area to the East around the notion of Sport City and an expanding tram network were just some of the reasons why Manchester had earned the reputation of being an entrepreneurial 'can do' kind of city. Yet the picture was always more mixed that the plaudits suggested. Lines continued to point the wrong way for those in the city concerned with addressing inequality, poverty and social exclusion. Residents for whom getting by was a struggle increased in number. Subjects whose entrepreneurialism in making a living, pulling together life's loose threads, jarred with the entrepreneurial rhetoric espoused by different branches of the State. The apparent renaissance experienced in Manchester was anything but all inclusive.

Ultimately the combination of the global economic recession of 2007 and 2008 and the UK coalition government's programme of austerity revealed the fragility of this transition. And Manchester was not alone. The often unspoken spatial assumption of Manchester's success was that what was good for the city was good for the wider city region of Greater Manchester. Growth would spread outwards. The likes of Oldham and Rochdale, Stockport and Trafford would perform flanking roles, supporting the growth underway in the centre of Manchester. It was classic agglomeration economics 101, with a clear spatial division of labour, between Manchester and the other nine boroughs. And it worked … for a while.

Between 2010 and 2016 the budgets of the ten Greater Manchester local authorities were cut by £1.7 billion. In addition to each Council cutting thousands of jobs, meaning for residents the closure of libraries, public toilets and swimming pools, provision in such front-line areas as adult and children services was reduced. For those who had at best received relatively little by way of benefit from the Manchester-centred growth model, austerity made an already unpleasant situation worse. Getting by, making do, and generally holding together paid and unpaid work was rendered harder by national changes in housing and welfare systems, while at the same time closer to home, local authorities made cuts in the kinds of services that supported lower-income families.

In this austere context the various devolution 'deals' involving Greater Manchester were something of a political lifeline for the ten Councils. While they involved no new money for the city-region, the increased powers and responsibilities have been presented locally as a means of the city region exercising greater control over its future. With echoes of Manchester City Council's earlier entrepreneurial turn, talk has turned to what can be done rather than what cannot, albeit across ten local authorities rather than one. Policymakers and politicians have, to paraphrase one of Manchester City Council's former strap-lines, jumped at the chance to 'make things happen'. There have been regular conferences and workshops on the subject of what has been termed 'Devo Manc'. To what end is not yet clear, however. There is no blueprint for devolution on this scale, at least not in the UK. Much of what happens is likely to be made up there and then, as the new Greater Manchester Combined Authority feels its way, gently and slowly, into an uncertain post-devolution future.

Those leading the Combined Authority have cast Manchester (often as shorthand for the wider city-region) at the leading edge of a revolution. Once again the city has been represented as a city of firsts. Control over some public sector budgets and the design, delivery and evaluation of some services was traded with central government for the election of a Mayor for Greater Manchester in May 2017. Other UK cities and towns have referenced the changes underway in Greater Manchester to make the case for their own particular combination of economic, financial and political devolution. The city-region's first mover advantage has not lasted long it seems. With parallels to the devolved landscapes of Northern Ireland, Scotland and Wales, cities, counties, towns and villages in England have combined in some cases with historical precedent, in other cases without, to form new governance structures. Not for the first time, talk of revolution, like the drizzle, is in the air of Greater Manchester.

Quite what this recent history has meant for those who call Greater Manchester their home is often not clear. In many cases accounts of the city's recent restructuring has tended to focus on those in elected or unelected positions of power: so, those whose day job it is to design and deliver policy in one shape or another, whether economic development or education, health or transport. From a focus on city hall and government, attention has turned to those other actors who are involved in shaping the future of cities such as Manchester. These include architects, activists, analysts, consultants, engineers, environmentalists, financiers and planners. Uncovering this increasing complex and opaque decision-making machinery has led many scholars of urban studies to interview those involved. This examines how particular policies were reached, whether they involved the attracting of inward investment or the physical regeneration of a new area. It requires interviewees to explain an already made decision as a means to uncovering the politics behind the realisation of a particular future for Manchester.

Theorising from the particular

It is here that *Realising the city* makes a telling contribution. It takes an alternative approach, stepping away from the emphasis on elites and away from interviews. It makes no grand claims to universalisation. Instead, it provides a different set of insights into how contemporary Manchester continues to be made and remade. In doing this, it seeks to advance an approach that draws attention to the ways in which residents in Manchester have been involved in the restructuring of the city. Not as dupes or pawns, but rather as agents in the making and remaking of identity and place. In this it speaks to an approach that sees people as infrastructure. It junks the binary that constructs those who make policy as all powerful, and those on whom policy is targeted as all powerless. Instead this book provides ethnographies on different aspects to city-making. These emphasise the everyday and often mundane work of all of those involved in the realisation of contemporary Manchester. Using a range of geographical locations, including those less studied to the east and north of the city, and viewing these relationships through a number of lenses – for example, culture, self-policing, sexuality – this book gets beyond those accounts of urban change that run the risk of being fleeting and passing. Through long periods in the field, and the use of detailed and rich ethnographic methods, the book provides a series of insights into the many ways in which those who live and work in and across Manchester co-exist. It reveals the tensions in areas which have suffered systemic economic and social dislocation. This book also makes clear that these same communities are also far from dysfunctional and failing in the way that they tend to be represented in local and national policy.

The discrete but related insights into the workings of the city are outlined in each chapter, as the fine-grained and rich material draws us, the readers, in. Whether it is lounging out at the airport or making your way around estates in East and North Manchester, in joining up accounts in this way an appreciation of the complexity and diversity of urban transformation is generated. While specifically about Manchester's recent history, the book does offer a means of studying cities per se. It does so with an acknowledgement of those urban ethnographies which have come before it but also with a view to making the case for future urban studies to pay attention to the various acts and works that go into making up contemporary cities the world over.

Jessica Symons and Camilla Lewis

The tensions in making and realising a city

In 2006, a magnificent oak table with fine Indian ink drawings sat in an artist's studio in Manchester in the north-west of England. Three metres in length, it displayed a relational network diagram of key decision makers in the city. The art piece, called *The Thin Veneer of Democracy* (UHC Collective 2007), sketched a web of connections drawing attention to the close relationships between individuals from public and private institutions in the city. The spidery diagram identified 'the names of 101 institutions, officials, companies and private individuals invested in Manchester City Council's Knowledge Capital project' (UHC Collective 2007). The artists behind the table were critical of these relationships. They emphasised the political dynamics in the city as a cosy arrangement between connected individuals and drew attention to how others felt left out. This brought disquiet to the people named on the table. They discussed the artwork with each other, saying that collaboration to regenerate the city was to be celebrated rather than criticised.

Fast forward to 2015. In this year the British government under a Conservative administration, and Manchester City Council under a Labour administration, announced a historic agreement to devolve spending power to the city region, including the city centre itself, affecting almost three million people. Devolved power allowed for independent decision making at city-region level and this agreement was the culmination of decades-long lobbying from the Manchester City Council Executive (Haughton, et al. 2016). Yet the final decision for devolution happened in private in a meeting between the UK Chancellor of the Exchequer George Osborne and the Leader of Manchester City Council, Sir Richard Leese. This was an 'elite co-option' (Smith and Richards 2016) and the outcome presented to the city region as a *fait accompli*. In the press release, Councillor Sir Richard Leese claimed the devolution plans were 'revolutionary' and a model that 'other cities around the country would want to adopt and copy' (Wintour 2014).

While the UK Government Select Committee explored the potential of the Manchester agreement as a 'model' for the devolution of powers to other cities (Communities and Local Government Committee 2015), a furore erupted over the fact that it was possible for just two men in a democratic system to agree in principle to a reformed governance system without consulting the Council members or the electorate. Previously in Manchester, a 2012 referendum had sought to replicate the London model of an elected Mayor post but it was rejected by public vote. However the 2015 devolution agreement included an elected Mayor position to receive powers including six billion pounds in funding for health and social care and responsibility for transport, housing and planning.

The decision was questioned by local press, one newspaper calling it a 'democratic travesty' (*Salford Star* 2016). A national constitutional lawyer unpicked its legality (Leyland 2016) and government ministers questioned its intent (Communities and Local Government Committee 2015). Three years previously, Councillor Leese had recognised a 'very clear rejection' from the public for a mayoral role (BBC 2012). Yet just a few years later, he privately agreed to a new Mayor for Greater Manchester.

This decision did not bode well for democratic representation (Smith and Richards 2016). Despite objections, the following months led to the appointment of a new Mayor by senior politicians without an election (BBC 2015), and by 2016 the devolution process was well underway. A growing body of research 'Devo Manc' focuses on the impact of sharing decision making about health and social care budgets (see, for example, Colomb and Tomaney 2016; Haughton, et al. 2016; Walshe, et al. 2016).

The proposal for devolution and the proposal for the art collective's oak table are symptomatic of Manchester's political dynamics. An 'entrepreneurial approach' to city development has been led by two charismatic and determined individuals – Sir Richard Leese and Sir Howard Bernstein. Together they had controlled the City Council for over thirty years as Leader and Chief Executive respectively. This historic agreement for devolution was a culmination of their long-sought autonomy from central government. However, such control over the democratic process has produced consternation as well as results and respect.

From the mid-1980s, political and economic activity in Manchester was driven by an 'entrepreneurial elite', who adapted to an antagonistic national political regime by collaborating with private companies locally (Quilley 1999; 2000). Leese and Bernstein were leading figures in New Labour; they operated within the rules but also worked to reshape the way in which local government operated (Fielding and Tanner 2006; Massey 2007; cf also Ward 2003). One former Councillor, Kath Fry, identified this new approach as Manchester's 1984 Revolution. Her autobiographical account reveals how individuals within the Council controlled change and made decisions. The majority of elected Councillors resided outside the inner circles and were not privy to decision-making processes (Fry and Cropper 2016).

This book gives ethnographic accounts of Manchester's urban challenges from 2002, journeying through the city over a fourteen-year period, into the halls of power and out to local communities to understand the effects of this style of 'entrepreneurial' governance. Each author in the collection presents empirical analyses of the city's life from their ethnographic fieldwork and through this process, gives insight into how people experience civic control.

The ethnographic accounts demonstrate how a city is constituted in the productive tension between *making* and *realising*, between directing activity and allowing for its emergence. The ethnographers worked independently across different sites in Manchester, and the combined analysis shows the tension between making and realising which helps us understand how the devolution agreement came about.

The analyses also show how the oak table of inscribed relations produced by UHC Collective illustrated a bubbling undertow of resentment and feelings of disempowerment among different groups in the city. 'Making' a city rather than allowing it to 'realise' through emergent activities is a challenge that civic decision makers struggle with daily. Urban planners, civic officials and politicians are elected or employed to make decisions that shape the city but they are also charged with representing the interests and aspirations of the citizens. The tension lies in how different versions of the city are realised and how they intersect.

Ethnography is based on fieldwork in socio-cultural settings. The ensuing analysis focuses on this grounded experience to explore broad themes ranging from kinship relations to the effects of globalisation, from birth and death rituals to migration and organisational structures (Eller 2016 provides a textbook for cultural anthropologists; Eriksen 1995 provides a good introduction to social anthropology). Disciplines including sociology, geography, politics, economics, architecture, urban planning, and fields such as community studies and Science and Technology Studies (STS) use ethnography as a methodological tool. In this book, we demonstrate the potential of ethnographic analyses that build directly on insights developed during fieldwork.

Ethnographers observe and participate in the daily lives of people, working alongside them, asking questions and watching as they go about their daily lives. Misunderstandings, fallings out and friction provide particularly fruitful moments for analysis, as they reveal underlying ambiguities in social understandings. Where 'classic' anthropology primarily focused on rural locations, urban ethnographers now construct a field by living and working alongside a group of people in urban locations. In cities, ethnographers also spend time in organisations and with people who have 'shared understandings' about how things are done. Urban contexts work well as ethnographic field sites and as multiple and overlapping 'communities of practice', a term used to describe how people learn from each other in situated contexts (Lave and Wenger 1991). Ethnographies are also valuable in research into material culture (Evans 2013; Harvey, et al. 2014), with non-humans (Candea 2010), research into finance, data and ontologies (Holbraad, et al. 2014; Riles 2013) and every other aspect of life.

The value of urban ethnography lies in the fieldworkers' ability to bring coherence to messy contexts and to 'understand urban dynamics empirically' (Pardo and Prato 2016: 3). In their Introduction to the collection *Anthropology in the City*, Pardo and Prato provide an extensive review of urban ethnographies which 'spell out the need to stay engaged empirically' (2016: 20), for example to maintain attention to what is happening on the ground.

In this book, we illuminate *who, how, where, why* and *what* happens in city making through observations from situated urban ethnographers living and working alongside civic actors. Their analyses provide comparative opportunities for researchers to interrogate the dynamics of other urban contexts. Cities are the 'locus of our most well-rehearsed national problems' with social arenas and 'interlocking processes of living, meeting, making, relating' (Amin, et al. 2000: 8). These processes are recorded through ethnography.

In the following ethnographic accounts, the researchers go beyond institutional frames, official rhetoric and marketing speak to find out how the city comes into being. They follow officials through the City Council and organisational networks, share the experience of workers and residents in communities, and explore negotiations over public spaces. They reveal the conflicting dynamics of a city where people both benefit from and are troubled by the political and civic administrative influence over their lives. Each ethnographer was immersed in their field site and produced insight specific to the particular circumstances. These insights combine effectively to produce a discursive manifestation of the city as it emerges in the productive tension of its collaborative development.

In this Introduction, we open up the city of Manchester as a site for analysis and comparative opportunities for other urban contexts.

Introducing Manchester

Greater Manchester, in the north of England, is the country's second most populous urban area, with a population of almost three million in the greater city region. Its status as the first city in the UK to achieve a devolution agreement with central government fits together with an ongoing civic ambition to be a 'city of firsts'.[1] When Peter Saville, a successful musician and producer was commissioned to develop a civic identity for the city, he proposed the notion of Manchester as the 'original modern' city. Saville's idea rested on representing the city as a world leader in innovation, which began with its emergence as the 'first industrial city' (Bramley and Page 2009; Leadbeater 2009; O'Connor 2007). Socialism, the co-operative movement and female emancipation are claimed as 'firsts' alongside the parks, libraries, sewers, railway stations and 'Baby' the original computer. New initiatives such as the Manchester International Festival, a biannual art event, use this notion to commission all original work. The discovery of graphene, a new carbon struc-ture, at the University of Manchester was celebrated as 'another first'.

City of Revolution, Peck and Ward's edited collection about the regen-eration of the city, tells the story of Manchester's transformation into its 'modern' status today (Peck and Ward 2002). It shows how the apparent success of Manchester is actually a story of contradictions – flourishing in some areas, decline in others that never recovered from the collapse of the manufacturing sector in the 1970s. This volume extends this analysis to share insight from fieldwork among the communities themselves as these changes have happened.

While its origins date back to Roman times, Manchester gained city status in the nineteenth century during the Industrial Revolution. The city boomed rapidly as 'Cottonopolis', a hub of technological and social innovation, and gained city status on the back of its industrial success. From the 1950s onwards however, the city's fortunes changed and its industries closed down as the outsourcing of mass production went to developing countries such as India and China. By the 1980s, the city was struggling with mass unemployment, poverty and social unrest.

Frozen out by a central Conservative Party, the predominantly Labour City Council began to leverage public–private partnerships to re-build a 'post-industrial city' (Peck and Ward 2002). During the New Labour period under Prime Minister Tony Blair, Manchester City Council strengthened their rela-tionships with the private sector, foregrounding a property-led strategy of urban regeneration in the city (Quilley 2000). Their aim was to harness the potential of private capital to be used for public good rather than solely for market gain. Manchester is now cited as a case of 'entrepreneurial urbanism'-a 'new urban politics', where the city is viewed by government and private companies as a business in its own right (MacLeod and Ward 2002: 155; Peck and Ward 2002; Ward 2003: 116).

This bold move heralded a strong re-entry onto the international stage as a regenerated city whose new wealth and success were based on property specu-lation, a growing services sector and the attraction of commercial business to a large vibrant city in the UK. A revitalised inner-city housing market was accompanied by flourishing business quarters, booming retail, and cafes, bars and restaurants, as well as multiple ambitious projects to regenerate some of the city's most deprived neighbourhoods (Peck and Ward 2002).

The apparent 'success' of the city's 'boom-bust-boom' trajectory and transformation has produced widespread recognition and emulation of a 'Manchester model' of regeneration (Sanjek 2000). However the post-industrial city transition narrative from 'a grimy, northern industrial city', to a 'hip, fashionable and dynamic place where people are excited to live' (Jones and Evans 2008: 163–164) does not account for the inequalities and divisions which remain and a growing unease about the future for some residents (Binnie and Skeggs 2004; Mellor 2002; Young, et al. 2006).

As Cochrane, et al. (1996) argued in the 1990s, Manchester City Council's bid to host the Olympic Games, the enthusiasm for 'boosterism', or developing city regions as an economic strategy, actually put the city in a compromised position. When obliged to deliver formerly national responsibilities, the city became constrained in unexpected ways. Danger resided in the replication of a command-and-control model at a city rather than national level. This issue continues to hold resonance with the devolution process. The 'Manchester model' and its 'Rolls-Royce reputation' may have succeeded *because* it had 'political and policy stability under a hegemonic Labour council' (Hebbert and Punter 2009: 3; Jones and Evans 2008). But it was this form of command-and-control that also produced accusations of exclusion, such as the art collective's oak table questions about why only some people have influence over the city's development.

The representation of civic decision makers as a clique of connected individuals manipulating power dynamics in the urban realm is a familiar one and not unique to Manchester. However, the critical role of city officials, activists and citizens, and how they contribute to the formation of the city, has not been given sufficient attention. The Chief Executives, city leaders, key civic administrators and media stars may be remembered but less so the democratic body made up of different parts of the Council, community groups and organisations, the influencers and the intermediaries.

This collection captures the day-to-day practical dynamics of the people who have been involved in making this vibrant and rapidly changing post-industrial city over two decades from 2000 onwards. These 'ethnographic moments' of Manchester explore the activities of city makers such as politicians, administrators, company leaders, workers, activists and residents. They show how a city will never be produced from a singular vision or set of activities, yet people act as if the city should be realised according to their individual aspirations. They also show that conflicted understanding gives the city dynamism but also creates disruptions and spaces of contestation or 'friction' (Tsing 2004). From residential neighbourhoods to cultural events in the City

Council, from businesses to the city's airport, people's decisions and actions co-produce the city daily and give it shape and its identity.

These ethnographies show that people have ideas and go about bringing new realities into being but how there is always a *politics* to this because what existed before either gets moved, forcibly, out of the way (generating resistance) or gets recruited into the vision of the 'way things will be from now on' (Evans 2013: 207).

Aims of the volume

Within and across these accounts is the potential for urban ethnography to provide insight into how a city comes into being and the role which different actors play in that process. In this way, ethnography can be compared to 'urban assemblage' analysis (Farías and Bender 2012) and compliments approaches to how infrastructure makes a city (Graham and Marvin 2001). In this volume, we consider the 'social infrastructure' of the city (Simone 2004).

The ethnographic accounts focus on particular places in Manchester to explore issues such as: the ethics of self-policing on a housing estate (Smith); loss in former working-class communities (Lewis); disenfranchised football fans (Poulton); negotiating sexuality and public space (Atkins); civic parades as nurturing for an emergent city (Symons); defining the commons in public spaces (Lang); conflicting futures thinking (Pieri); networked urban governance (Knox); and how airport design shapes behaviour (O'Doherty). Their specificity provides grounded contexts for identifying ideological patterns, structural processes and the contingency of everyday life. These accounts demonstrate the potential of ethnographies to go beyond the particular and into the theoretical and philosophical realm.

As each ethnographer describes their experience in Manchester; as they focus on different parts of the urban environment at a similar period in time and under the same civic administration, it becomes possible to identify common threads across these settings. A broader perspective emerges, one that points to a tension between attempts to direct a city and a desire to allow it to emerge.

These accounts show the everyday effects of urban policy on social relations and the ways in which urban policies come to fruition through their multiple entanglements of people, places and things. They illuminate the social, spatial and temporal reorganisation of a city under post-industrial conditions (Smith and Hetherington 2013). By putting the accounts together in an edited volume, they provide an 'urban portrait' – an 'essence of the city' (Hannerz 1980). In particular, they show how people attempt to realise (to make real) imagined versions of a city. Each act has an affective outcome and it is in the combination that the characteristics of the city emerge. Here is a comparable example of distributed urban dynamics, attendant to the unexpected insights that emerge through an open and discursive ethnographic process. Others can use these analyses to shape research into their own cities.

In this way, we suggest that a city's future may be planned but it does not materialise as the perfect representation of its blueprint drawings, strategies or vision documents. Instead it emerges through the accumulative efforts of thousands of people over time and with what Scott (1998) describes as 'metis', meaning people's local, experiential wisdom. As anthropologist Harvey suggests, 'The trick for ethnographers and local people alike is not to be beguiled for too long by the State's own version of itself and look instead at the details through which things come to seem as they do' (Harvey 2005: 139). In this volume, through urban ethnography, a nuanced story of urban dynamics of the city emerges, which complicates accounts of Manchester as an entrepreneurial city of renaissance.

The emergence of urban ethnography

Urban ethnography contributes to analyses of cities across multiple disciplines. Since ethnography is designed to accommodate communities of practice that operate within and across organisations, it is well designed as an analytical tool for complex circumstances. In the following section, we explore the emergence of urban ethnography across disciplinary fields. We focus here on how trajectories of ethnographic work orient around the city rather than provide a comprehensive review of all urban ethnographies.

A precursor to urban ethnography could be Engels' account of industrialising Manchester; a comparison made by historian Tilly (1978). *Conditions of the Working Class in England* (Engels 1993 [1845]) explores in intimate detail the desperate living and working conditions of urban factory workers in Manchester and other industrialising cities. Engles' work remains inspirational for urban scholars today exploring the relationship between political and urban change and, crucially, the conditions of the working poor in industrialised cities.

Industrialisation across the world has resulted in growing migration to cities, and anthropologists have followed them there, sharing often devastating accounts of urban experiences. For example, Scheper-Hughes' seminal text *Death Without Weeping* provides a harrowing account of people's life in a Brazilian urban slum (Scheper-Hughes 1992); Kleinman, et al. write about urban violence as 'social suffering' (Kleinman, et al. 1997); Bourgois shares experiences of selling crack in inner-city America (Bourgois 2003). Many anthropologists now practise ethnography in cities alongside other disciplines (See Low 1999 for a summary). Ethnographic work by visual anthropologists has brought images, film, sound and sketches together with text-based narratives, often in urban settings (See Pink 2013 [2001] for an overview of visual ethnography).

Sociology also used ethnography as an analytical device for urban dynamics early on in the discipline's development. While Malinowski (1922) was in the Pacific, sociologists from Chicago in the 1920s and 1930s adopted ethnography for research in urban areas of the USA (Pole and Morrison 2003). The Chicago Schools founder, Robert Parks, designed a 'laboratory metaphor' for the city as a 'laboratory' where social processes could be studied. For him, the city contained 'ecological niches' occupied by 'human groups' in concentric rings surrounding a central core (Low 1999). The studies produced by Parks and his students provide detailed understandings of social groups and their related behaviours (Emerson 2002).

Parks' students focused on studying the 'exotic' members of their own societies, looking at the commonplace with 'new eyes' (Duneier, et al. 2014). Like anthropologists, these sociologists adapted their behaviour to blend in with the locals and experience their lives first hand (Pole and Morrison 2003). They focused on unfamiliar people living in close proximity – 'the strangers next door'. This emphasis led to the 'case-study method' closely associated with urban ethnography (Duneier, et al. 2014).

William Foote Whyte's *Street Corner Society* (1943) documents life in an Italian slum through close observations of the lively conversations on the street. Foot Whyte and his contemporaries' monographs are richly detailed and historically sensitive urban studies that attend to politics and power, describing daily life in these urban localities (Sanjek 2000). A second generation of Chicago School urban ethnographers, including Hannerz (1969), further developed this approach, revealing the potential for social scientists to penetrate and interpret social worlds in their own cities (Jackson 1985). For further discussion on how ethnography developed in anthropology and sociology, see Hammersley (2016).

Meanwhile in 1950s London, the Institute for Community Studies was exploring slum clearances and rehousing. Young and Wilmott's *Family and Kinship in East London* (1957), provides a detailed study of the impact of slum clearances in the post-Second World War period, stressing the continuation of social ties among changing urban communities.

While the Chicago School viewed the city as a configuration of ecological niches, these scholars approached the city as a collection of urban communities based on extended networks of family relations and kinship networks (Low 1999). Community studies in Britain have traced the impact of urban policies on working-class communities showing how networks of informal support have strengthened an attachment to place and sense of identity (Lewis 2016 explores this further). Rather than industrialisation and urbanisation leading to a loss of social ties, community studies showed how personal relationships were consolidated and reconfigured as a result of urban change.

Informed by these founding schools, ethnographic accounts of urban lives have proliferated among anthropologists, social workers, political scientists, urban studies specialists and sociologists. These accounts provide important contributions to the conceptual vocabulary of scholars and social theorists, journalists and social critics (Duneier, et al. 2014). They have inspired collaborations with disciplines such as Science Technology Studies (STS), architecture and art (see, for example, Blok and Farías 2016; Corsín Jiménez and Estalella 2016; Farías and Bender 2012; Yaneva 2016).

In the 2000–2010s, there was growing recognition that these contextual analyses of cities should be valued for their particularity; for the fact that they acknowledge the complexity of diverse urban cultures and the need for situated, grounded research. Recent debates in urban studies call for a new 'epistemology of the urban' (Brenner and Schmid 2015; Walker 2015). These discussions make distinctions between and wrestle over the difference between grounded and theoretical or philosophical analyses. Ethnographic approaches are unique as they provide perspectives on urban challenges which focus both on the particular – groups of people in specific geographic locations in the city focused on different themes – but also explore broader social, environmental and economic issues. The theory comes from the particular.

Ethnographic moments: creating a portrait of the city

In this volume, nine ethnographic accounts bring to life the day-to-day activities of actors living, working and shaping the city of Manchester. Three thematic sections open up the city as a site for ethnographic analysis with perspectives on urban organisations, public spaces and local communities. Drawing on ethnographic methods, the authors interrogate the relationships between government officials, private sector companies and people living and working in the related areas. They share ethnographic methodological approaches including observation, participation and interviews.

All the researchers explored their communities by 'hanging out', helping with projects, attending meetings, following email and verbal conversations, uncovering histories, reviewing documents, and participating in events and social activities. Over time, they developed working relationships and made friends with people 'in the field'. These practices underpin ethnographic work. Through day-to-day conversations, they gained insight into how things were done – customs and rituals, established understandings, common practices. Interviews towards the end of their fieldwork provided opportunities for clarification, eliciting quotes and further detail about particular observations. Each chapter presents an ethnographic account which orients around a particular people, place and insight revealed through the process of fieldwork.

Part I, 'Realising urban organisations', explores the process through which organisations take their shape from the constituent parts of a city, with people as its 'social infrastructure' (Simone 2004). It is the way relationships weave through organisational structures that shapes the dynamics of how a city operates.

Hannah Knox describes how Manchester's civic administration has responded to calls to reduce its carbon emissions. Creating 'real' spaces for action depends on establishing collaborations between individuals and organisations who act as proxies for and extensions of the local authority in areas that exceed the Council's shrinking domain of responsibility. Knox argues that these changes extend the capacity of state actors to effect change, and offer a form of engagement that reformulates what it might mean to be a citizen of the contemporary state and the mechanisms through which a sustainable world might be pursued. She also shows how people will engage with initiatives that they do not necessarily agree with, in order to realise broader objectives.

Jessica Symons argues for an 'emergent city' urban policy, inspired by organisers of civic parade in Manchester, which involved over 1,800 participants from ninety community groups. She compares the top-down process of cultural strategy development in the city with the nurturing emergent approach of the organisers commissioned by the Council to produce a civic parade. Drawing on parade making as a cultural trope, Symons describes how the parade makers held back, allowing the parade shape to develop rather than over-directing it. She suggests that city decision makers can learn from this restrained approach.

Damian O'Doherty follows the practices of architects, designers, project managers and quantity surveyors working on a new experience airport departure lounge at Manchester Airport. As he traces the development of the lounge and an attendant notion of 'loungification', he seeks moments where decisions are made and instead finds obfuscation.

Part II, 'Realising urban spaces', explores tensions in how organisational processes and community aspirations are negotiated through physical sites in urban spaces. The authors show how these places are manifested into something in particular in the confluence of multiple trajectories.

Michael Atkins argues that combining narratives of success and community with imagery and maps actually characterises and regulates Manchester's Gay Village as a distinct, bordered, hedonistic and particularly tolerant place. This chapter provides collaboratively produced graphic stories, created using combinations of drawings, text, photographs and found images. These 'ethno-graphics' describe lived experiences of men seeking sex in public and engaging in exchanges of intimacy, money, goods and services that challenge the master narratives that are openly recognised and spoken about in the village.

Luciana Lang explores three different interventions on public land in Cheetham Hill, an area of North Manchester often regarded as a place of community disengagement. Amid austerity measures and cuts to public services, the author argues that the 'commons' are made as people adjust to new scenarios brought about by historical disruptions, collapse of work opportunities, and breakdown of state support. 'Commoning' provides a space for productivity and, in the process, people's sense of belonging emerges as they envisage, realise and retrieve their right to the city.

Elisa Pieri focuses on Manchester city centre to argue that exploring the futures that different stakeholders envisage for the city centre reveals tensions that are otherwise glossed over. Critically engaging with urban futures, as mobilised by institutional stakeholders, and how other actors envisage the future, highlights whose interests are currently being prioritised and whose are traded off. Engaging in an analysis of these urban futures reveals not only important tensions connected to future developments and imagined uses of the city centre, but also opens up to scrutiny the present experiences and uses of the city centre and competing interests.

Part III, 'Realising urban communities', explores how people's lives interact with the dynamics of urban transformation and development in their daily experiences. The impact of city administrative or political activity can be traced through ethnographic analyses, in particular as a presence that affects people's ability to realise their own ambitions.

George Poulton analyses urban economic transformation through his fieldwork among a group of football fans who, in 2005, formed a breakaway club 'FC United of Manchester' in response to a transnational debt-leveraged buy-out of Manchester United Football Club. Poulton shows how notions of locality and community had become increasingly politicised amongst these fans. With Manchester United's growing international presence, local fans perceived that the club no longer needed a relationship with them. In response, the fans increasingly articulated a moral claim about Manchester United's responsibility to its local 'community', which Poulton relates to anthropological theories of gifts and commodities. This analysis contextualises the subsequent formation of FC United and its enduring reciprocal obligations to its 'community'.

Camilla Lewis shows how, despite millions of pounds worth of urban regeneration, high levels of unemployment and welfare dependency continue to characterise East Manchester. The rapid disappearance of industry brought about not only a dramatic reduction in jobs, but also a deep sense of uncertainty about the future, and a strong sense of loss for former ways of life. This chapter argues that the industrial past continues to shape older people's sense of place, through physical reminders in the material environment and also discursively, through sharing memories of previous places of employment. It reveals, however, that place attachment has become ruptured for long-standing residents who are highly conscious of the discontinuities between their own experiences and those of previous generations.

Katherine Smith explores self-policing of urban violence in Harpurhey, Manchester. She argues that ethical decision making is practiced regularly in the process of policing the actions and behaviours of others. Through an encounter on this social housing estate, she suggests that self-policing is not an outcome of neo-liberal ideologies of self-management, but an ethical engagement with the quotidian aspects of everyday life.

In the Afterword, Symons considers these chapters together to argue that cities are made in the tension between attempts to make a city according to particular visions and the entity that emerges – realises – is made real in the resultant foment of activity.

In summary

These ethnographies show that people have ideas and go about bringing new realities into being but there is always a *politics* to this because what existed before either gets moved, forcibly, out of the way (generating resistance) or gets recruited into the vision of the 'way things will be from now on' (Evans 2013: 207). Such conflict gives the city its dynamism but also creates disruptions and spaces of contestation or 'friction' (Tsing 2004). These accounts help make sense of how Leese and Osborne could meet in a room in Manchester and personally agree devolution – a significant change to the city's governance. They show why the art collective might be motivated to make a substantial oak table decorated with the network of relations between individuals in the city. They go some way to answering the question 'Who are city makers really?'

Notes

1 www.marketingmanchester.com. Accessed 8 February 2017.

References

Amin, Ash, Doreen B. Massey, and Nigel J. Thrift. 2000. *Cities for the Many Not the Few*. Bristol: Policy Press.

BBC. 2012. "Manchester votes against a directly elected mayor". BBC News.

— 2015. "Tony Lloyd appointed Greater Manchester's interim mayor". BBC News.

Binnie, Jon and Beverley Skeggs. 2004. "Cosmopolitan knowledge and the production and consumption of sexualized space: Manchester's gay village". *The Sociological Review* 52 (1): 39–61.

Blok, Anders and Ignacio Farías. 2016. *Urban Cosmopolitics: Agencements, Assemblies, Atmospheres.* London: Routledge.

Bourgois, Philippe. 2003. *In Search of Respect: Selling Crack in El Barrio.* Vol. 10: Cambridge: Cambridge University Press.

Bramley, Warren and Ra Page. 2009. *Manchester Forward.* Manchester: Marketing Manchester.

Brenner, Neil and Christian Schmid. 2015. "Towards a new epistemology of the urban?" *City* 19 (2–3): 151–182.

Candea, Matei. 2010. "'I fell in love with Carlos the meerkat': engagement and detachment in human–animal relations". *American Ethnologist* 37 (2): 241–258.

Cochrane, Allan, Jamie Peck, and Adam Tickell. 1996. "Manchester plays games: exploring the local politics of globalisation". *Urban Studies* 33 (8): 1319–1336.

Colomb, Claire and John Tomaney. 2016. "Territorial politics, devolution and spatial planning in the UK: results, prospects, lessons". *Planning Practice & Research* 31 (1): 1–22.

Communities and Local Government Committee. 2015. Devolution in England. In Department for Communities and Local Government. London: House of Commons.

Corsín Jiménez, Alberto and Adolfo Estalella. 2016. "Ecologies in beta: the city as infrastructure of apprenticeships". In *Infrastructure and Social Complexity.* P. Harvey, C.B. Jensen, and A. Morita, eds. London: Routledge.

Duneier, Mitchell, Philip Kasinitz, and Alexandra Murphy, eds. 2014. *The Urban Ethnography Reader.* Oxford; New York: Oxford University Press.

Eller, Jack David. 2016. *Cultural Anthropology: Global Forces, Local Lives.* London; New York: Routledge.

Emerson, Robert M. 2002. *Contemporary Field Research: Perspectives and Formulations.* Wiley Online Library.

Engels, Friedrich. 1993 [1845]. *The Condition of the Working Class in England.* Oxford: Oxford University Press.

Eriksen, Thomas Hylland. 1995. *Small Places, Large Issues: An Introduction to Social and Cultural Anthropology.* London: Pluto.

Evans, Gillian. 2013. "What documents make possible". In *Objects and Materials: A Routledge Companion.* P. Harvey, H. Knox, G. Evans, N. Thoburn, E. Casella, E. Silva, K. Woodward, and C. Mclean, eds. pp. 309–409. London: Routledge.

Farías, Ignacio and Thomas Bender. 2012. *Urban Assemblages: How Actor-Network Theory Changes Urban Studies.* London: Routledge.

Fielding, Steven and Duncan Tanner. 2006. "The 'rise of the Left' revisited: Labour Party culture in post-war Manchester and Salford". *Labour History Review* 71 (3): 211–233.

Foot Whyte, William. 1943. *Street Corner Society: The Social Structure of an Italian Slum*. Chicago: University of Chicago Press.

Fry, Kath and Karen Cropper. 2016. *Manchester 1984*. Manchester: Creative Commons.

Graham, Stephen and Simon Marvin. 2001. *Splintering Urbanism: Networked Infrastructures, Technological Mobilities and the Urban Condition*. London: Routledge.

Hammersley, Martyn. 2016. *Reading Ethnographic Research*. London: Routledge.

Hannerz, Ulf. 1969. *Soulside: Inquiries into Ghetto Culture and Community*. New York: Columbia University Press.

— 1980. *Exploring the City: Inquiries Toward an Urban Anthropology*. New York. Guildford: Columbia University Press.

Harvey, Penelope. 2005. "The materiality of state-effects: an ethnography of a road in the Peruvian Andes". In *State Formation: Anthropological Perspectives*. C. Krohn-Hansen and K.G. Nustad, eds. pp. 123–141. London: Pluto Press.

Harvey, Penny, Eleanor Conlin Casella, Gillian Evans, Hannah Knox, Christine McLean, Elizabeth B. Silva, Nicholas Thoburn, and Kath Woodward. 2014. *Objects and Materials: A Routledge Companion*. London: Routledge.

Haughton, Graham, Iain Deas, Stephen Hincks, and Kevin Ward. 2016. "Mythic Manchester: Devo Manc, the Northern Powerhouse and rebalancing the English economy". *Cambridge Journal of Regions, Economy and Society* 9 (2): 355–370.

Hebbert, Michael and John Punter. 2009. "Manchester: making it happen". In *Urban Design and the British Urban Renaissance*. J. Punter, ed. pp. 51–67. London: Routledge.

Holbraad, Martin, Morten Axel Pedersen, and Eduardo Viveiros de Castro. 2014. "The politics of ontology: anthropological positions". *Cultural Anthropology* 13. https://culanth.org/fieldsights/461-the-politics-of-ontology.

Jackson, Peter. 1985. "Urban ethnography". *Progress in Human Geography* 9 (2): 157–176.

Jones, Phil and James Evans. 2008. *Urban Regeneration in the UK: Theory and Practice*. Los Angeles, Califoria: Sage.

Kleinman, Arthur, Veena Das, and Margaret M. Lock. 1997. *Social Suffering*. Berkeley; London: University of California Press.

Lave, Jean, and Etienne Wenger. 1991. *Situated Learning: Legitimate Peripheral Participation*. Cambridge: Cambridge University Press.

Leadbeater, Charles. 2009. "Original Modern: Manchester's journey to innovation and growth". National Endowment for Science, Technology and the Arts.

Lewis, Camilla. 2016. "'Regenerating community'? Urban change and narratives of the past". *The Sociological Review* 64 (4): 912–928.

Leyland, Peter. 2016. "Devolution, Greater Manchester and the Revitalisation of Local Government". In *UK Constitution Legal Blog. Online: International Association of Constitutional Law*.

Low, Setha. 1999. *Theorising the City: The Urban Anthropology Reader*. New Brunswick: Rutgers University Press.

MacLeod, Gordon and Kevin Ward. 2002. "Spaces of utopia and dystopia: landscaping the contemporary city". *Geografiska Annaler: Series B, Human Geography* 84 (3–4): 153–170.

Malinowski, Bronislaw. 1978 (1922). *Argonauts of the Western Pacific: An Account of Native Enterprise and Adventure in the Archipelagoes of Melanesian New Guinea.* London, Routledge.

Massey, Doreen. 2007. *World City.* Cambridge: Polity.

Mellor, Rosemary. 2002. "Hypocritical city: cycles of urban exclusion". In *City of Revolution: Restructuring Manchester.* J. Peck and W. Kevin, eds. pp. 214–235. Manchester: Manchester University Press.

O'Connor, Justin. 2007. "Manchester: the original modern city". *The Yorkshire and Humber Regional Review*: 13–15.

Pardo, Italo and Giuliana B. Prato. 2016. *Anthropology in the City: Methodology and Theory.* Aldershot: Ashgate.

Peck, Jamie and Kevin Ward. 2002. *City of Revolution: Restructuring Manchester.* Manchester: Manchester University Press.

Pink, Sarah. 2013. *Doing Visual Ethnography* (3rd ed.) London: Sage.

Pole, Christopher and Marlene Morrison. 2003. *Ethnography for Education* (Doing qualitative research in educational settings). Buckingham: Open University Press.

Quilley, Stephen. 1999. "Entrepreneurial Manchester: the genesis of elite consensus". *Antipode* 31 (2): 185–211.

— 2000. "Manchester first: from municipal socialism to the entrepreneurial city". *International Journal of Urban and Regional Research* 24 (3): 601–615.

Riles, Annelise. 2013. "Market collaboration: finance, culture, and ethnography after neoliberalism". *American Anthropologist* 115 (4): 555–569.

Salford Star. 2016. "Greater Manchester devolution democracy slated by Commons Select Committee". *Salford Star.* http://salfordstar.com/article.asp?id=3122. Accessed 26 May 2017.

Sanjek, Roger. 2000. "Urban history, culture and urban ethnography". *City & Society* 12 (2): 105–113.

Scheper-Hughes, Nancy. 1992. *Death Without Weeping: The Violence of Everyday Life in Brazil.* London; Berkeley: University of California Press.

Scott, James C. 1998. *Seeing Like a State: How Certain Schemes to Improve the Human Condition Have Failed.* New Haven: Yale University Press.

Simone, AbdouMaliq. 2004. "People as infrastructure: intersecting fragments in Johannesburg". *Public Culture* 16 (3): 407–429.

Smith, Martin John and David Richards. 2016. "Devolution in England, the British political tradition and the absence of consultation, consensus and consideration". *Representations*: 1–18.

Smith, Robin James and Kevin Hetherington. 2013. "Urban rhythms: mobilities, space and interaction in the contemporary city". *The Sociological Review* 61 (S1): 4–16.

Tilly, Louise A. 1978. "The social sciences and the study of women: a review article". *Comparative Studies in Society and History* 20 (1): 163–173.

Tsing, Anna. 2004. *Friction: An Ethnography of Global Connection*. Princeton, NJ: Princeton University Press.

UHC Collective. 2007. *The Thin Veneer of Democracy*. Table handpainted with map of Manchester power relationships. Manchester.

Walker, Richard. 2015. "Building a better theory of the urban: a response to 'Towards a new epistemology of the urban?'" *City* 19 (2–3): 183–191.

Walshe, Kieran, Anna Coleman, Ruth McDonald, Colin Lorne, and Luke Munford. 2016. "Health and social care devolution: the Greater Manchester experiment". *British Medical Journal*: 1–5. https://manchester.idm.oclc.org/login?url=http://search.proquest.com/docview/1777837174?accountid=12253. Accessed 26 May 2017.

Ward, Kevin. 2003. "Entrepreneurial urbanism, state restructuring and civilizing 'New' East Manchester". *Area* 35 (2): 116–127.

Wintour, Patrick 2014. "George Osborne overcomes obstacles to pull off Manchester devolution deal". *Guardian*. https://www.theguardian.com/politics/2014/nov/03/george-osborne-manchester-devolution-deal. Accessed 26 May 2017.

Yaneva, Albena. 2016. "Politics of architectural imaging: elements of architecture". *Assembling Archaeology, Atmosphere and the Performance of Building Spaces*. Mikkel Bille and Tim Flohr Sorensen eds. pp. 238–255. London; New York: Routledge.

Young, Craig, Martina Diep, and Stephanie Drabble. 2006. "Living with difference? The 'cosmopolitan city' and urban reimaging in Manchester, UK". *Urban Studies* 43 (10): 1687–1714.

Young, Michael and Peter Willmott. 1957. *Family and Kinship in East London*. London: Routledge.

PART I

REALISING URBAN ORGANISATIONS

Figure 1.1 Molecule Man by Jonathan Borofsky

1

Inclusion without incorporation: re-imagining Manchester through a new politics of environment

Hannah Knox

Introduction

In this chapter I provide an ethnographic description of political relations in the city of Manchester by focusing on recent attempts to distribute responsibility for reductions in the city's carbon emissions. Building on approaches from the anthropology of policy, I attempt to move beyond descriptions of political relations in the city that have depicted a disjuncture between a ruling political elite and a general population. Instead I focus on the situated practice of doing politics. I describe how political, institutional and financial uncertainty have informed the formation of professional identities and relationships that traverse and complicate dualisms between: central and local government; institutional politics and political activism; and political actors and local populations. Instead of clear divisions or distinctions between different realms of political subjectivity, I argue we find a struggle taking place across these different groups between the importance of inclusion and a simultaneous resistance against or questioning of a politics of incorporation. I argue that paying attention to the struggle over how to achieve inclusion without risking incorporation might provide new directions for understanding the nature of urban politics in Manchester.

Background to the field site

The particular field of policy practice that I focus on in this chapter is the formation of the city of Manchester's environmental policy: specifically that which came in response to the 2008 Climate Change Act. The chapter emerges from ethnographic research that I conducted in Manchester between 2010 and 2013. This research was conducted in order to better understand the relationship between the science of global climate change and the nature of contemporary political relations. I was particularly interested in understanding the way in which the science of global climate change is affecting, reworking, reconfiguring and reinforcing how people imagine their place as agents of social change.

At the time when I started this project I had already been conducting ethnographic research in Manchester for several years. My doctoral research had been a study of an attempt by local businesses, European funded projects and local authority actors to stimulate a 'new media' industry in the city in the early 2000s. I also conducted research at Manchester Airport from 2003–2005, looking at the role of information systems in managing and running the airport as an organisation. In 2009 I conducted a small ethnographic project with the engineering firm ARUP, looking at the way in which they were developing city models in Manchester to assist with practices of urban planning and strategy, and it was here that I first became aware of work that was occurring in the city to reduce the city's carbon emissions. One of the city-models that ARUP was working on was a model to monitor and predict the carbon emissions of the city's buildings. It soon became clear that this modelling work was part of a broader conversation that was underway about the challenge that climate change posed to the city, and how that challenge should be responded to at a city level.

In 2009 Manchester, like many other cities, had signed up to a climate change action plan, which, in line with the UK Climate Change Act, committed the city to reduce its carbon emissions by 41 per cent by 2020 from a 1990 baseline. I was fascinated to discover that the action plan, entitled *Manchester: A Certain Future*, was established from the outset as a plan for the city and was an explicit attempt to produce a space of intervention that was not to be solely the responsibility of Manchester's local authority. Rather the action plan was to be a plan for the whole city, outlining actions that would have to be taken by a variety of different actors, from citizens to charities to private corporations. The action plan was to be overseen by a steering group that would provide direction, galvanise people into action, and monitor progress against the 41 per cent reduction target. The steering group was to be constituted by representatives of key sustainability organisations in the city, including universities, the local authority, Housing Associations, environmental charities, consultants, freelancers and business people.

I was struck immediately by the way in which the steering group seemed to rework forms of governance that I had seen in my earlier research. In my doctoral research, the language deployed had been that of economic stimulus, of a concern with what kind of support could be providing for already existing economic processes in order to allow them to flourish. People were broadly concerned about what kinds of 'trickle down' benefits the stimulation of a high-tech industry sector could have on some of the more impoverished residents of the city (Knox 2003: 22).

This form of urban intervention was consistent with Manchester's approach to economic development since the 1980s, which has been written about extensively. Since Peck and Ward's *City of Revolution* (2002), many scholars have described the transformation of Manchester from its heyday as an industrial powerhouse, to the doldrums of post-industrial decline and, most recently, to the meteoric rebirth of the city into a flourishing cosmopolitan centre (Quilley 2000; Young, et al. 2006). Both celebrants of Manchester's economic renewal and its many critics frequently attribute the city's transformation to the actions of politicians, in particular the leader of the City Council Richard Leese, and the Chief Executive Howard Bernstein. With Leese presiding over a chamber of predominantly Labour Councillors, and Bernstein over a local Council which at its peak employed nearly 20,000 people, these two men have been seen as largely responsible for establishing Manchester as arguably England's second most important city (see also chs 2 and 3, this volume).

The policies that were put in place after the 1980s, when Richard Leese and Howard Bernstein both took up important roles within the city, are often characterised, following David Harvey (Harvey 1989), as those of the 'entrepreneurial city' (Jonas, et al. 2011; Quilley 2000; Ward 2003a; Ward 2003b; While, et al. 2004). According to Harvey, the entrepreneurial city privileges public–private partnerships as a way of delivering public services, at the same time as focusing on wealth generation rather than the direct provision of local public services.

One of the reasons for this focus on entrepreneurial governance has been a concern with the relationship between this form of urban governance and its impact on local populations. Supporters of an entrepreneurial approach to urban politics in Manchester have argued that public–private partnerships have been the basis for a generally positive transformation of the city, measured primarily in terms of an increasing measure of GVA (Gross Value Added). From this perspective, public–private partnerships, or the transfer of responsibility for public services to private providers, is seen to provide a welcome check and balance on the bureaucratic inertia and institutional conservatism of public sector organisations. It is seen to allow the dynamics of market competition to weed out underperforming participants and incorporate a wider range of people into decision-making processes (Bache and Flinders 2004). It is also seen as holding the potential for economic redistribution via the previously mentioned 'trickle down' effect. Critics of this approach, in contrast, argue that public–private partnerships are undemocratic, exclusionary and serve the interests of the powerful at the expense of the poor (Hall and Hubbard 1998; Quilley 1999; Tickell and Peck 1996). Deep social and economic inequality in Manchester remains evident for anyone who ventures beyond the redeveloped city centre with its jobs and new buildings into nearby residential areas, such as areas of Salford and East Manchester, which still suffer from endemic underemployment. This seems to many to underscore the failure of the ambitions of entrepreneurial city policies to bring about improvement for all (Cooper and Shaheen 2008; Ward 2003b).

With this focus on charismatic leadership, public–private partnerships and the effects of these governmental structures on local populations, both the supporters and critiques of entrepreneurial governance produce a picture of the city which sets up an opposition between those who are doing the work of government with those who are being governed. Whilst this was certainly a key feature of my earlier research on economic development, my more recent work on environmental politics in the city unsettles and challenges this dualistic description of political relations in this city.

It was in the context of this understanding of the manner in which politics had been pursued in the city that I encountered the *Manchester: A Certain Future* steering group. I was immediately struck by how, in contrast to the economic development practices I had observed in my earlier research, the steering group seemed to enact a rather different and less dualistic set of political relationships. Here was a group, working on behalf of the city, involving the City Council but not led by them, whose aim was to bring about a form of urban transformation that would support a move towards a sustainable future, not just for the city centre, nor even for a broader sense of the city itself but also for the global population. Here the city (including its population of residents) was to act as a political collective in order to realise a sustainable social and environmental future for all. To achieve this end, what had been devised was an explicit exercise in collaborative government. This was an experiment towards ways of producing a form of political organisation that, like entrepreneurial government, would distribute responsibility for societal change away from institutionally located governmental actors to communities, citizens and activists of different kinds.[1] But it was to do so in a way that also problematises the characterisation of governance partnerships as simply about neo-liberal governmentality.

The ethnographic approach

The steering group in many ways sat at the centre of my ethnographic study, and provided a pivot around which the research revolved. I interviewed and talked informally to several members of the steering group throughout the course of the research. Some became friends and some became colleagues. I spoke to those who were not involved in the group about what they felt about this organisational form. I attended three steering group meetings and also attended one of the steering group strategy away days where the future of the climate plan was discussed. I did fieldwork in four organisations represented on the steering group – spending approximately four months shadowing members of a university research project, five months researching climate change mitigation activities in the City Council, four months in a local environmental business and a week shadowing the environmental officer at one of the city's Housing Associations. I also attended several planning meetings about the *Manchester: A Certain Future* plan, and participated in a one-day 'refresh' of the *Manchester: A Certain Future* document in 2013.

My ethnographic focus was thus less a particular and well-defined community of individuals and rather the set of social relations and practices that came to cohere around a particular policy intervention for which the steering group was responsible – the aim to reduce the city's carbon emissions by 41 per cent by 2020. The purpose of taking this approach was to achieve a study of politics in the making (Shore and Wright 1997; Shore, et al. 2011). As Susan Wright has pointed out, 'the study of a policy process acts as a window into changing forms of government and regimes of power' (2006: 22). This chapter describes the manner in which collaborative government was being organised, and the hopes, concerns and ambitions of those who were working to find a viable mode of doing politics in the city at this time. The chapter thus deploys an ethnographic description of policy making in order to investigate what kind of understandings about the nature of urban politics are made visible when we pay close attention to the practice of this kind of distributive governance. Whilst the description is specific to this particular network of people, conversations with others that I met during my research leads me to suggest that the findings have broader relevance for understanding of how political work is done in urban settings. The contribution of this chapter is both an exploration of the value of an ethnographic analysis of policymaking as a way into understanding cities as objects and sites of political practice, and a diagnosis of some of the key issues that constitute urban politics in contemporary Manchester.

Environmental policy in the Council

I begin this exploration of the practice of doing climate change policy by considering how the work of reducing carbon emissions was being approached from within the local authority itself. Although the steering group was officially responsible for the reduction of carbon emissions in the city, the local Council also had a group of Council Officers employed as members of an environmental strategy team. This team had a central role in supporting and directing the work of responding to the challenges of climate change.

The environmental strategy team, however, inhabited rather a vulnerable position within the local authority. The idea that the local Council should have an environmental policy team at all was a relatively recent development. One of those involved in putting environmental issues at the heart of Council policy explained to me the process through which the establishment of an environmental strategy team had been achieved, telling me how it emerged in relation to a proposal to introduce a congestion-charging scheme in the city in the early 2000s. One side effect of the work that went into putting the case together for the congestion charging scheme was that Council Officers and politicians had built up strong relationships with non-governmental environment groups in the city such as Friends of the Earth. The congestion-charging scheme had been put to a referendum in 2004, but the population voted 'no', leaving the scheme to be disbanded. By this time however, the relationships were in place to ensure that environmental concerns in general, and climate change in particular, were 'on-the-radar' as far as the local Council was concerned.

The success of establishing an environmental strategy team within the local authority was not then seen as inevitable nor the result of some kind of creation of consensus amongst Councillors, activists and the population about the importance of environmental issues. Indeed, in many ways the anti economic-growth ethos of many environmentalists went directly against the dominant political currents at the time.[2] In Council meetings Councillors repeatedly reported that their constituents were more concerned about waste collection and dog muck than any more general sense of the environment. The establishment of the environmental strategy team was thus not a response to general public concerns but rather a result of specific social ties that had allowed conversations to emerge and policies to gain credence in order, to quote one of the city's Councillors, to 'edge things forward'.

An important moment in ensuring that this 'edging forward' could continue came when Richard Leese, the leader of the Council, made several public announcements regarding his support for the local authority's climate change activities. These included a foreword to the *Manchester: A Certain Future* document, his presence at the annual *Manchester: A Certain Future* conference and his involvement in the launch of an initiative called the Manchester Carbon Literacy project. Howard Bernstein was also appointed as chair of the Council's environment committee – something that was seen as another important indicator that people working at the very highest levels of the local administration were taking environmental issues, and in particular climate change, seriously. This combination of the strengthening of social ties across groups, the buy-in of the leaders, and also statutory conditions such as the creation of National Indicator 186, which required local authorities to reduce their own carbon emissions, meant the circumstances were there for an environmental strategy team to be established. These circumstances were not, however, an indicator of the unquestionable power of Manchester's charismatic leaders, but were rather experienced as a somewhat fragile agreement based on support that was constantly at risk of being taken away.

By the time I began my fieldwork, the viability of this team of officers was already under strain. National Indicator 186 had been disbanded when the Conservative/Liberal Democratic coalition government came to power in 2010 and this had left the environmental strategy team with no statutory responsibility to fulfil within the Council. Cuts had already been made to an energy advice centre that had been the responsibility of the team. During the course of my fieldwork, further cuts were made and in January 2013, the local authority received a 'settlement' from central government that outlined further massive cost reductions to be made to the local authority budget over the coming year.[3] Discussions were common at this time among the environmental strategy team about the bleak future that they faced. People who already felt that they had to fight their case for recognition within the local authority saw a future where they would be one of the first services to be cut.

Links to 'the centre'

This was the context for my first ethnographic insight about the way in which people working in this area of government went about doing the work of politics. Overwhelmed by a feeling of uncertainty and doubt about the circumstances of their employment – people often said that they felt they were 'living in a climate of constant change'. In order to be able to work in this climate, these Council offers had to become adept at finding creative ways of making things happen in a constantly shifting operating environment. It was clear to everyone I spoke to that there was no money available from the local authority itself for environmental work, so the team had to find other ways of being self-sustaining. One important way of doing this was by finding ways of gaining grants and loans from central government and the European Union. A former executive member for the environment told me: 'I think my biggest success was when I flew from the City Airport to Luxembourg to meet the top people at the European Investment Bank and came away with a commitment of €200 million to put in to our waste project'. Others meanwhile highlighted how getting involved in central government or European initiatives was key to being considered for involvement in other upcoming grants for funds.[4]

One of the sources of funding that was established during the course of my fieldwork was an organisation called the 'Low Carbon Hub'. It was understood among members of the environmental strategy team whom I spoke to, that city leaders had been able to negotiate central government money to establish Greater Manchester as a centre for low carbon investment and development. The Low Carbon Hub was one part of a broader agreement called the City Deal which had been brokered by Leese and Bernstein to ensure central government support for Manchester's continued growth strategy. The leaders had argued the case that the city was likely to be a key component of overall UK growth, promising to create some 40,000–70,000 new jobs over the coming few years. They had argued that central government needed to support the city in achieving this success. The precise set of negotiations by which the Low Carbon Hub had been set up as a spin off from this City Deal was somewhat opaque to most members of the environmental strategy team. Nonetheless, they were hopeful that this might open up other relationships and links between Manchester and central government, giving them, for example, 'a route into the new Green Investment Bank' (quote from member of the environment team).

As well as having established the City Deal, Manchester was also one of ten cities in the UK that were part of a 'core cities'[5] group, another policy tool that enabled Manchester 'to work as [a] partner with the government of the day to ensure the successful delivery of improved outcomes for our cities and the economy'.[6] A central aspect of this kind of relationship with Whitehall was that it had the effect of establishing Manchester as a trusted location where central government policy could itself be tested out. One example of this kind of arrangement in the field of environmental policy came in 2013 when Manchester was chosen to trial a new central government initiative called the Green Deal.

The Green Deal was a proposal to transform funding for making homes more energy efficient from a grants-based scheme that already existed, to a complex loan-based mechanism which aimed to marketise carbon reduction by incentivising householders to invest in home-energy saving technologies. The project was in its pilot stage and a number of people working in Greater Manchester in local authorities, Housing Associations, charities and co-operatives had been working hard to put together a case for why Manchester should be one of the test locations for this project under a scheme called 'Green Deal Go Early'. Much future funding for carbon reduction activities in the city rested on the Green Deal bid being successful.

Involvement in initiatives like the Green Deal appear on the surface to fulfil the criteria of policy entrepreneurship discussed above. They involved partnerships across the public and private sector, they entailed the devolution of power away from local authorities to other, perhaps less accountable actors, and they channelled funds in ways that could be argued to be beneficial to the centre of capital (large property owners, energy suppliers) but not to local populations. However, simply characterising this practice as policy entrepreneurship glosses over the everyday experience of those people involved of in this work. Most people I spoke to about their involvement in the Green Deal scheme started with an admission that they were uncomfortable about their involvement in this initiative. They recognised that for Manchester to receive any funding it was necessary for the city to have links and relationships with the Department for Energy and Climate Change, but at the same time people worried about being seen as supporters of a means of funding carbon reductions which they did not agree with and did not expect to work. This was exacerbated by a tension between on the one hand a Manchester local Council that by 2015 was entirely made up of Labour Councillors, and on the other a central government that was led by a party of right-of-centre Conservatives.[7]

Here then we have our first hint at the need that people felt to be included in processes even when they themselves were highly uncomfortable with the nature of the policies with which they were having to be aligned. To explore this further I move in the next section to consider how officers and Councillors dealt with this tension by inhabiting a position that enabled them to be included in these discussions without becoming incorporated in the politics that these projects seemed to represent.

The activist officer

> The good thing was that, he was immediately more trusted because he didn't come with a local government background, he came with a voluntary sector background with really strong environmental credentials. (Interviewee, Manchester City Council)

In order for officers working for the City Council to be able to do the work of ensuring inclusion discussed above, it was important for them to define their role as officers of the local authority, inhabiting a neutral position of public servant and not one of an individual with vested interests (for more on this see other anthropological studies of bureaucracy e.g. Hertzfeld 1993; Hull 2012; Mathur and Bear 2015). However at the same time, many of the people in the environmental strategy team had been employed precisely because they brought other, more radical and activist-driven kinds of knowledge, expertise and connections to their role as Council Officers. A senior member of the environmental strategy team, for example, came to the Council after a long career working for an environmental charity. Another was seconded from the Department for Energy and Climate Change, another had a degree in geography and environmental sciences, and several others had worked for environmental charities, universities and think tanks. One of the anxieties often expressed by these officers was how they could reconcile this biographical identity, which they often saw as instantiating quite radical political hopes and ambitions, with the requirement of inclusion into central government policies and schemes outlined above and the daily practice of working in a bureaucratic organisation.

One way they did this was by defining their own role as distinct from, but complementary to, environmental charities and environmental activists working for pressure groups in the city. Any latent activism was expressed not in terms of personal political beliefs, but rather extended through networks of relations with other organisations in the city, which could do the work of enacting radical activism whilst leaving Council Officers to do the work of negotiating with 'the centre'. Indeed, the broader field of environmental politics in the city was often characterised by pointing to an important but uneasy relationship between 'activists' and 'officers'.

Partnerships with other organisations outside the Council had been written into the *Manchester: A Certain Future* document, and offered the potential for officers to work with activists to translate policy into practice. Here, bureaucratic or regulatory work was supported by or linked with interventions that could be carried out by people untethered by the institutional rhythms and structures of the local authority. But this idea of partnership with non-governmental others belied a more complex and ambiguous anxiety that people felt about the appropriate means by which they themselves as political actors might practice politics. Whilst a distinction between officers and activists was often asserted to point to a division between those working inside the Council and those with whom they partnered, this distinction was often more ambiguous than it initially seemed. Day-to-day conversations with those working within the Council suggested instead that this distinction served to disguise an ambiguity felt by some Council Officers about what kind of political agency they had, and what it meant to be a specific kind of political actor.

People working within the local authority were often involved with other groups outside the Council who were trying to intervene in changing the city in ways that were somewhat different to the kinds of links into the central government and European initiatives I have already discussed. Several Council employees, for example, attended events associated with a group called Steady State Manchester, which was trying to establish a form of urban policy that would not be based on GVA measures of economic growth, but would find other ways of valuing the city as a place to live and work. Awareness and involvement in such activities led some Council Officers to question and reflect on the relationship between their political commitments and the actions available to them within their role as local authority officers. The following quote is typical of the way in which people working in the Council environment team would reflect on their work:

> The reason why I love [the Council] is because I actually think that value-wise it is driven by the right things. I think it does want to drive economic growth for the greater good of the greater number. I do think it's about there being a safety net below which nobody should fall. I do think it's trying to embrace the green agenda. It might be limited but I think it's trying to do these things, and I can forgive it a lot of its foibles on the basis that it's a value-driven organisation.

It was also through these kinds of reflections that ambivalence about the implications of involvement in central government schemes like the Green Deal was articulated.

'Aligning' with the public

Whilst officers and Councillors working on carbon reduction in Manchester had to find ways of linking their activities to central government, they were also concerned about the need to make their activities relevant to other people and institutions in Manchester. The local authority had formal systems for consulting with local populations but these were frequently seen as highly problematic and ineffective. Commenting on a regular public accountability session held in the City Council offices, called the Environmental Scrutiny Committee, one Councillor lamented:

> We want to align with the public but we can't. The reports that make decisions are subject to public scrutiny and public view but the sad thing is that, of course, participation in general is quite low. The number of times we get people in the public gallery for these meetings is … small.

The failures or limits of public engagement or public consultation as a means of producing public involvement in political process have been widely critiqued (see, for example, Blakeley 2010 for discussion of citizen participation). However, my purpose of drawing attention to public consultation is less to critique its failure, than to highlight the existence of a desire to involve the public and an awareness of the challenge of doing so. Recognising this allows us to see that the work of these Council employees required that they work in a space in-between relationships that would enable them access to large grants, and the commitment to serve a local population.

In Manchester, the key way in which this was achieved was in fact not through consultation, but rather through a more relational practice of partnering. To be able to justify the local political relevance of their work, Council Officers found themselves needing to cultivate something akin to the 'flex nets' or flexible networks described by Janine Wedel (2011) in her study of the 'NeoCon core' in America. Difficulties of engaging a general public were mitigated in part by relating to another public, instantiated in the form of relations with charities, universities and other local institutions.

The environmental strategy team at the City Council, like other Council departments, was working continuously in partnership with several universities, Housing Associations, local co-operatives, school, energy companies, and IT companies throughout the time I spent there. The partnerships led to the provision of research into projected local climate change and into local food chains, the creation of a carbon literacy project, provision of energy saving advice through a telephone hotline, the provision of insulation in many houses, and so on. Through partnerships with these external organisations, the Council offers were able to bring about changes that would never have been financially supported by Council funds. Many of these projects were made possible by grant funding from research or innovation funds that supported just these kinds of partnerships.

If public consultation is a form of engagement that often seems to distance local government from the populations it simultaneously tries to incorporate, partnering was a way of incorporating others from outside the local authority directly into the process of providing Council services. The way in which this 'partnering' work was described was as a means of extending capabilities that were curtailed by the responsibilities that came with being situated within an institution like a local authority.

The *Manchester: A Certain Future* steering group was a perfect manifestation of this complex relationship between the local authority and a more distributed form of local politics. Whilst in official documentation the *Manchester: A Certain Future* steering group was described as a being for 'the whole' city, it was not uncommon to hear the same steering group referred to as a 'stab vest for the Council'. The critique being made by this accusation was that the steering group had merely been set up as a way of devolving responsibility for climate change mitigation away from otherwise accountable local government officials onto non-elected others. By creating the institutional form of the 'steering group' under the guise of participatory governance, the Council were seen to have created a means of protecting themselves against charges of inaction or a lack of effectiveness. Here, by attempting to incorporate others into the work of politics that should rightfully belong to Council Officers, they were seen to be trying to defend themselves from criticisms about their political effectiveness.

Operating 'inside the tent'

This leads us to the final section of this discussion, to consider how the organisations who were being invited to be incorporated into this distributed form of politics responded to being part of this 'stab vest' organisation. If there was a difficulty with these partnerships from the perspective of those who were meant to be doing the work of the Council, the difficulty paralleled the same tension that we saw as people in the Council tried to work with central government. Here in these partnerships, local authorities needed non-governmental organisations not only to be included in decision-making processes but to become incorporated into the very work of doing local government itself. Caricaturing the involvement of activist partners in Council-led initiatives run with external funding, one Council employee tellingly characterised these external organisations as needing to be brought 'inside the tent'. Unsurprisingly however, this was not a straightforward process.

So far I have described how the work of being a Council Officer working on environmental issues involved a consideration of political actions in terms of the importance of retaining a relationship with 'the centre' – be that Europe or Whitehall, and the related importance of partnering with others who help pull the work of the Council into another more activist form of local political engagement. In this final section I want to provide a brief discussion of this process of inclusion from the perspective of some of those people working in partnership with the local Council. As I described at the beginning of this chapter, Manchester's climate change action plan was always written as a plan 'for the whole city'. To institutionalise this ambition, the steering group was established, as a governmental form which existed outside local government. Many of the people involved in the steering group were those same people or representatives of the same organisations that were partnering with the City Council on carbon reduction activities – representatives from Housing Associations, environmental charities and co-operative organisations.

As an institutional form that was neither continuous with the Council, nor fully external to it, the steering group was a fascinating site of engagement where issues of inclusion versus incorporation were being worked out. To describe this position, those who sat on the steering group often articulated their relationship to the local authority as one of 'critical friend'. This term itself seemed to perfectly capture the tension between incorporation and inclusion that I have been exploring throughout this chapter. Friendship, in this case, indicated the existence of a relationship. It pointed to a mode of relating where individuals and institutions might be called upon to participate in funding bids, to come to events, to disseminate information and ideas and to support one another in the work that they were doing. But this friendship was not to be mistaken for consensus of opinion or intention. For whilst those around the table of the steering group meetings were in once sense open to partnership, they were simultaneously aware of the dangers of a form of incorporation that would erase difference in personal and institutional histories, intentions and desires.

Members of the steering group were from varied backgrounds. There were people from commercial property development firms, universities and small business, as well as individuals with a history in direct climate action. This meant that, interestingly, a situation had emerged where people with relatively radical left-wing political agendas found themselves working in partnership with private corporations and a Conservative government, as well as with a local government structure which itself was seen at times as incapable of bringing about the kinds of radical social transformations needed to tackle climate change. The effects of collaboration were far from resolved, as the tension in the term critical friendship perhaps alludes. People I worked with asked on a daily basis what the implications of their partnerships were. What space, for example, was there for critique, when radical left-wing activists were being incorporated and entangled into something like the highly neo-liberal Green Deal? While people involved in these kinds of relationships with local government – gaining funding from grants, and doing the work that used to be the remit of local authorities – have been termed policy entrepreneurs – considering these activities in the context of a left-leaning environmental politics, rather than in terms of urban regeneration, complicates the idea that these actions are in fact entrepreneurial at all. Instead it behoves us to pay greater attention to the ambivalence and complexity of entanglements between different kinds of political action and to the place of this ambivalence or complexity in the constitution of a field of political action in a city like Manchester.

Conclusion

As I have shown, people involved in Manchester's urban politics struggle on a daily basis with the question of how to align themselves with others whose interests and agendas might differ from their own. Whilst collaboration and partnership is pursued in various different forms, collaborative relationships reveal the importance of questions about identity and belonging, about the relationship between pragmatism and ideology and concerns over authenticity and trust. As we have seen, the call for partnership and collaboration raises issues for people both inside and outside the Council who want access to resources to get things done but for whom there is a tension between inclusion in channels of communication, information circulation, meetings, initiatives and incorporation. This means that people find themselves becoming unavoidably aligned with those who do not necessarily stand for the same things that they stand for.

I suggest that the experiences I have recounted here have key relevance for understanding the on-going transformations of urban politics, particularly under current conditions of 'austerity' politics. As we attempt to understand urban politics in terms of the way in which people both within and beyond the offices of local government negotiate an environment of 'constant change', we would do well to further trace the tension between the importance of inclusion and the dangers of incorporation that I have described in this chapter. This, I suggest, will enable us to extend descriptions of political process in urban settings like Manchester beyond the 'usual suspects' to a much broader array of people involved in political processes. Once we extend beyond government offices to look at the constitution of these broader networks of relations, the possibility even opens up of extending these networks to incorporate non-human actors. In this chapter I have focused on social relations between people, but once we attune ourselves to the relationships through which political work gets done, then such an approach also opens up the prospect of unravelling how policies, documents, percentages, meetings, plans, buildings and infrastructures are also at play in this process of inclusion without incorporation that I have begun to describe in this brief incursion into environmental politics in the city of Manchester.

Notes

1   See MacLeod 2011 for further discussion on the post-democratic city.
2   One active group at the time was called 'Steady State Manchester' and they were advocating for a non-growth focused development strategy for the city.
3   It was announced in January 2013 that some £80m of savings would have to be found between 2013 and 2015. This came on top of cuts of £170m that had already been made over the preceding two years, which had led to some 2000 job losses.
4   The City Council was invited to become part of a 'core cities' group at the time of my fieldwork, which offered a way of extending relationships that had been established through the low-carbon hub.
5   The other cities that are part of core cities are: Birmingham, Bristol, Cardiff, Glasgow, Leeds, Liverpool, Newcastle, Nottingham and Sheffield.
6   Quote from core cities website www.corecities.com/what-we-do/working-government. Accessed 20 December 2016.
7   One member of the environmental strategy team, for example, commented that since the coalition government had come into power in 2010, the relationship between local and central government had changed and that you didn't 'have a direct route into government the same way as you did before'. People responded to this problem of potential suspicion, mistrust and lack of a 'direct route' to local government by working in coalition with other councils in Greater Manchester (such as Stockport Council, which did have a Conservative majority) who would be better placed to develop this conversation with national politicians.

References

Bache, Ian and Matthew Flinders. 2004. "Multi-level governance and British politics". In *Multi-Level Governance*. I. Bache and M. Flinders, eds. pp. 130–136. Buckingham: Open University Press.

Blakeley, Georgina. 2010. "Governing ourselves: citizen participation and governance in Barcelona and Manchester". *International Journal of Urban and Regional Research* 34 (1): 130–145.

Cooper, Malcolm and Faiza Shaheen. 2008. "Winning the battles but losing the war? Regeneration, renewal and the state of Britain's cities". *Journal of Urban Regeneration and Renewal* 2 (2): 146–151.

Hall, Tim and Phil Hubbard. 1998. *The Entrepreneurial City: Geographies of Politics, Regime, and Representation.* Chichester: John Wiley & Sons.

Harvey, David. 1989. "From managerialism to entrepreneurialism: the transformation in urban governance in late capitalism.' *Geografiska Annaler.* 71: B (1): 3–17.

Hertzfeld, Michael. 1993. *The Social Production of Indifference: Exploring the Symbolic Roots of Western Democracy.* Chicago: University of Chicago Press.

Hull, Matthew S. 2012. *Government of Paper: The Materiality of Bureaucracy in Urban Pakistan.* Berkeley, California; London: University of California Press.

Jonas, Andrew E.G., David Gibbs, and Aidan While. 2011. "The new urban politics as a politics of carbon control". *Urban Studies* 48 (12): 2537–2554.

Knox, Hannah Catherine. 2003. "'Blocks to convergence' in the new media industries: an anthropological study of small and medium sized enterprises in Manchester". Unpublished PhD thesis, University of Manchester.

Mathur, Nayanika and Laura Bear. 2015. "Remaking the public good: a new anthropology of bureaucracy". *The Cambridge Journal of Anthropology* 33 (1): 18–34.

Peck, Jamie and Kevin Ward. 2002. *City of Revolution: Restructuring Manchester.* Manchester: Manchester University Press.

Quilley, Stephen. 1999. "Entrepreneurial Manchester: the genesis of elite consensus". *Antipode* 31 (2): 185–211.

— 2000. "Manchester first: from municipal socialism to the entrepreneurial city". *International Journal of Urban and Regional Research* 24 (3): 601–615.

Shore, Chris and Susan Wright. 1997. *Anthropology of Policy: Critical Perspectives on Governance and Power* (European Association of Social Anthropologists). London: Routledge.

Shore, Cris, Susan Wright, and Davide Però. 2011. *Policy Worlds: Anthropology and the Analysis of Contemporary Power.* New York: Berghahn Books.

Tickell, Adam and Jamie Peck. 1996. "The return of the Manchester men: men's words and men's deeds in the remaking of the local state". *Transactions of the Institute of British Geographers* 21 (4): 595–616.

Ward, Kevin. 2000. "Front rentiers to rantiers: 'active entrepreneurs', 'structural speculators' and the politics of marketing the city". *Urban Studies* 37 (7): 1093–1107.

— 2003a. "Entrepreneurial urbanism, state restructuring and civilizing 'New' East Manchester". *Area* 35 (2): 116–127.

— 2003b. "The limits to contemporary urban redevelopment: 'Doing' entrepreneurial urbanism in Birmingham, Leeds and Manchester". *City* 7 (2): 199–211.

Wedel, Janine R. 2011. *Shadow Governing: What the Neocon Core Reveals about Power and Influence in America. Policy Worlds: Anthropology and the Analysis of Contemporary Power.* New York: Berghahn Books.

While, Aidan, Andrew E.G. Jonas, and David Gibbs. 2004. "The environment and the entrepreneurial city: searching for the urban 'sustainability; fix' in Manchester and Leeds". *International Journal of Urban and Regional Research* 28 (3): 549–569.
Wright, Susan. 2006. "Anthropology of policy". *Anthropology News* 47 (8): 22.
Young, Craig, Martina Diep, and Stephanie Drabble. 2006. "Living with difference? The 'cosmopolitan city' and urban reimaging in Manchester, UK". *Urban Studies* 43 (10): 1687–1714.

Figure 2.1 Parade day, Manchester, 2012

2

NURTURING AN EMERGENT CITY: PARADE MAKING AS A CULTURAL TROPE FOR URBAN POLICY

Jessica Symons

The city inside us all

I pedalled my bike down the back of Castlefield, past the canals and converted mills, over the footbridges, by the geese pecking in the grass, sun glinting in the water, refracted across the apartment windows. I barely passed a soul those early summer weekdays as I wended my way through to the industrial units which sat behind the flats. The sound of laughter and music greeted me as I locked my bike up and wandered into the expansive space, crowded now with huge birds, airplanes, a giant human lying prone, his legs propped up. I walked around these legs and over to Bob, who was always in the parade workshop and who always greeted me with good cheer and a job to help with. As we worked alongside each other, our chats about the world and everything included the difference between artists and prop makers. 'Artists', he told me, 'have something inside them that has to come out'. He stood underneath a massive bamboo and fibreglass structure, ten metres long and four metres wide with a pink head and hands shaped from foam. 'I just make stuff and when it leaves the workshop, I'm not interested in it anymore', he continued.

Bob's statement preoccupied me throughout my fieldwork over two parades in Manchester. His technical mastery of large parade structures was admired by many, and he designed and built the leading sections. I contemplated his words as I worked alongside artists, those who were 'not sure' and others who were 'not artists'; comparing and thinking about the differences between their work. During both parades, I observed and participated, helping people 'make stuff' as artists, prop-makers, parade organisers, City Council workers and community groups.

Gradually I developed the insight that artists are trained to use the 'something inside of them' as creative inspiration. They learn how to 'bring it out' in a structured, productive way. The inspiring, creative people I met making these parades in Manchester clearly understood this process and recruited parade artists to draw out the creative potential of non-artists – the 1800 people in ninety community groups across the city who made the parade. The parade organisers did not 'produce' the parades, controlling all the words spoken and actions taken. Instead they developed a nurturing approach, encouraging community groups to develop their own ideas and then providing artistic support and resources to bring them out and make them shine. Returning to Bob's observation, I argue that we all have something inside us, we just need help to draw it out. Artists have training in how to do this.

As cities grow exponentially in increasing complexity, civic decision makers face the impossible task of designing coherent plans and processes. My fieldwork among civic parade makers has revealed a way of supporting an 'emergent city'. They have developed an effective process for nurturing and supporting the development of local ideas. Let's learn from them.

Introduction

Created by Manchester People. Commissioned by Manchester City Council. Produced by Walk the Plank. (Manchester Day Parade website, 2012)[1]

In this chapter, I draw insight from fieldwork in Manchester where a nurturing approach by an events organisation, working with multiple community groups and stakeholders in the creation of a major civic parade, led to an emergent entity rather than a directed one. This cultural moment provides an opportunity for learning through analogy: nurturing a parade works as a synecdoche for how 'the city' as a conceptual frame can be approached by decision makers.

In urban research, cities may be understood as complex organisms but there is a tendency to depict a city as an agent in its own right: London does this; Manchester does that. Theorists often take an anti-capitalist stance representing urban decision makers and commercial organisations as villains of the piece. For example, Harvey explores control in cities by identifying 'monopolies' over production and surplus (2012). For him, 'bureaucratic capitalist governmentality' dominates urban contexts. He raises Fletcher and Gapasin's question of 'how to organise the city' without socialist urban success stories and his reply is 'we simply do not know' (Fletcher Jr and Gapasin 2008; Harvey 2012: 140). This notion of the failed socialist project hangs heavy over urban debates. In 1970, Lefebvre argued that the city was too complex to grasp, and so its distributed nature produced passivity; inertia borne from helplessness (Lefebvre 2003 [1970]). A similar sense of the impossible grips people today.

Yet city dynamics are only manifestations of layered processes and pathways, decisions taken, events that happen, people and places that take on a particular shape based on their historical experiences – a palimpsest where every morning sunrise is a new page of city life. Insight beckons from getting our hands dirty, spending time with city decision makers, observing and participating in their daily activities and preoccupations, sharing in the complexity of their challenges. The mirage of a tightly controlled, malevolent capitalist force evaporates close-up. The passivity induced by this realisation can be ameliorated with participant observation. Ethnography provides a structured method for analysing how and why situations develop as they do.

Many anthropologists use De Landa's concept of assemblages when designing ethnographic research in a city. He argues that everything is made up of combined assemblages, interconnected parts or 'constellations' (De Landa 2006: 49). These constituents of life start with cells, some containing DNA and proteins, and build up from there into people, objects, buildings, cities, nation states up to Earth itself. Each assemblage has component parts, materials such as body limbs, plants and vehicles and expressive parts such as language or sensual 'impressions'. These assemblages have distinct functions, as well as contributing to the functions of larger assemblages.

Assemblage theory supports analyses of a city's component parts, looking at how different aspects fit together, and their distinctive characteristics in operation, including cultural understandings and practices that are assumed and unspoken. When Harvey (2012) asks, 'how to organise a city', an ethnographic approach insists on understanding how each city is organised first. While all cities are different, the process for analysing how they work can be methodologically the same – through participant observation. Analysing a city's cultural mechanics provides pathways, connections between aspirations for the right to the city and *who* can enable this and help make it happen.

Manchester provides a good site for exploring these challenges. The local government administration had a settled leadership for over thirty years, whose method of operating was controversial for some and praised by others (see Introduction, chs 1 and 3, this volume). Local civic officials brought about significant change in the city, particularly in response to the post-war decline of its manufacturing base. Their activities stimulated Manchester's renaissance to become a leading 'second city' in the UK after London. Yet the cultural dynamics of the city administration manifests differently depending on who you speak to. These inner workings of the local Council and connected organisations and individuals are traceable through social relationships. By revealing the assemblages that constitute Manchester's cultural agenda and the people involved in its development, it is possible to understand the dynamics of the city and how it takes on its particular shape (see ch 1, this volume).

Manchester Day Parade was the only civic event commissioned directly by the Council in 2011 and 2012. Analysis of its development provides 'design trace' through which urban dynamics of the city can be followed and its constituting parts considered. This approach helps break down the dualisms and turns 'capitalist agents' into real people with aspirations and allegiances, ideas and flaws. In the following analysis, I lay bare how a cultural entity was produced in the city and what can be learned from the making process.

Ethnographic approach

Over eighteen months, from 2011–2013, I spent time with civic officials and key organisations involved in the development of the Manchester Day Parade. Entry into the 'field' came through a phone conversation with the Head of Events at Manchester City Council. She invited me to a parade meeting where I met Walk the Plank, the organisation commissioned to develop a civic parade for local residents in the city centre on a summer's day in June. Three women – the Director of Walk the Plank, the Producer, and the Design Co-ordinator of the parade welcomed me into their world, allowing me to participate in meetings with the Council, parade artists and community groups. I spent time in the Town Hall and Walk the Plank's office but mainly in the warehouse where the parade artists worked putting the parade sections together, and with two community groups as they developed their ideas for the parade. In each case, I asked permission to participate, introducing myself as an anthropologist researching the creative process in making a parade. Some people talked about themselves and their lives, others ignored me; most treated me as a friend and colleague.

As 'parade day' drew closer, I would turn up at the warehouse and hang around, asking people if they needed help. In the first year, the Walk the Plank team asked me to organise a parade section for a participating organisation. In the following year, I volunteered with two community groups working along-side them as they developed their parade sections. This included making rat heads, tails and a bin-bag ballgown using wire, sacking, paint, glue and glitter. My fieldwork reached its crescendo when participating in the parade itself. In my second year of fieldwork, I walked the route alongside fellow rats in a parade section designed by a leading London sculptural artist celebrating the community group's city centre cafe.

The following six months focused on interviewing the key participants in the making of the parade, to understand their backgrounds, how they came to be involved, and what was important to them about their work. I also took photographs and short films to capture the aural and visual splendour of the parade, both in its making and on the day itself.

The cultural, political and socio-economic history of Manchester provided important contextual understanding of the city dynamics, together with eth-nographies and studies of parades and festivals in other cities. For comparison, I interviewed key people involved in the Manchester International Festival, a

Figure 2.2 Walking in my bin-bag ballgown with fellow rats towards
the parade start

major biennial art event in the city. I also drew on theoretical understandings
of anthropology, art, creativity, idea development and urban dynamics to
make sense of my findings.

In the following analysis, I tease apart the constituting entities that brought
the parade into being. As the combined output of the city's 'cultural strategy'
and cultural expression by community groups, the parade event was a 'string
of circumstances, held together by social interactions. a hybrid imagined in
a socially extended state' (Strathern 1996: 521). By looking at these 'strings
of circumstances' it is possible to make sense of how the groups of people
making the parade brought their own cultural contexts and preoccupations to
its co-construction. Understanding how the parade was made in Manchester

shows how the city itself is continuously being made every day in a collaborative effort between civic officials and the communities that constitute the city.

Contextualising the parade

In 2010, the Manchester Day Parade launched down the city's main street to the theme of 'Out of this World'. A spectacle of dancing, stilt walking, bright colours, live music, huge trolley and bike mounted structures, the parade involved over 1,800 participants from 90 community and social groups across Manchester, supported by freelance artists, co-ordinated by the arts charity, Walk the Plank, and funded by Manchester City Council. I started fieldwork a year later and followed the development of two parades over eighteen months. As I spent time with people from these different organisations and cultural contexts, I noticed how they each engaged with the same event in different ways. The parade became a 'thing' that was made to work based on who was representing it, why and how. Contemplating the 'techniques of representation' in making the parade reveals its constitutive processes and the kinds of political representation people seek in assembling a parade, both as initiators and participants (Latour and Sánchez-Criado 2007). This kind of analysis also reveals underlying assumptions and ambitions involved in organising it.

Manchester's local governance processes have been analysed extensively (see Introduction, this volume, and also Cochrane, et al. 1996; Green and Harvey 1999; Hatherley 2011; Leadbeater 2009; Peck and Tickell 1995; Peck and Ward 2002; Quilley 1999, 2000; Symons 2015, 2016; Ward 2003). While the authors may differ on the appropriateness of the political interventions and the differing emphasis (or not) on empowering communities, they evidently agree on the highly active and engaged nature of local government involvement in shaping the city's dynamics. In this analysis, I situate the parade and therefore the city as a 'distributed object' (Gell 1998), constituted of multiple assemblages. This approach allows acknowledgement of the many different agendas and perspectives in, and of, the city that overlap, intermingle and compete, whilst also locating these activities in a specific place and time.

The notion of a distributed object comes from anthropologist Gell (1998), who focused on art objects and how they were constituted by the social relations that surround them. Gell presents art objects as 'vehicles of complicated ideas' which are best understood both by the effects that produce them and what effect they have. For Gell, Malangan carvings, Maori meeting houses and the artist Duchamp's body of work retain and embody stylistic characteristics from the production process and through their impact on others. Each entity emerges from its cultural setting borne by and entangled with its context. As 'art objects', they retain their own agency, complimenting and conflicting with others.

In his analysis, Gell describes the relations surrounding a painting of *Rokeby Venus* by Velázquez. Hanging in the National Gallery in London, this painting was slashed as part of a protest by suffragette Mary Richardson. The sabotaged painting was photographed and then restored. Almost a century later, the protest was described by Freedberg and Gallese (2007) and then by Gell to illustrate his point. Gell observes that the painting was acted upon and had an impact on others. When describing these relations, it becomes an 'index' (Gell 1998: 60–62). The painting 'indexes' the artist Velázquez's motivation in producing the work as well as Mary Richardson's anger, the museum's consternation at a damaged painting, and the 'public sensation' that its sabotage caused. It also indexes the academic intention of both Freedberg and Gell who develop arguments based on its relational contexts. The painting as index represents the 'congealed residue of performance and agency in object form, through which access to other persons can be attained, and via which their agency can be communicated' (Gell 1998: 68).

This approach provides a process for analysing how objects emerge from cultural contexts whilst not being singly representative of them. It adds to the assemblage theory proposed by De Landa (2006) by showing how objects, people and concepts are connected by the relational force they exert on each other. The Manchester Day Parade analysed together as an assemblage of material and expressive entities, and also as an 'art object' with relational force, reveals the assumptions, understandings and contexts that guided how people engaged with the parade production and its constituent parts. The parade is also an aspect of urban dynamics within Manchester as a city, and therefore acts an index embedded in, constituted by and impacting on other relationships, objects and indices.

While the combination of assemblages and indices may seem initially quite complex, they provide conceptual but flexible framings to tease out the constituting elements that make up a city. They allow the researcher to go beyond organisational boundaries such as the 'City Council' and 'Walk the Plank'. She can follow people and entities as they relate to each other and see how ideas and understandings travel between them. Obviously working from DNA in cells up to city level is beyond the scope of any study, so it is necessary to focus on certain aspects for analysis. In this context, I wanted to consider the cultural dynamics in Manchester's city administration and so trace the contours of particular assemblages that seemed to have an influence over decision-making processes. In the following section, I identify two indices that shaped how the parade came into being and the wider relations that defined its purpose in the city.

The first index is Manchester's 2002 *Cultural Strategy*. This document encapsulates the local Council's positioning of the city as a 'cultural destination' delivered through 'a programme of cultural events' (Manchester

Cultural Strategy Team 2002). To this end, a 'Cultural Strategy Team' was established in 2003, with a remit for 'increasing participation in culture by the people of Manchester and *using culture* as a means to improve the profile of the city, with the aim of attracting people to live, work and play in Manchester' [my italics].[2] This statement made 'culture' abstract, an entity to be mobilised for economic and social gain. It was the latest 'hook' to be used by an ambitious local government committed to developing Manchester through economic stimulus that began with physical regeneration of infrastructure, housing stock and commercial development (see Introduction, this volume). However this expressed aim of *using culture* caused consternation among the very people whose creative expression had turned Manchester into a cultural destination, particularly musicians.

During the 1980s and 1990s, a thriving counter-culture music scene flourished in the city. Hatherley (2011) describes how punk and rave music communities grew up in run-down areas such as Hulme, just as other parts of the city were regenerating into urban chic dwellings. However, the Council Executive were not well regarded by many of these musicians who were 'subjected' to building development in the name of 'regeneration' (Hatherley 2011: 115–156). Council rhetoric focused on creating jobs, improving financial wealth and attracting others to 'live, work and play' in the city. This did not resonate with the aspirations of local musicians, poets and environmental activists (see chs 1, 8 and 9, this volume). They perceived their activities as largely ignored by the Council until the early 2000s when Manchester was selected by Richard Florida, a cultural geographer, to join his highly influential list of creative cities worldwide (Florida 2003, 2005).

Florida used certain criteria to identify a 'creative class', including people working in digital media, artists, musicians, lesbians and gay men (Florida 2005). Much like the Council adoption of the Green Deal (see ch 1, this volume), the Council Executive embraced the 'creative city' rhetoric and developed a cultural strategy to bring the city's 'cultural activities' into an economic productivity agenda. Yet rather than celebrate Council support for local creatives, Hatherley condemns this move. He describes how key figures in the Manchester music scene were 'kept outside' by the Council for years and then when the economic value of these cultural legends became more apparent, they were 'brought in' and involved in Council machinations (Hatherley 2011: 115–156). Peter Saville[3] was co-founder of Factory Records, an iconic record label from the 1980s (Redhead 1997). By 2000 he was working as the city's 'consultant creative director' and devised the Original Modern concept representing Manchester as the 'first' industrial city.[4]

Quilley (1999; 2000) describes political and economic activity in Manchester from the mid-1980s as driven by an entrepreneurial elite (Fielding and Tanner 2006; Massey 2011 [2007]; cf also Ward 2003). This depiction chimes with

Tickell and Peck's representation of a 'so-called Manchester Mafia' dominated by a male chauvinism related to the industrial era when 'Manchester Men' were renowned for 'ruthless economic individualism' (Tickell and Peck 1996: 605). In the 2000s, the economic agenda dictated who gained support from the Council to carry out activities in the city. Atkins demonstrates in his study of the transformation of Manchester's gay scene (ch 4, this volume) how the less salubrious side of the Gay Village was pushed out of sight, under bridges and down alleyways, when the Village became a popular tourist destination. Pieri shows how Council staff aspirations shaped the design and development of the city centre, despite the wishes of local residents. The cultural strategy reveals (indexes) an instrumental approach at the Council towards 'cultural activities' as potential assets to be exploited. This approach led local actors feeling like instruments to be used rather than individuals to be supported.

The second index to provide insight into the city's relational dynamics is the *Manchester International Festival*. The Council's development of new cultural activities alongside the existing arts and music scenes led to accusations of appropriation and alienation of artists in the city. This became most evident during the development of the Manchester International Festival (MIF hereafter), 'the world's first festival of original, new work and special events'.

Council Leader Richard Leese was proactive in developing MIF, recruiting Director Alex Poots and supporting the organising team to produce a world-class event and raise the profile of the Festival nationally and internationally (Alex Poots, interview 2011). The first two MIF festivals cost £18.3 million, with the Council providing some funding and also supporting MIF to gain sponsorship from private sector sources, such as Bruntwood, a commercial property company with a wide portfolio of interests in the Manchester area. This process of pulling together networks of public and private partners to sponsor cultural activities followed an existing pattern of practice developed initially for Manchester's Olympic Bid in 1985 (see Fry and Cropper 2016 for a perspective from inside the Council).

However, while public–private relationships were established to 'reduce pressure on the public purse' (Alex Poots, interview: 2011), disparate communities with no financial leverage or access to senior politicians were rarely included in Council executive planning. Just as the music scene was left 'in the cold' during the 1980s and 1990s, discontent arose almost immediately with the launch of the first MIF. In 2007, a new grassroots arts collective, called 'Not Part of the Manchester International Festival', emerged in reaction to the commissions-only festival. This collective 'decided to create from scratch a wholly unpretentious and open arts festival for everyday people to display the products of their hard work' (Not Part of the Manchester International Festival 2007). It was established to run alongside the MIF because 'a lot of the creators who form Manchester's day-to-day artistic pulse were not part of it'.

As MIF developed, the organisers started to include local artists and by 2013, the 'Not Part of' alternative festival no longer existed. However, the protest against MIF demonstrates, indexes, evident local anger towards the Council among the artist community. These issues echo experiences in other parts of the city, such as East Manchester, where communities were frustrated by Council-led physical regeneration in the areas they lived (see ch 8, this volume). Council-led cultural production and its mobilisation for economic gain did not sit easily with Manchester artists, musicians and local communities.

These two indices – the 2002 Cultural Strategy and the Manchester International Festival – combine with others such as the public–private partnerships, the role of city leaders and the counterculture music and arts scenes to reveal the relational dynamics involved in this city. They indicate a tension between Council-led direction of city dynamics and local cultural autonomy. The genesis of the Manchester Day Parade must be considered within these contexts.

At first glance, the Manchester Day Parade appears to be part of the City Council's structured and strategic approach to developing a cultural 'offer' to match the city's other financially focused activities. The parade was commissioned by the Council, and the press releases emphasised the parade's value to the local economy.[5] However, during fieldwork, I did not uncover a preoccupation with 'cultural strategies' or 'economic gain for the city' among the key people involved. Instead the parade was initiated by two Councillors keen to 'celebrate all things Manchester'.

Councillor Pat Karney was Executive Member for the City Centre and Councillor Mike Amesbury Executive Member for Culture and Leisure at Manchester City Council during my fieldwork. They initiated the Manchester Day Parade as part of a broader ambition to create a 'Manchester Day' in the city, as an expression of civic pride. A celebration of Manchester was something the city press officer claimed few cities would have the 'brass neck' (courage/cheekiness) to do (Interview 2011). Mancunians like to be renowned for their pride in their city (Quilley 2000).

So, while the Councillors were part of the Chief Executive team at the Council, they did not emphasise the Manchester Day celebration for its economic potential. I attended several meetings where they were present or when their priorities were discussed by the parade organising team. Audience numbers were important to demonstrate interest in the parade, and economic success was necessary to gain internal and press support for the event, but the priority at every turn was a focus on 'celebrating all things Manchester'. The Councillors were concerned with local people – 'Mancunians' – and their achievements.

It seems that the Councillors were also concerned with cultural production in its own right, reacting to the economic emphasis on the city as a 'destination' with an 'international cultural offer', much like the musicians in Hulme and the artists objecting to MIF. The press officer at the Council described the Council's position on Manchester Day Parade as follows:

> We're not just economists, we're also people who believe that culture is a good thing. As well as being good for economic health of a city, it's good for the social fabric of a city and that's something that we've seen with [the parade], that it's brought together community groups ... So we see events as being something that drive the city's success economically but also have a less tangible impact on the social fabric of the city, which is why we do it, and both those things are equally important. (Interview, PR officer, 2011)

This insight counters the 'Manchester Men' rhetoric (Tickell and Peck 1996: 605) and demonstrates multiple visions of Manchester in the Council and broader obligations beyond economic productivity. However it also demonstrates the *extent of control* sought by officials over civic activities. In their enthusiasm for city making, the civic officials privileged Council versions of Mancunian cultural identity over spontaneously emerging ones. While their aim was to celebrate Manchester, the Councillors still chose the mechanism through which this process was developed – a 'Manchester Day', a parade. They also approved the topical themes proposed by the parade organisers and who could participate.

Navaro-Yashin discusses the 'production of the political in public life' through an expression of cynicism (2002: 1). She argues that in Turkey, people create 'fantasy-led' versions of the State through cynical observations on state-led activities. In Manchester, different groups both within and outside the City Council create versions of the city and then compare their perspectives with others. Artists, musicians, Council executives, press officers all have an understanding of Mancunian identity and seek to realise this through their activities. Often their activities are established in opposition to each other.

The Manchester Day Parade began as a 'fantasy-led' enactment by Council officials on what they wanted to see celebrated, what they believed should constitute 'cultural life' in the city centre. This perspective had the potential to produce more tension over who had the right to define culture in the city. However, the parade organisers at Walk the Plank developed a way of working which deftly knitted together the priorities of different parties, enabling, allowing, nurturing all these versions to sit alongside each other – literally and metaphorically like a parade.

During steering group meetings and other encounters in the field, I noticed how civic officials and parade organisers worked to fit a vibrant parade event into the Councillors' requirement that the parade celebrated Manchester. When the Councillors queried parade aspects asking 'and what does this have to do with Manchester?', the parade organisers would talk about producing an exciting parade, as well as one that celebrated the city. One year the Councillors became attached to a parade theme of 'A City of Heroes' to celebrate a clean-up operation spontaneously organised by citizens after the Manchester riots of 2012. I followed the discussions and negotiations as the Parade Director sought to persuade them that a heroic theme would produce a parade 'full of David Beckhams' rather than a diverse range of characters. She worked with civic officials exploring strategies for encouraging the Councillors to change their point of view. The compromise was a parade theme of 'The Sky's the Limit ... a celebration of heroic achievement'.

These relational dynamics indicate a tension in the role of elected and civic officials. The cultural strategy and MIF were intended to make Manchester and to make culture. For the parade the civic figures imagined themselves to be supporting people to celebrate their own selves and their identities. However, these intentions were dominated by senior members of the Council insisting on certain priorities. They were attempting to make the public much like parade structures to be fashioned from bamboo and coloured fabrics.

The dynamics within the Council reveal a 'moral moment' where political values, social idioms and questions of justice fold onto one another (Corsín Jiménez 2007). In his analysis of 're-institutionalisation', Corsín Jiménez aims to capture the moments where flows of affect, morality, power and knowledge are revealed within any one particular organisational context (Corsín Jiménez 2007: 7). He foregrounds the ways that particular concepts of social relationships manifest themselves in organisations, shaped by and shaping how people and objects interact.

This idea helps think through 'how people organise their social life in virtue of the image they have of themselves and of their human capacities' (Corsín Jiménez 2007: 7). How the Councillors engaged with cultural events in the city provides an ethnographic moment to understand urban dynamics at a broader scale. It shows both the agency of civic officials and their power, but also how they were reliant on public participation in order for their visions for and of the city to materialise. The parade as an index demonstrates democracy at work – how elected officials articulate and engage with their civic responsibility. In the following section, I show how the event organisers of the Manchester Day Parade managed to work productively within these constraints to *realise* a co-production, rather than *make* it.

Co-producing a parade

Walk the Plank was a small public arts charity focused on outdoor event production. They provided a niche service that combined large-scale parade structures, outdoor performance and pyrotechnic firework specialism. They worked across Europe producing outdoor events such as parades, firework displays / fire gardens, civic celebrations and performances. Based in a small office in a converted house in Salford, they were very busy in 2011 and 2012 with major events such as Turku's Opening Ceremony in Finland and build-up events to the London Olympic Games. For them, the Manchester Day Parade was just one of many events.

Manchester City Council was the large, sprawling local government organisation responsible for the physical infrastructure of the city, as well as social, educational and increasingly cultural development. The Major Events team oversaw hundreds of activities over the annual calendar, working primarily with external events providers who produced activities such as the Chinese New Year, Christmas Lights, parades, marathons, festivals and much more. In the years of 2011 and 2012, the Manchester Day Parade was the only event directly commissioned by the Council and championed by two Councillors in the Chief Executive team.

The Major Events team commissioned Walk the Plank to develop a proposal on how to celebrate Manchester Day with a parade. This proposal led to a contract to develop and deliver three consecutive annual celebrations. The parade organisers designed a production strategy which enabled the parade to be planned and developed with community participation. Their independent status as an arts charity also facilitated a spontaneous 'happening' ethic. This flexibility ranged from hiring freelance artists to work with community groups, to developing sections for the parade, to linking together the different parts of the Council from road, litter and infrastructure management teams to community liaison officers and the Councillors themselves. They also brought a creative glamour to the Council and its various sponsors from retail, engineering and property development and services. The most highly valued attribute of Walk the Plank, however, was their ability to respond and adapt to changing circumstances, a process which I argue defines their creative purpose (Symons 2016).

In this organisation three women were critical to the parade formation. The charismatic Director, Liz Pugh,[6] had a performing arts background and strong relationship with the Council's Major Events team. She defined the parade themes each year and negotiated what were at times tricky relationships with senior staff from participating organisations. The Design Co-ordinator, Candida Boyes, had previously worked in theatre and TV production set design, gradually moving into larger mobile settings to provide creative direction. She worked with the artists commissioned by Walk the Plank to support the community groups' parade sections. The Producer, Billie Klinger, had previously worked in the Events team at the Council and also for MIF. She liaised with the Council's civic officials and the production team, as well as project managing the parade.

These experienced women brought a consensus-based, collaborative and productive approach to parade development, protecting the artists' and community groups' freedom to be innovative. They had a very particular approach to creative development, which focused on encouraging ideas to emerge rather than over-dictating the productive process. I discovered their process one bright cold January day in 2012 when they met to discuss the community group submissions for Year Three, themed 'The Sky's the Limit … a celebration of heroic achievements'.

The parade ideas review meeting took place on a Dutch barge in Salford docks. We sat around a large wooden dining table for a marathon six-hour meeting. Over tea and cake, the Walk the Plank trio verbally spun the parade into a shimmering mirage before us. Candida would pick each submission up, outline the idea (written in 'no more than 500 words'), talk about how it might work and which artists could develop the idea into something tangible for parade day. Liz and Billie would pitch in with their ideas, verbally sketching the section out. Shape, colour, movement and sound spun in the air as they worked through the pile of papers. Multiple versions of the parade danced before us. Yet there was no expectation of a final parade looking like the structures imagined in the room. Each idea was anticipated and imagined on its own terms.

During the discussion, potential consequences for the proposed structures were discussed. One application described a Viking ship with shields decorated to celebrate a successful campaign to eliminate a debilitating disease. We imagined the ship in different forms. We discussed practicalities. In the previous year, themed 'A Voyage of Discovery', the lead structure was a huge ship, whose sails had proved challenging in high winds during the parade itself. A different ship might also be 'another nightmare'.

The conversation moved on to a different application, from a community group of older people who posed a risk due to their frailty. Where would the older people sit before the parade? Would they be able to walk the parade route unaided? How could some wheelchairs be decorated to accommodate the less able?

With each idea, the team discussed possibilities for how to develop a parade 'section' to match the idea described by the community group. The options were comprehensively developed but left without conclusion. Intention and consequences were discussed, but there was no finality in the discussion, no decisions on the final design or structure made. Each submission was placed on Yes, No or Maybe piles based on the team's view of their own ability to deliver on the idea and group's expectations, not on a judgment of quality. Then the next form was picked up.

Parade making by the trio from Walk the Plank substantiates the imaginative production suggested by Hastrup (2005) as a succession of imagined scenarios anticipated without becoming expected. 'Society is a suspended form that precipitates particular actions, through which the illusion is gradually *realized*' (Hastrup 2005: 198 her emphasis). Hastrup argues for a dialogue between agency and imagination – where agency is driven by a succession of imagined and anticipated scenarios. She draws a distinction between describing an event and its consequences to argue that creativity resides in the ability to act 'without incorporating an anticipated consequence into the perception of the action' (Hastrup 2005: 201). She states that 'Imagination is what makes present actions meaningful by making anticipation possible ... and also makes the creative agent perceive that intention and consequence are not one and the same' (Hastrup 2005: 204). This avoidance of finality in the early stages was critical to the development of the parade. The anticipation was there, the imagining was there, each section of the parade was created in the room on the barge but there was not a direct and responsive action. The parade organisers as 'creative agents' anticipated the ideas as intentions and possibilities, but did not expect them to emerge as exact manifestations. By the end of the meeting, I emerged blinking in the evening dusk, my head swimming with the glorious spectacle of not just one parade, but many possibilities of the parade.

As Parade Producer Billie Klinger says,

> What's hard is having freedom to put some things together and see what happens [rather than] put things together and make sure that will happen. If you put creative people together ... sow the seeds, stand back, let it happen ... it is a voyage of discovery ... And the more you do, the more you understand: if you make a decision too early, you won't enable that to happen.

This 'holding back' in the co-production of the parade imaginary allowed the parade to develop gradually. As artists were paired with community groups and worked on ideas, the parade possibilities became more focused. Decisions were made on content, colour, materials, participants and movement, which affected the design of the parade sections. Time, weather, the size and height of the workspaces, the flexibility of the materials chosen and many other factors also narrowed the options.

Gradually a 'parade shape' emerged as a 'sculptural form', according to Design Co-ordinator Candida Boyes. She described her role as 'knitting together' the different ideas, encouraging, nurturing and supporting the parade artists and groups to produce parade sections with colour, shape and movement and at a scale clearly visible on the street. Candida dashed around for months in the build-up of the parade, moving between the community groups. She and Billie worked alongside parade artists, choreographers, production staff and project managers. They all worked together solving problems, advising, challenging and encouraging people in the community groups to realise their ideas into something tangible for parade day. An open, discursive approach to developing the ideas was apparent throughout.

For Walk the Plank's Director, Liz Pugh, the parade theme was an 'organising metaphor'. It provided groups with an 'opportunity for imaginative journeying', following their own inspirations and being guided by an artist rather than led by one. She understood the role of her organisation as providing a suitable framework for this process to happen. Her team took pleasure in imagining the parade's eventual constitution, but without expecting it to be that way. They held in tension an open anticipation of *expected* consequences with an anticipation of *possible* consequences to guide their work. This approach contrasts with a directive approach where activities are defined from the outset and then developed based on these definitions. Macdonald's ethnography of the London Science Museum describes how attempts to make a new gallery were hampered by over-control by the development team (Macdonald 2002). By perceiving intention and consequence as separate states, expectations can become more fluid and responsive.

Through my conversations and fieldwork among parade organisers, it became apparent that the parade *emerged*, therefore, as a 'distributed object', constituted of multiple assemblages each with their own characteristics and dynamics, and managed through a combination of highly experienced professionals with a willingness to respond and adapt to rapidly changing circumstances. The final parade that marched down the city centre of Manchester was a realisation, a physical manifestation of the city's relational dynamics at that particular time. When the Parade Director argued that the very fact of walking down the streets in a parade makes a community group a 'celebration of Manchester', she was referring to this realisation.

Green, et al. describe in relation to ICT how Manchester City Council sought to develop networks to stimulate a digital sector in the city (Green, et al. 2005). The independent behaviour of organisations and individuals who established their own activities came as a surprise and also caused some chagrin among Council officials. They wanted to engage with citizens in a proactive manner but they also wanted to retain control over the particulars of that engagement. The authors' analysis holds some remarkable parallels with Council engagement of the Manchester Day Parade participants. The organisational structures of the local authority prohibited or enabled different forms of engagement leading to outsourcing the parade production. Walk the Plank's emergent, open way of parade making allowed the Councillors to construct their version of a Manchester celebration but at the same time gave people in the city an opportunity to realise their own visions of themselves. Each group participated on their own terms with their own understanding and version of what the parade itself meant.

Conclusion: 'the emergent city' – a governance approach?

The Manchester Day Parade was a Council-led project. It was commissioned by two politicians – Councillors – one of whom was so passionate about the event that the words 'Manchester Day Parade' were written in red across his face on the day. They paid parade organisers to work with community groups in the city to bring the parade into being. The parade organisers applied an open and nurturing approach both in communities and in the Council, helping realise the ambitions of the Councillors and working with restrictions of time, funding and bureaucratic obstacles.

Returning to Harvey's (2012) concern with how to organise the city, there is benefit in taking an emergent approach – extrapolating it to another scale to think about how decision makers can allow a city to emerge. Similarly the parade organisers' attitude can inspire those who feel frustrated by intractable urban problems; for the parade makers would not be deterred by anything. Their organising attitude was that problems could and would be surmounted, people's concerns addressed, possible consequences anticipated and mediated. During one particular knotty situation where Walk the Plank's Director was negotiating between several different parties and waiting for approval to move forward in the next phase of parade development, she described her challenge as 'like a log jam'. 'There are lots of logs all jammed together and I keep pulling away logs and nothing is happening. Eventually, I will get the right log out and a whole load will come down at once.' For Liz, the 'logs' were blockages – issues such as waiting to see people, to have the right conversation to make things happen and to get certain people together for the 'decision to be valid'. Parade day was inevitable and her response to problems was to work with them.

As urban decision makers try to fold people's activities into their urban planning processes, they must engage with the messy, complex and conflicting realities of day-to-day city dynamics. These are revealed through detailed ethnography of the organisational processes that shape different aspects of a city. Rather than trying to hold still the rapidly changing, distributed entity that constitutes a city to make decisions, take actions and allocate resources, a nurturing, emergent approach may work better. A responsive and adaptive approach to city development is to let it go: to provide structure and then nurture the emerging entities.

Manchester has an existing emphasis on govern*ance* rather than govern*ment* (Cochrane 1993; Peck and Tickell 1995). City executives have worked for years with large corporates in public–private partnerships developing mutually beneficial aspirations for the city. The city's renaissance can be attributed to the combination of structure and autonomy, to letting a city's potential emerge rather than overly controlling it. However, there is work yet to be done on how to nurture citizens more directly – supporting musicians, artists, community groups and individuals is a tougher nut to crack.

Holding back and allowing a city to emerge is risky for urban decision makers. They are accountable to their citizens, to local companies and organisations, to central government and to their reputation as 'decision makers'. Born's analysis of jazz and other forms of improvised music helps here (Born 2005). She presents jazz as an unusual form of music because its constitution comes from the process of making.

> The jazz assemblage, in contrast, is lateral and processual. Jazz entertains no split between ideal musical object and mere instantiation, no hierarchy between composer as Creator and performer as interpreter of the Word. There is no final, untouchable work that stands outside history. This is not to deny jazz's specific capacity for self-idealization, evident in a pronounced metaphysics of (co-)presence. But jazz's ontology is primarily material and social focused on the movement or oscillation between two phases, two crucibles of creative practice. (Born 2005: 27)

Drawing on Born's argument, city makers' attempts to realise their own particular visions of a city are actually just co-productions running alongside the activities of other urban actors. The City Council as 'Creator' and community members as 'performers' of the 'Word' is no longer an appropriate conceptualisation of urban decision making. Furthermore, as government resources decline, the dynamics of 'who is in charge' becomes increasingly pertinent and the release of control to a more dialectic approach may well come as a welcome relief. However, alongside governments fostering a greater sense of independence, must also be a willingness to reduce attempts at controlling civic expression.

The co-productive process in the development of the parade points to an emphasis on enabling creative activity. Ethnographic analysis of key events co-produced by civic officials and community members provides a process for embracing unintended outcomes. The nurturing emergent parade making process could be developed into a constructive nurturing emergent city making process to address the dichotomous task of both representing the city as democratically appointed officials and enabling and supporting citizens to realise their own ambitions.

Acknowledgements

I would like to thank all the people involved in the making of the Manchester Day Parade for opening up their imaginations with me and sharing their daily lives.

Notes

1 http: //manchesterday.co.uk/. Accessed 9 February 2017.
2 From website: www.manchester.gov.uk/info/500001/supporting_culture_in_manches ter/1594/about_cultural_strategy_team/1. Accessed 9 June 2011.
3 From website: www.marketingmanchester.com/original-modern/peter-saville.aspx. Accessed 4 October 2013.
4 www.marketingmanchester.com/original-modern/peter-saville.aspx.
5 From website: www.bbc.co.uk/news/uk-england-manchester-13829003. Accessed 4 January 2016.
6 These names are provided in agreement with the parade organisers to recognise their contribution to the civic event.

References

Born, Georgina. 2005. "On musical mediation: ontology, technology and creativity". *Twentieth-Century Music* 2 (1): 7–36.
Cochrane, Allan. 1993. *Whatever Happened to Local Government?* Buckingham: Open University Press.
Cochrane, Allan, Jamie Peck, and Adam Tickell. 1996. "Manchester plays games: exploring the local politics of globalisation". *Urban Studies* 33 (8): 1319–1336.
Calhoun, Craig. 2016. "Brexit is a mutiny against the cosmopolitan elite". *New Perspectives Quarterly* 33 (3): 50–58.
Corsín Jiménez, Alberto. 2007. "Introduction: re-institutionalisations". In *The Anthropology of Organisations* (The international library of essays in anthropology), pp. xiii–xxxii. Aldershot: Ashgate.
De Landa, Manuel. 2006. *A New Philosophy of Society: Assemblage Theory and Social Complexity*. London: Continuum.
Fielding, Steven and Duncan Tanner. 2006. "The 'rise of the Left' revisited: Labour Party culture in post-war Manchester and Salford". *Labour History Review* 71 (3): 211–233.
Fletcher Jr, Bill and Fernando Gapasin. 2008. *Solidarity Divided: The Crisis in Organized Labor and a New Path Toward Social Justice*. Berkeley and Los Angeles, California; University of California Press.
Florida, Richard. 2003. *Boho Britain*. London. Demos.
— 2005. *Cities and the Creative Class*. New York: Routledge.
Freedberg, David and Vittorio Gallese. 2007. "Motion, emotion and empathy in esthetic experience". *Trends in Cognitive Sciences* 11 (5): 197–203.
Fry, Kath and Karen Cropper. 2016. *Manchester 1984*. Manchester: Creative Commons.
Gell, Alfred. 1998. *Art and Agency: An Anthropological Theory*. Oxford: Clarendon.
Green, Sarah and Penny Harvey. 1999. "Scaling place and networks: an ethnography

of ICT 'innovation' in Manchester". Internet and Ethnography Conference at Hull, UK.

Green, Sarah, Penny Harvey, and Hannah Knox. 2005. "Scales of place and networks: an ethnography of the imperative to connect through information and communications technologies". *Current Anthropology* 46 (5): 805–826.

Harvey, David. 2012. *Rebel Cities: From the Right to the City to the Urban Revolution.* London: Verso Books.

Hastrup, Kirsten. 2005. "Performing the world: agency, anticipation and creativity". *Creativity and Cultural Improvisation* 44: 5–19.

Hatherley, Owen. 2011. *A Guide to the New Ruins of Great Britain.* London; New York: Verso Books.

Latour, Bruno and Tomás Sánchez-Criado. 2007. "Making the 'res public'". *Ephemera: Theory & Politics in Organization* 7 (2): 364–371.

Leadbeater, Charles. 2009. "Original Modern: Manchester's journey to innovation and growth". National Endowment for Science, Technology and the Arts.

Lefebvre, Henri. 2003 [1970]. *The Urban Revolution.* Trans. Robert Bononno. Minneapolis: University of Minnesota Press.

Macdonald, Sharon. 2002. *Behind the Scenes at the Science Museum.* Oxford: Berg.

Manchester Cultural Strategy Team. 2002. *The Cultural Strategy.* Manchester City Council.

Massey, Doreen. 2011. *World City.* (2nd ed.) Cambridge: Polity.

Navaro-Yashin, Yael. 2002. *Faces of the State: Secularism and Public Life in Turkey.* Princeton, NJ; Oxford: Princeton University Press.

Not Part of the Manchester International Festival. 2007. "Not Part of, History page". http://notpartof.org/history/. Accessed 9 June 2011.

Peck, Jamie and Adam Tickell. 1995. "Business goes local: dissecting the business agenda in Manchester". *International Journal of Urban and Regional Research* 19 (1): 55–78.

Peck, Jamie and Kevin Ward. 2002. *City of Revolution: Restructuring Manchester.* Manchester: Manchester University Press.

Quilley, Stephen. 1999. "Entrepreneurial Manchester: the genesis of elite consensus". *Antipode* 31 (2): 185–211.

— 2000. "Manchester first: from municipal socialism to the entrepreneurial city". *International Journal of Urban and Regional Research* 24 (3): 601–615.

Redhead, Steve. 1997. *Subculture to Clubcultures: An Introduction to Popular Cultural Studies.* Oxford: Blackwell.

Strathern, Marilyn. 1996. "Cutting the network". *Journal of the Royal Anthropological Institute* 2 (3): 517–535.

Symons, Jessica. 2015. "Shaping the flow: ethnographic analysis of a Manchester parade event". *Ethnos* "Anthropology and Festivals": 1–15.

— 2016. "Untangling creativity and art for policy purposes: ethnographic insights on Manchester International Festival and Manchester Day Parade". *International Journal of Cultural Policy*: 1–15.

Tickell, Adam and Jamie Peck. 1996. "The return of the Manchester men: men's words and men's deeds in the remaking of the local state". *Transactions of the Institute of British Geographers* 21 (4): 595–616.

Ward, Kevin. 2003. "Entrepreneurial urbanism, state restructuring and civilizing 'New' East Manchester".

Figure 3.1 Escaping the lounge, Manchester Airport

3

LOUNGE MANCHESTER:
THE NEW POLITICS OF LOUNGIFICATION

Damian O' Doherty

The Escape Lounge

Passengers arriving at the sliding glass door entrance to the new Escape Lounge at Manchester Airport are bathed in a warm ambient glow as they momentarily pause at the threshold to what the architects call the 'feature entrance sequence'. Broken into shards of crystal luminescence by the highly reflective surfaces of polished steel and glass doors, the light also flickers and sparkles in ways that might prompt a certain unease or agitation. Surfaces are being broken up and entities scattered, clear outlines of subjects and objects are giving way, as we enter a more 'plastic' dimension of organisation. 'It's a different world in here, isn't it (?)' Edie, one of the lounge hostesses tells me (or asks) as I take up my seat for the day, next to the television area – or what is known in the formal design literature as 'the snug'. She has just graduated from a personal grooming training programme provided for lounge staff, and she moves gracefully, attentively and with a studied deference. She can fetch you drinks, she explains, or offer advice on the menu. 'You know, we have a Wii game in 'the attic', and free Internet access in the study ... What time does your flight board, Sir?' As you peruse the Escape Lounge, you might catch a glimpse of the ghosts of Sir Richard Leese (the elected leader of Manchester City Council) and Sir Howard Bernstein (Manchester City Council's Chief Executive) reflected in the depths of the surfaces and mirrors that bounce the light around. Or, you will do ... if you have been fully loungified.

Introduction

Based on ethnographic research conducted at the Manchester Airport Group 2009–2012 this chapter follows some of the actors and practices involved in the making of the Escape Lounge. This chapter explores what Pickering (1995) might call a 'mangle of practice' that stretches across a range of disparate times and spaces in which the airport is implicated (Adey 2006, 2009; Fuller and Harley 2004; Schaberg 2012). It deploys the concept 'loungification' that allows analysis to collect a heterogeneous range of materials and practices that extend across the city of Manchester linking up with practices that extend across Europe and even further afield. In following these practices we find no stable producer or consumer that forms the lineaments and co-ordinates of something like an economic 'market', and into which a product or service like the Escape Lounge could be moved (Callon 1998; MacKenzie 2006; Mitchell 1998). Moreover, the lounge does not take place in any discrete space and time or organising – airside in terminal 1 for example. Instead, it remains better understood as one instantiation of a wider movement of loungification. With this concept we become implicated in the enactment of the phenomena, or – rather – we acknowledge what is an inevitable reflexive entanglement in the problematic of study.

There is an important politics to the city here, but one that is easily ignored in most studies of city politics and its organisation. As this chapter shows, the city is being made-over by this loungification – which begins to assume the role of a new political actor, but one not yet fully formed or domesticated within the established institutions and parliamentary forums of city politics (Latour 1993). Values and attitudes are changing, new ways of living are silently taking hold, established power relations, hierarchies and organisational configurations are being destabilised as new lounge expertise are in the ascendency and old skills and knowledge-practices decline. Akin to Sloterdijk's (2014) spheres in the world interior of capital, the lounge is becoming a potent actor and we must learn to negotiate with its practices and demands. This chapter draws out one important feature of this loungification that allows us to see the ties that bind together a range of actors typically positioned in different formal organisations and at different 'levels' or scales of formal institutional politics routinely divided, for example, between the macro and micro. This feature is what is known as the 'Manchester vibe', but to feel this vibe we must re-sensitise our methods and concepts of ethnography so that we can explore dimensions of organising that are prior to such separations.

Ethnographic approach

Two and a half years of ethnographic fieldwork at the Manchester Airport Group opened up the politics of the city only insofar as the ethnographer was prepared to sacrifice and largely forget – or actively forget as Nietzsche (Nietzsche 1967 [1887]) wrote in *The Genealogy of Morals* – an inherited body of knowledge. Entering the field as a 'Professor' from the Business School invited all kinds of projections from management and staff, at times understandably suspicious and at other times invested with appeals to authority (see

O'Doherty 2017: 29–63). I would struggle to articulate a rationale or defence when asked to prove the value of my participation to airport management in terms of 'commercial value', a question that is ever-present during research and is well-known particularly amongst those ethnographers who work in corporate ethnography (Cefkin 2010; Denny and Sunderland 2016). Yet, as I soon discovered, management and other members of organisation were also in search of commercial value, and of its definition, and also perhaps preoccupied with a little anxiety of their own about their capacity to justify minute-by-minute their own net contribution to commercial value or shareholder capital. As the distance between my interlocutors and myself began to diminish I began to experience ever-greater dimensions of complexity associated with the constitutive and reflexive entanglements of ethnography in its object of study. Ethnography is not a way of looking, it's a way of being in the world, or a way of practicing (reproducing and creating) modes of being in the world. This insight was achieved slowly because in the first year it was all too easy to collect ethnographic data as illustrations of evidence of what was already known, but this led to frustration and a sense that the research was inhibited and reductive, missing out on what was happening in the wider 'organisation'. To capture organisation 'as it happens' (Knox, et al., 2015; Schatzki 2006) where more open and expansive or 'enacted' organisation is in process (Mol 2002) demands the relinquishment of established categories of social scientific analysis. Moreover, to extract the specificity of what is happening, or how organisation happens demands a mode of ethnographic conduct that seeks to return to the surface, to the 'pure immanence' (Deleuze 2001) of organisation.

One requires new site-specific concepts for this labour of empirical philosophy. As this chapter progresses the ethnography is worked to assemble and explore a whole series of different actors, agencies, materials and artefacts associated in the construction of the Escape Lounge at Manchester Airport. We will explore some of the origins of the Escape Lounge as we follow a thread that is woven by commercial managers at Manchester Airport, taking us from the practice of completing airport quality service questionnaires to the agency ostensibly responsible for their design and administration head-quartered in the pretty Swiss lakeside town of Lac Leman. We then trace the use that airport management sought to make of geo-demographic consumer data. As we become progressively more entangled in these kinds of materials and their mediated enactment, we lose sight of the big macro actors often presumed to be behind the scenes orchestrating 'local' management actions: neo-liberal capitalism, capitalists, government and political economy. In this conception chief executive officers, business leaders and senior managers are considered to be subordinate to wider system pressures.

As the owners of the airport, the combined authorities of Greater Manchester might appear to evidence the direct implication of politics in economics. This is what traditional MBA syllabi refer to as the 'political context'. Here is where power lies, at the 'top' of society, in roles of responsibility and governance. From this we might deduce that an airport lounge forms part of a political strategy to promote the city of Manchester; the Escape Lounge becomes a vehicle for this, a reflection of 'wider' political ambitions to manage cities as political, economic and cultural phenomena. However, in the ethnography from which this chapter draws we discover that politics and cities are not context or agents, but are also partial outcomes of things that are often deemed so marginal, insignificant and frivolous even (indeed evidence of these things moves fast – following Deleuze (1990) they are on the 'surface' of congealed institutions and their equivalent conceptual baggage) that they are ignored. They are also things that *act*.

Loungification is coined to prevent the splitting of the empirical into conventional dualisms of structure and agency and to sensitise empirical research to things that move 'fast'. Here we begin to trace the actorial status of things like 'Manchester vibe' and thereby show how politics and the State are being reassembled around things like loungers, t-shirts, graphic design and fashion. Power is being mobilised and harnessed around this apparent trivia and insignificance; nor is this just decorative. It is better conceived as constitutive. Hence, this ethnography presents the first speculative account of a new politics of loungification. Whether this means 'the State' is any more relaxed than it was in the past must remain moot, but our ethnographic approach must itself learn to relax and become responsive to matters that neither appear enduring or evanescent, serious or frivolous, high or low. As verb and noun 'loungification' rewires the networks of cause-effect, of actor and acted-upon, to trace a more immanent dimension of city politics and the likely tensions and lines of contestation this engenders. In these ways we might see that not only politics, but the State too, is a 'becoming-vibe' and on that little resembles the body of a leviathan as imagined since Hobbes.

The high street lounge

Up and down the UK a fleet of fashionable lounges are currently being launched. Located in various business parks and 'business centres' these lounges and their promotional websites create the impression of a vibrant and busy world of business and commerce. On the website promoting Media City in Salford Quays, Greater Manchester for example, there are lounges full of people dressed in business suits who are variously captured in poses of studied attention, attending presentations and 'network events', talking on mobile phones, huddling around tables in break-out rooms – presumably in earnest discussion about important business matters – reclining in leather sofas and sitting at desks making use of the digital facilities in the 'post production club'. 'It's a digital space for like-minded creative people and food lovers, with opportunities for private hire and deal-making privacy', reads the website.[1] Not to be outdone, Richard Branson's Virgin group has also been developing the concept, re-lounging the high street retail bank through its network of 'Virgin Money lounges'. Resembling a cross between a cocktail piano bar and a business centre, these lounges are available for drop-in customers and pre-booking private hire. Facilities include complimentary refreshments, a free cash machine, free Wi-Fi connection, iPads, iMacs, phone chargers, TV, newspapers and magazines, and a dedicated children's area complete with books, art materials and a games console.

It seems we may all be sitting in lounges watching 'Friends' sit in their own various lounges creating a vertiginous loop of reflexivity that threatens to materialise some of the most lurid spectacles imagined by Jean Baudrillard. The lounge has found new life in higher education as well. Academics are no longer immune from this viral-like spread of the lounge. A spate of recent developments show that universities are currently transforming libraries and seminar rooms into lounges and various combined study areas/lounges that emphasise informality and casualness. University websites promote campuses using images of a range of lounge spaces and other comfortable areas around university buildings that – variously furnished with couches and bean-bags – appear to be designed for 'relaxing, studying or "just hanging out"'. At the University of Manchester, senior management have recently launched something a little more democratic in the form of its 'Library Lounge'. Incorporating its own branded 'Café@TheLibrary Lounge' this space is being advertised as a new venue where students and faculty are invited to 'unwind, relax and perhaps have something to eat and drink'. The Carol Anne Letheran 'Fireplace Lounge' at the Bronfman Business Library at Montreal's York University, for example, which is devoted to the collection and display of classic management texts, represents the equivalent of a gentlemen's private club or a VIP lounge.

Making the customer: the airport services quality initiative

But how have we come to inhabit the city as a 'lounger'? Who or what is responsible for these spaces? Origin stories are always treacherous but ethnography allows one thread to be followed at the airport. Following the members of the project team working on the Escape Lounge at Manchester Airport I am introduced to people responsible for what is known as 'The ASQ'. The 'Airport Services Quality' initiative is a little-known programme outside of a specialist group of custodians in the aviation industry but which has been cited in a lot of the documentation and project management meetings responsible for the launch and tracking of the design and construction of the Escape Lounge. The ASQ is an international quality assessment regime that draws up league tables of airports against service quality performance (Bezerra and Gomes 2015; Halpern and Graham 2013: 78). It is a vast machine that involves survey techniques, paper and pens, algorithms, software development, award ceremonies, annual conferences, presentations and intellectual property rights.

One morning at the airport I follow Mary, who is responsible for the handing out and completion of the ASQ questionnaire. It is 5.30am and we are handing out questionnaires to passengers milling around the shops and restaurants in the departure terminal. The survey is conducted according to a complex methodology and a set of rules that mean only passengers on particular flights are asked to complete the questionnaire. Mary tells me that the terminal provides no space within which one can easily identify passengers because there are no clearly demarcated departure gates around which passengers gather. She explains that this makes the task of distribution and collection difficult because you can waste a lot of time going up to people who are travelling on an airline or destination that are not part of the sample plan for the day. The people to whom we need to distribute the questionnaires could be anywhere in the space, at the shops, or the adjoining cafes and restaurants. Mary is contracted for four hours of work this morning and so she must focus her efforts efficiently in order to collect the requisite number of completed questionnaires. She asks me to help in the distribution and collection. 'You're not supposed to speak to the passengers and you definitely cannot fill out the form for them even if they ask you'. However, they do need some guidance and instruction, she explains, but it's not clear at what point one is likely to stray into forms of assistance that might actually influence and therefore 'pollute' the data we are trying to collect. These seem to be shaky foundations upon which to build a lounge and its loungers.

The questionnaire is basically composed of thirty-four 'Key Performance Indicators' (KPIs) arranged in the form of a tabular Likert scale tick-box exercise that evaluates each KPI on a range from excellent to poor. These include things like: ground transportation to/from the airport (A); availability of parking facilities (B); value for money of parking facilities (C); the courtesy and helpfulness of inspection (I) and airport staff (R); and the quality of the shopping facilities (V). On one level such exercises might be interpreted as evidence of the disciplinary and 'surveillance society' (Lyon 2001) to which a broad body of work, ranging from studies of 'the mystery shopper' (Ball 2010), financial accountancy (Hoskin and Macve 1986; Robson 1992) the electronic panopticon of call-centre technologies (Bain and Taylor 2000) and techniques of personnel management – including career management (Grey 1994) and performance and appraisal (Townley 1994) – have contributed. However, whilst such techniques and technologies put pressure on management and workers to deliver greater service quality, they also help constitute airport experience in ways that help passengers think of themselves as customers, and more specifically customers of airports. Through such techniques, a customer of the airport is being made, then, at the same time that the airport is being made-over as a service provider or delimited object or space of consumption. We are talking here about airport consumers, not passengers in an airport who consume in its franchised retail outlets. However, the devil, as always, is in the detail. To forge a subject and object of airport consumption is a long, fraught and bewilderingly complex process, and one that is never complete, bearing with it untold consequences and outcomes.

To understand how this questionnaire is made to work we must follow it as it travels in space and time, through airport terminals in Manchester to a data-processing centre in Leeds and on to the offices of a company called 'DKMA'. With its head office in the picturesque Swiss rural hamlet of Gland nestled on the banks of Lac Leman, DKMA might be considered the authors of the ASQ. In tracing these circulations, however, we discover that the questionnaire does far more work than we might imagine and cannot simply be thought of as something that allows Mary to collect data so that airports can be benchmarked in terms of quality. We discover, for example, that it takes considerable time and effort for the questionnaire to stabilise in the form of that object which is routinely handled by Mary and airport customers. For some the ASQ is not just a questionnaire survey, it forms part of a fully-fledged business proposition for DKMA, even an entrepreneurial venture, and possibly a speculation or financial investment. It is, however, for others, a contested object of dubious proprietorial status. There are also some for whom it remains an experiment – of dubious methodological standing – with possibly deleterious consequences for the airport. Senior executives responsible for security or airfield operations, for example, had little time for the ASQ at Manchester Airport Group. Despite their suspicions and protestations, however, it eventually formed part of a wider strategy of airport service quality management at Manchester Airport, advanced by an emerging team of 'commercial management' (O'Doherty 2017: 141–184).

Devising the Escape 'Lounger': geodemographics

If the ASQ is an institutional apparatus responsible for the measurement and promotion of certain kinds of 'quality service' at an airport, members of the project team turn to other resources for help in trying to imagine how to devise and design products and services that might enhance customer experience and service quality.[2] However, even after the commissioning of the design, it appears that one very basic question remains. 'We need to know who are the dinkies[3] and when they travel' declares one of the senior commercial executives at the airport during one meeting. There is a palpable sense of unease in the meeting. Members of the project team are worried that this senior project executive may be getting frustrated. Perhaps the team have not achieved the level of detail and precision he is looking for, and the meeting itself is difficult to pin down or 'minute'. He has forced an interruption and cut across the conversation as he tries, as he says, to 'nail down the specifics'. We need the 'nitty gritty', and much more 'data crunch'. It seems that some of the design proposals are too ambitious. 'We can't get away from the fact that the airport is 80 per cent departing leisure passenger' he continues, 'that is the kind of airport we are. The lion's share of our business is family/leisure and that we are trying to develop a product that has a sense of being *designed just for you*'.

Other people have referred to the passengers at Manchester Airport as 'buckets and spades',[4] and it would seem that there may be some dis-alignment between the aesthetics and design of the lounge and what it is Manchester Airport customers might want or be willing to pay for. In response to these problems the project team has called on the services of the customer insight manager, who has been working on the ASQ survey for the past two years. He has recently begun to promote the use of the Mosaic geodemographic consumer classification system that was in part devised by British sociologist Richard Webber and is now marketed and developed with the global information services group Experian. Drawing on census data and other commercial and non-commercial databases Mosaic applies a form of cluster analysis to derive a spatial distribution, based on postcodes, of patterns of consumption, habits and lifestyle (Harris, et al. 2005). It organises these patterns into 11 distinctive demographic 'groups', which then break down into 61 more finely grained patterns at the level of what it calls 'types' (see Burrows and Gane 2006; Savage and Burrows 2007; cf. Webber 2009). 'Alpha Territory' are one such group, for example, and make up around 10 per cent of the population. The types of people in this group are identified as the 'global power brokers', 'voices of authority', 'business class' and 'serious money'. With this data, characters such as 'Piers and Imogen' begin to circulate in the airport, described as people

> likely to purchase bespoke luxury items such as expensive brands of jewelry, cars, kitchens and furniture. They are most likely to pay for private education and healthcare, and to employ staff to clean their homes, tutor their children and maintain their gardens. If not found on their own private yacht, then they are most likely to be seen in the business or first class cabins of airlines, to holiday in their own foreign property and to enjoy the service of exclusive hotels and restaurants. (Experian 2010: 8)

Representing a far bigger proportion of the airport catchment area than Piers and Imogen are those identified as 'suburban mindsets', people like Surinder and Bina. 'The most common feature of these people is their industriousness', the Experian catalogue informs us. With 'modest incomes', suburban mind-sets are usually in work but have most of their financial wealth invested and tied up with their property, of which they are apparently 'justly proud' (Experian 2010: 8). They also tend to develop and apply their own skills to home improvements and gardening rather than employing specialist trades people. Experian also find from their data that suburban mindsets have 'unpretentious' tastes in consumption and tend to buy popular branded goods from 'nationally known retail chains'.

According to some data circulating during the Escape Lounge project, 'suburban mindsets' is an important category representing a base volume of 644,347 individuals within a 90-minute drive of the airport and representing 12.4 per cent of the overall demographic. Subsequent calculations provide the basis to establish what is called a 'mid-market customer' who is estimated to represent 21 per cent of the catchment area for the airport. Commercial management at the airport also begin to aggregate Mosaic data to establish another category of likely consumer that represents 24 per cent of 'the market' made up of what they call 'upmarket couples', This category includes those classified as 'business class' and 'serious money', but also 'mid-career climb-ers', 'footloose managers' and 'soccer Dads and Mums'. Upmarket couples are therefore a hybrid of Mosaic categories. It is a term taken from Mosaic litera-ture (where it is not used as an aggregator) but then translated and re-applied to generate a more capacious type of lounge customer available to Manchester Airport. A couple called 'Graham and Caroline' also begin to circulate in doc-uments at this time. They are deemed representative of this lounge customer. They are described as people who consider themselves to have 'expensive tastes and are happy to pay more for quality goods. They are interested in the arts and other cultures and prefer to take holidays off the beaten track. Family orientated, they enjoy entertaining at home or pottering round the garden'. They are not, in other words, the same as Piers and Imogen. How Piers and Imogen might feel about being aggregated into a group that includes Graham and Caroline was not available to this ethnography in any direct way, but it would be worthy of further study.

Hence, in designing the lounge, management is trying to forge a product that will appeal to a number of different types of 'market'. But, as can be seen here, they are also trying to extract or construct a hybrid type of customer – a new aggregation of customer that management can be reasonably confident will be mobilised or enticed by a new lounge product. There has never before been an Escape Lounge at the airport, and in this sense there is no established customer base. Management is trying then to both isolate empirically what is a likely to be 'the market' for the lounge, whilst at the same designing the product. And, no product, no market; they are in effect implicated in the construction of a new market. The risk this involves partly explains why, from early on in the project, it was understood that the lounge would be 'zoned' in an attempt to accommodate a range of different submarkets or categories of 'lounger'. As the next section shows, the process of design and construction involves major interventions and constructions of 'lifestyle' that might amount to a veritable experiment in social engineering. What is it that the Escape Lounge offers which is distinctive and new, and which might appeal to people like Piers and Imogen, or Graham and Caroline? Here we find fantasies and imaginaries of the wider city becoming important actors in this social experiment.

Mindsets and the 'Manchester vibe'

Drawing on an internal survey of terminal users commissioned by management, the lounge design team further identify three 'mindsets', which aggregate and cut across the Mosaic types to form different patterns and distributions; these are the 'time to relax' passengers, the 'harried and hassled', and the 'airports are boring' types. Central to the appeal of the lounge was what was deigned to be a 'Manchester Experience' or a 'Manchester vibe'. This was a concept that emerged iteratively and remained throughout the project a source of considerable debate. In comparison to the recently opened Virgin clubhouse at Heathrow airport, members of the project team repeatedly made reference to the fact that the Escape Lounge had to be 'quirky' and 'different', anti-corporate even. Clear resonance might be found here with the City Council's attempt to enact/mobilise a 'Manchester vibe' by circulating as a slogan (often through the city's official marketing agency 'Marketing Manchester') Tony Wilson's famous quip that 'This is Manchester, we do things differently here'.

The final design presentation before drawing up detailed tender documents was hosted in December 2009, during which the architects made an effort to summarise the design. The presentation was dramatic and colourful, each slide packaged together with the strapline 'so this is our Culture & this is how we do it'.

The presentation is replete with a series of images of city centre hotels featuring contemporary-styled lobby areas, public spaces and restaurants. 'They are very similar spaces to the spaces in airports', one of the design consultants tells us. 'We have looked at a whole range of hotels that embrace and celebrate Manchester', including 'hotels that are "true to its roots"'. Apparently, the Lowry art gallery is 'great' for this, the design for which included the commissioning of local art to decorate the space. We are shown images of the Lowry, during which the consultant informs us that we are looking at space that is 'quite dark and moody'. 'You see?' It has more of a 'club-feel to it'. Following this, interior photos of the city-centre Radisson Edwardian hotel are projected. In one image, stripped and polished oak floors lead the eye through what appears to be an endlessly receding series of marble galleries in which deep burgundy red sofa chairs and other contemporary seating has been arranged in ways that form lines and patterns that break up the monotony of a rectangular box. Lit with subdued lighting, a table with immaculate white linen sits centre stage, upon which sit two crystal champagne flutes and a graceful and delicate three-tiered porcelain stand displays a colourful range of petit fours.

At this point, there appears to be some discomfort in the air. The two commercial managers visibly shift in their seats; I wonder if they are thinking about budget and costs but also whether this is consistent with what they imagined to be the look and feel of the lounge and the type of customer they thought possible and commercially viable. Previous meetings have been wrangling over the type of passenger at Manchester Airport and the kind of person that is likely to use the lounge. However, moving on, one of the design team invites the audience to share the club-feel as this has been integrated with a traditional hotel lobby area. 'And it's very Manchester … edgy, different, etc.'. We then look at images of the Hilton. By contrast, she explains, 'You could be in any city … it lacks a Manchester vibe'. She goes on to explain that this Manchester vibe, 'doesn't have to be Happy Mondays on the wall, or a picture of Bez all mong'd out'

In this presentation the design team are reporting a synthesis of various findings, data and input compiled during the initial research for the outline design. An important part of this exercise had involved brainstorm meetings with the airport commercial team, during which a consensus seemed to have emerged that what was wanted was a 'Northern attitude' that would help convey this 'Manchester vibe'. It was this, they believed, that would make Escape distinctive and thereby attract the Alpha Territory people, as well as the Dinkies and people like Surinder and Bina and Graham and Caroline. But how had the commercial team arrived at these concepts, possibilities and insights? In one important meeting the design team had introduced an exercise called 'BRATA', which is an acronym that stands for Benefits – Role – Attitude – Territory – Attribute. Designed to encourage free-associative thinking and the creation of concepts, it was during this meeting that thinking about the lounge had found expression in terms such as 'experience' and 'vibe'.

The design specialists inform members of the wider project team that BRATA is a methodological tool to encourage and 'free up' thinking in a way that resembles other popular tools of 'imaginization' (Morgan 1986). BRATA invites members of the airport management team to think of the lounge in terms of its 'Benefits' and 'Role', its 'Attitude', 'Territory' and 'Attribute'. As the exercise begins, the architects find they have to provide considerable explanation and encouragement to help their client team apply these methods.

When discussion turns to 'Attribute' the architects try to explain that this means addressing 'What is the clearly identifiable *signature* or *character* of the Escape Lounge?' The lead BRATA consultant tells us that he is looking for a 'word' or 'vision'. 'Is it a clubhouse, or an informal, 'chilled', relaxed space, he asks, or do you want 'an energised feel?'. 'Yes', one of the commercial team responds, 'but in a Northern way'. Discussion then proceeds about what this 'Northern' is. Is it Manchester? The North-West? Or is it also Yorkshire? What about Scotland, 'that is also Northern' one of the commercial team adds, and 'there's a good catchment area there for our passengers'.

With all this discussion and free-associative work, it is difficult to keep up. The architect tries to summarise. 'So, is it like the Virgin lounge, but more true to its roots?' The senior project manager proffered an equally valid summary when he declared in a somewhat ironic comment following the conclusion of the meeting that the key attribute of the lounge was a 'gritty Virgin'.

There is now a 'concept' for the lounge – 'more true to its roots' or a 'gritty Virgin' it is never made clear – which the architects translate into a series of outline designs for the lounge presented during the meeting in December 2009. The final report prepared for this meeting concludes that there are 'several key spatial elements and devices with an Escape Lounge' (cf. Callon, et al. 2007; Marres and Lezaun 2011; McFall 2009). Above all, we are told, 'The Escape Lounge should not be fussy, cluttered or irrational, nor should it be too hard or soulless'. The accompanying workbook describes the proposal as 'a bold response and confident visual aesthetic', and details each of the zones in the lounge. There is 'a reception', 'the deli/bar', a 'den' ('akin to a members club or smart hotel lounge area'), the 'study', and 'the attic'. The attic, for example, is described as a 'fun space for both adults and children! This facility truly reflects the Escape brand – to be different and fun … in a grown up manner'. This is where we will eventually find a Wii play station and a 'giant' Scalextric racing-track and where 'there are more vivid colours and graphics displayed to subtly portray a chilled out and fun space'. A 'vapour trail' theme is also picked out for us by the design team, which we are told will inform the shape and look of the feature walls and ceiling; this is important because it 'is supposed to contrast with "daily life in a box"'.

In this report the architects show how each zoning will appeal to what had been earlier identified as the three main mindsets. The report includes images of Piers and Imogen, and Graham and Caroline, with accompanying text that explains specific design features and how they are likely to stimulate and arouse various desires. Escape 'calms and services' those 'harried and hassled', for example, by features such as 'The welcome', which offers – as described in the form of a bullet point list: 'Calming straight away. Luggage taken care of. Warm, friendly greeting. A quick tour of the lounge to set you at ease'. The deli and bar area is designed as a place to 'get away from the crowds and sit with your family and wait to be served'. For those who are 'bored with the airport', the deli/bar area is being designed in a slightly different way where it will be 'not just the place to collect your food – but a place for entertainment in itself'.

The BRATA exercise is clearly not the origin of the concept of a 'Manchester vibe', and nor does it provide a method in which this vibe could be translated into a visual aesthetic and set of allied experiences. So, where might one find an illustration or experience of this Manchester vibe? Who are its spokespersons and its delegates? Who has the legitimate authority to decide what counts as the Manchester vibe? As I pursue these questions, I follow a trail that takes me into the hallowed chambers of city hall and its politics.

City politics and the 'Manchester family'

During the project, senior executives at the airport had encouraged me to explore the work of an agency called 'Marketing Manchester'. This is one of a number of different quasi-public institutions in Manchester that form part of what is known amongst some students of city politics as 'the Manchester family', which also includes agencies such as MIDAS (Manchester's Inward Investment and Development Agency) and New Economy (Headlam 2014). Charged with responsibility for the promotion of the city on a national and international stage, the publications and activities of Marketing Manchester prove instructive. Their highly stylised publications and promotional material are full of the language of creativity, energy, vibe and spirit – albeit not without criticism from within the marketing industry (Sarbutts 2011). These apparent virtues have been aggregated into the marketing strap line 'Manchester: Original Modern', a phrase that (according to their 'Original Modern' e-book) explains Manchester's spirit, its indefatigable energy for progress and change, that 'do something' attitude, that desire to be different that always has and always will exist within the City (see also Introduction and ch 2, this volume).

This chimed with a whole series of public documents in circulation including the City Centre Strategic Plan 2009–2012 produced by Manchester City Council's 'City Centre Regeneration Team'. Here the authors write that the image we have of the city will have been formed 'through quintessentially Mancunian bands such as The Fall, Happy Mondays, The Smiths, New Order, Ting Tings and Elbow – or through enjoying the city's often edgy club scene' (MCC 2009: 13). It was during this stage of the research that I was told the airport is effectively Sir Richard Leese's (the elected City Council leader) and if I wanted to understand the role of the airport in the wider strategic shaping of Manchester as a city I should speak to him and Sir Howard Bernstein, the Chief Executive of Manchester City Council.

The Chief Executive emerges from behind his desk and walks towards me; dressed in black and wrapped up in his characteristic thick black neck scarf, despite the heat pumping from the radiators. He appears smaller and more vulnerable than I had imagined. He smiles. Pale thin fingers. Handshake. He gestures and I am invited to take a seat. I sink into a brown leather Queen Ann style armchair. We lounge, and tea is served. 'How is the airport?' he asks me. This charismatic epicentre of 'politics' in the city is gracious and unassuming. Following the exchange of pleasantries I begin to ask my questions, opening with a broad one: 'What is the importance of the airport to the economic ambitions you have for the region?' It is important, he tells me. I have to elaborate. 'I am interested in the new make-over of the airport, particularly the construction of the new Escape Lounge ... I want to know about the way Manchester and particularly this thing the 'Manchester Experience' has become an instrument or component of commercial endeavour in the airport. What is the role of the City Council in shaping this object? How do you in your position influence the way Manchester, the Manchester Experience, is developed and taken up in the airport?'

At this point the Chief Executive leaves the room and returns with an armful of books: *The Mancunian Way* (Price 2002); *Manchester Forward* (Bramley and Page 2009); *Original Modern* (Creative Concern 2009), published in collaboration with 'Marketing Manchester'; and *Manchester: Shaping the City* (MCC 2004), published by the Royal Institute of British Architects in collaboration with 'Manchester City Collaboration'. As he sits down again I flick through the pages and find a smorgasbord of publicity images and photographs, renovated city centre districts, cafes and bars, clubs, art, music, all showcasing and promoting the city of Manchester. Alongside marketing copywriters these publications contained text and images from commissioned artists and writers once considered counter-culture and certainly 'fringe' and avant-garde in terms of popular tastes and fashions. They are very similar to the PowerPoint presentation slides that the architects have been presenting during the Escape Lounge project. Here I am at the presumed centre of power, the apex of decision making in the North-West economy. Yet I am led back to texts and images that are sourced elsewhere and which circulate in ways that cannot be explained in simple hierarchical and linear terms. Our meeting lasts little more than thirty minutes. He is a busy man and I leave.

Written by graduates of business schools and degree programmes upon which I had taught, I was seeing the uncanny return of teaching and study to which I was a contributor. Trying to find a clear demarcation of cause and effect or to isolate and distinguish a source for something like the 'Manchester vibe' is a problem that finds itself entangled with the problem of identifying a clear separation of State and civil society. In this regard, it is something of a fallacy to say that it is Sir Richard Leese's airport. Strictly the owners are the people of Manchester, it is a public asset. And there is no place or office at which we can find 'the State', where we might find the architects of the city or the strategic visionaries of commercialisation at the airport. The local state is enacted and produced through these very activities, building airports, constructing lounges, circulating documents, economic reports, local newspaper editorials and publishing texts. We can also find the local state in the writings of Cath Staincliffe, for example, commissioned to write for *The Mancunian Way*, where she describes the regenerated Northern Quarter of Manchester in ways that implicate the State in activities to which official representatives might balk:

> Beyond here stretches the northern territories, poor, flat lands running up to the hills of Oldham and Rochdale. The wrong side of the tracks. Northern Quarter – time as this was a sorry place; neglected, low rents, vacant lets. The warren of streets and crumbling buildings offered a whiff of opportunity to entrepreneurs, specialists, idealists, fanatics, desperadoes, collectors, revels, pioneers. Risky business. Fashionable now. The edge of town, spitting distance. Des Res. Though there's still an edge. (Staincliffe 2002: 130)

Writing in a typical Ellroy-esque style, Staincliffe also invites us to think how the State stretches into the 'wrong side of the tracks', the 'northern territories'. Here it begins to fray, immersed in a terrain of inversions and reversals in which the once counter-culture becomes the dominant culture (see also chs 4, 8 and 9, this volume). Lemm Sissay, Peter Saville and the DJ Dave Haslam are amongst some of the other former counter-culture characters assembled and mobilised to help articulate Manchester as the 'original modern' city.

If the State is being re-forged through the lounge, then Manchester too is being made over. Interestingly, the period of cultural vitality to which these texts refer reflects a period of time marked by the transition from post-punk 'Manchester' to the far more self-consciously styled *second generation* of 'Madchester'. This was also a time of local Labour Party transition as 'effective control was established at the centre by a younger cohort of 'new realist' politicians [Stringer, Bernstein, Leese] in place of the earlier old Labour generation' (Robson 2002: 36). Patronising the changing fashions of newly emergent pop-culture, and promoting its creativity and urban sensibility, helped provide an important resource through which this new rising cadre of politicians in Manchester promoted a new image of the city. As Manchester became an object of greater self-conscious design and promotion, so too did the new local Labour Party as it sought to partner new private capital and post-industrial enterprise in its efforts to manage and maintain 'the city'.

Conclusion: the loungification of society

The double articulation of city and politics – new image politics, new image city – marks out a space that we might want to call a wider 'cultural politics', and one that has been self-consciously fashioned and harnessed in part for the purpose of attracting investment capital to the city (Cochrane, et al. 1996; Deas 2014; Symons ch 2, this volume; Quilley 2000). But this is a difficult and somewhat unstable assemblage made up of the constant circulation of things like paper questionnaires, Pearson statistical correlation techniques, PowerPoint presentations, fashion magazines, methods and coaching to inspire creative management, and a whole panoply of materials synthesised in the construction and design of the lounge – including various metals and fabrics, Irish bog oak, RSG structural supports, plaster, paint and glue. Some of these elements are themselves dogged by forces of disorder and decay – at one end of the traditional dualism questionnaires go missing, or get filled in incorrectly, whilst at the other, local state politics gets extended through avant-garde art and other practices that might threaten the sobriety and seriousness upon which such institutions have historically relied (O'Doherty 2017: 185).

To what extent the design of the Escape Lounge is held together by the achievement of a 'Manchester vibe' is difficult to establish, but what is certain is that the lounge provides a vehicle through which the elements that form the polarities of the traditional dualism in social scientific research get 're-mangled' (cf. Pickering 1995). Here, the dualism which posits a 'macro' against a 'micro' becomes subsumed by a more unstable amalgam of practices out of which clearly demarcated polarities struggle to emerge. We have seen how state patronage of this 'vibe', for example, is extended and elaborated through the micro-practices of image generation and reproduction, and the circulation of books and text, all of which might expose 'the State' to greater contingency and fragility as it risks an overstretch across complex capillary-like network of practices and materials. Cultivating association with a wider network of artistic and creative practice in Manchester, for example, might well animate energies and activities that could prove difficult to contain, for which surprising and unforeseen consequences might follow. 'Gunchester' T-shirts that mimic the official 'I [heart] Manchester', for example, might give licence to values and attitudes that might trouble the sobriety of the State and valorise things like the decadent lounger or a fashionable anti-establishment nihilism. Drawing on things signalled in the discourse of 'northern territories' and the 'edgy club scene', for example, was not without a certain anxiety and apprehension amongst members of the lounge design team. They worry about the effects of free drink, for example, or what might happen if a flight is delayed and the airport is left with a group of 'tired' travellers who refuse to leave the lounge – 'Bez and all mong'd out', perhaps. How we are to lounge, then, or how we are to lounge well in these spaces, becomes a problem of training and discipline, but one that will remain entangled in the generation of new resistances and what Foucault (1980) once called the 'intransigence' of the will.

The work of people like Mitchell (1991; 2002; 2006), Taussig (1997), and Navaro-Yashin (2009) has helped to show how 'the State' is better treated as an on-going and contingent practical accomplishment immanent to a whole range of materials and artefacts, embodiments and affective imaginaries. Despite an emerging critique that the Manchester city-region growth strategy reflects a 'post-political' mode of governance (Deas 2014; MacLeod 2011; Swyngedouw 2009), we can add to this work by extending our treatment of politics to include consideration of what might appear to be the humble space of an airport departure lounge. However, if we were to deploy established categories and definitions of politics and the State, studies of cities are likely to miss this politics or dismiss it too quickly as inconsequential. In tracing the contours of an emerging loungification we are given chance to consider the possibility that we are entering a period of what we might best describe as a state-becoming-vibe, defined in part by the 'Manchester vibe', but it is partly unruly and its consequences uncertain.

Notes

1 http://thelanding.org.uk/our-facilities/the-landing-post.aspx. Accessed 10 December 2013.
2 In fact, DKMA do provide managerial consultancy that seeks to help airport management secure ASQ improvement. Both trainer and judge, this places DKMA in a uniquely powerful position.
3 'Dinkies' is a colloquial marketing term for couples with 'Double INcomes and No KIds'.
4 A shared transgression was frequently indulged amongst management at the airport, particularly in the use of the term 'buckets and spades' to describe passengers. That I was able to hear the use of this term was some indication of my growing nativity in the airport.

References

Adey, Peter. 2006. "Airports and air-mindedness: spacing, timing and using the Liverpool Airport, 1929–1939". *Social & Cultural Geography* 7 (3): 343–363.
— 2009. "Facing airport security: affect, biopolitics, and the preemptive securitisation of the mobile body". *Environment and Planning D: Society and Space* 27 (2): 274–295.
Bain, Peter and Phil Taylor. 2000. "Entrapped by the 'electronic panopticon'? Worker resistance in the call centre". *New Technology, Work And Employment* 15 (1): 2–18.
Ball, Kirstie. 2010. "Workplace surveillance: an overview". *Labor History* 51 (1): 87–106.
Bezerra, George C.L. and Carlos F. Gomes. 2015. "The effects of service quality dimensions and passenger characteristics on passengers' overall satisfaction with an airport". *Journal of Air Transport Management* 44: 77–81.

Bramley, Warren and Ra Page. 2009. *Manchester Forward*. Manchester: Marketing Manchester.

Burrows, Roger and Nicholas Gane. 2006. "Geodemographics, software and class". *Sociology* 40 (5): 793–812.

Callon, Michel. 1998. *The Laws of the Markets*. Oxford: Blackwell.

Callon, Michel, Yuval Millo, and Fabian Muniesa. 2007. *Market Devices*. (Sociological Review monographs). Oxford: Blackwell.

Cefkin, Melissa (ed). 2010. *Ethnography and the Corporate Encounter: Reflections on Research in and of Corporations* (Studies in Public and Applied Anthropology; Vol. 5). New York: Berghahn Books.

Cochrane, Allan, Jamie Peck, and Adam Tickell. 1996. "Manchester plays games: exploring the local politics of globalisation". *Urban Studies* 33 (8): 1319–1336.

Creative Concern. 2009. *Original Modern*. Manchester: Manchester City Council.

Deas, Iain. 2014. "The search for territorial fixes in subnational governance: city-regions and the disputed emergence of post-political consensus in Manchester, England". *Urban Studies* 51 (11): 2285–2314.

Denny, Rita Mary and Patricia Sunderland, eds. 2016. *Handbook of Anthropology in Business*. Abingdon, Oxon: Routledge.

Deleuze, Gilles. 1990. *The Logic of Sense*. Trans. Mark Lester with Charles Stivale. London and New York: Continuum.

— 2001. *Pure Immanence: A Life*. Trans. Anne Boyman. New York: Zone Books.

Experian. 2010. *Optimise the Value of Your Customers and Locations, Now and in the Future*. Nottingham; Edinburgh; London: Experian.

Foucault, Michel. 1980. *Power/Knowledge: Selected Interviews and Other Writings, 1972–1977*. New York: Pantheon.

Fuller, Gillian and Ross Harley. 2004. *Aviopolis: A Book About Airports*. London: Black Dog Publishing.

Grey, Christopher. 1994. "Career as a project of the self and labour process discipline". *Sociology* 28 (2): 479–497.

Halpern, Nigel and Anne Graham. 2013. *Airport Marketing*. Abingdon, Oxon: Routledge.

Harris, Richard, Peter Sleight, and Richard Webber. 2005. *Geodemographics, GIS and Neighbourhood Targeting*. West Sussex: Wiley.

Headlam, Nicola. 2014. "Liverchester/Manpool? The curious case of the lack of intra-urban leadership in the twin cities of the North-West". In *European Public Leadership in Crisis?*, J. Diamond and J. Liddle, eds. pp. 47–61. Emerald Group Publishing Limited. Published online: 20 October 2014 http://dx.doi.org/10.1108/S2045-794420140000003012.

Hoskin, Keith W. and Richard Macve. 1986. "Accounting and the examination: a genealogy of disciplinary power". *Accounting, Organizations and Society* 11 (2): 105–136.

Knox, Hannah, Damian O'Doherty, Theo Vurdubakis, and Christopher Westrup. 2015. "Something happened: spectres of organization/disorganization at the airport". *Human Relations*, 68 (6), 1001–1020.

Latour, Bruno. 1993. *We Have Never Been Modern*. Cambridge, MA: Harvard University Press.

Lyon, David. 2001. *Surveillance Society: Monitoring Everyday Life*. Buckingham: Open University Press.

MacKenzie, Donald. 2006. *An Engine, Not a Camera: How Financial Models Shape Markets*. Cambridge, MA: MIT Press.

MacLeod, Gordon. 2011. "Urban politics reconsidered: growth machine to post-democratic city?" *Urban Studies* 48 (12): 2629–2660.

Marres, Noortje and Javier Lezaun. 2011. "Materials and devices of the public: an introduction". *Economy and society* 40 (4): 489–509.

MCC. 2004. *Manchester: Shaping the City*. Manchester: RIBA/MCC.

MCC. 2009. *A Strategic Plan for Manchester City Centre 2009-2012*. Available at http://cityco.com/city-centre-strategic-plan-2009-2012/. Accessed 23 May 2014.

McFall, Liz. 2009. "Devices and desires: how useful is the 'new' new economic sociology for understanding market attachment?" *Sociology Compass* 3 (2): 267–282.

Mitchell, Timothy. 1991. "The limits of the State: beyond statist approaches and their critics". *The American Political Science Review*: 77–96.

— 1998. "Fixing the economy". *Cultural Studies* 12 (1): 82–101.

— 2002. *Rule of Experts: Egypt, Techno-Politics, Modernity*. Berkeley: University of California Press.

— 2006. "Society, economy, and the State effect". In *The Anthropology of the State*. Aradhana Sharma and Akhil Gupta, eds. pp. 169–186. Malden, MA; Oxford: Blackwell.

Mol, Annemarie. 2002. *The Body Multiple: Ontology in Medical Practice*. North Carolina: Duke University Press.

Morgan, Gareth. 1986. *Images of Organization*. Beverly Hills: Sage Publications.

Navaro-Yashin, Yael. 2009. "Affective spaces, melancholic objects: ruination and the production of anthropological knowledge". *Journal of the Royal Anthropological Institute* 15 (1): 1–18.

Nietzsche, Friedrich. 1969 [1887]. *On the Genealogy of Morals*. Trans. Walter Kaufmann and R.J. Hollingdale. New York: Random House.

O'Doherty, Damian. 2017. *Reconstructing Organization: The "Loungification" of Society*. London: Palgrave Macmillan.

Pickering, Andrew. 1995. *The Mangle of Practice: Time, Agency, and Science*. Chicago: University of Chicago Press.

Price, Jane (ed). 2002. *The Mancunian Way*. Manchester: Clinamen Press.

Quilley, Steven. 2000. "Manchester first: from municipal socialism to the entrepreneurial city". *International Journal of Urban and Regional Research* 24 (3): 601–615.

Robson, Brian. 2002. "'Mancunian ways: the politics of regeneration'". In *City of Revolution: Restructuring Manchester*. J. Peck and K. Ward, eds. pp. 34–49. Manchester: Manchester University Press.

Robson, Keith. 1992. "Accounting numbers as 'inscription': action at a distance and the development of accounting". *Accounting, Organizations and Society* 17 (7): 685–708.

Sarbutts, Nigel. 2011. "Muddled Marketing Manchester: brand alert communications intervention". Accessed 21 April 2014.

Savage, Mike and Roger Burrows. 2007. "The coming crisis of empirical sociology". *Sociology* 41 (5): 885–899.

Schaberg, Christopher. 2012. *The Textual Life of Airports: Reading the Culture of Flight.* London: Continuum.

Schatzki, Theodore R. 2006. "On organizations as they happen". *Organization Studies* 27 (12), 1863–1873.

Sloterdijk, Peter. 2014. *In the World Interior of Capital: For a Philosophical Theory of Globalization.* Cambridge: Polity Press.

Staincliffe, Cath. 2002. "Northern Quarter". In *The Mancunian Way.* J. Price, ed. pp. 130–139. Manchester: Clinamen Press.

Swyngedouw, Erik. 2009. "The antinomies of the postpolitical city: in search of a democratic politics of environmental production". *International Journal of Urban and Regional Research* 33 (3): 601–620.

Taussig, Micheal T. 1997. *The Magic of the State.* New York: Routledge.

Townley, Babara. 1994. *Reframing Human Resource Management: Power, Ethics and the Subject at Work.* London: Sage.

Webber, Richard. 2009. "Response to 'The coming crisis of empirical sociology': an outline of the research potential of administrative and transactional data". *Sociology* 43 (1): 169–178.

PART II

REALISING URBAN SPACES

Figure 4.1 Negotiating public and private spaces in Manchester's Gay Village

4

UNDER THE SURFACE OF THE VILLAGE: PUBLIC AND PRIVATE NEGOTIATIONS OF URBAN SPACE IN MANCHESTER

Michael Atkins

Introduction

There is a risk that any form of city imaging can destroy its soul. The city is commodified, its form and spirit remade to conform to market demands, not residents' dreams. (Holcomb 1999: 69)

Between 2009 and 2014 I conducted ethnographic fieldwork with men who used the Manchester Gay Village. Prior to and during the early years of my research, I had worked as a street-based outreach worker delivering housing support and sexual health services to men in and around the streets and towpaths of the village, with the charity 'The Blueroom'. The focus of this work had been men aged 16–25 who came to the area to 'do business', but my work also brought me into contact with men of all ages who 'cruised' the area for fun. These colloquial expressions described various exchanges of sex, intimacy, money, goods and services that, although being part of the gay community and Gay Villages for many years, I had been completely oblivious to. These activities were usually conducted discreetly, involving ambiguous verbal and nonverbal communication. They formed part of everyday relationships, movements and social rituals of those involved, yet they were not explicitly visible to the many others that used the village.

The Manchester Gay Village city zone includes a stretch of the Rochdale canal along the well-known Canal Street, three parallel streets adjoining alleyways, and a small urban green called Sackville Gardens. During my research, I would often stand at the edge of the village where Canal Street meets Minshull Street, a main road into the city centre. This vantage point provided a good view of the row of brightly lit bars. It was also the point where the towpath of the canal diverged from street level and descended into a series of tunnels that provided discreet cover for men seeking anonymous sexual encounters with one another. The 'working lads' whom I had met through my outreach experience would often wait at this point, being able to keep an eye out for regular punters coming down the street and catch the eye of others going down into the cruising area. Although they would drink and socialise during their visits to the village and the canal, their ultimate objective was always to make money, get drinks or find a place to stay. Emulating the strategies of these men, I would wait at the top of the street. I knew it was at these key points I would always run into someone I knew. I had learned a way of seeing the village and recognising movements and activities that just a few years before had been totally invisible to me.

Often called 'the gay capital of the north' Canal Street sits on a raised canal bank. At night the many bars and street lights are reflected in the dark glassy water. Rainbow flags and images of naked male torsos line the windows of the drinking venues that dominate the street. Traditional looking British pubs stand alongside glass-fronted dance bars with neon signs and titles proclaiming their open-minded credentials. In one bar, a large billboard advertises the LGBT (Lesbian, Gay, Trans and Bisexual) Foundation displaying the message: 'We're here if you need us'. Tucked along the back streets is a hotchpotch of diverse venues, including a quirky tearoom, multiple taxi ranks and take out joints and two male only venues. These dim, windowless, basement bars have a more sleazy edge, advertising underwear nights and playing porn above the bar, safely out of sight of passing tourists. The small urban green of Sackville Gardens bears markers of a 'gay history': a memorial flame dedicated to victims of the HIV and AIDS epidemic that ravaged the male gay community in the 1980s and 1990s, and a brass figure of the scientist Alan Turing on one of the benches, his left hand holding the cyanide-laced apple which killed him.[1] The village has a public reputation or 'image' as an area where alternative gender identities, sexual orientations and lifestyles are celebrated. This reputation has been produced and reproduced through images and stories deployed locally and in wider marketing and administrative strategies of the city such as tourist maps and policing. The 'Manchester Gay Village' is one of the 'most visible compact and gentrified gay spaces in the UK' (Binnie and Skeggs 2004: 48). It has featured on national television shows, most notably the *Queer as Folk* fictional series about gay men in the city,[2] but also more mainstream soap operas such as *Coronation Street*.

Although its gay credentials were proclaimed clearly, at weekends people of all sexual orientations flooded into the few streets and alleyways around Canal Street to enjoy the twenty-four-hour weekend night life and party atmosphere. Above street level, former warehouses were converted into office buildings and expensive apartments as part of high-end accommodation which was built in the 1990s after the area's reputation as 'Gay Village' grew. The influx of non-LGBT residents and partygoers tested the limits of the area's reputation for permissiveness, tolerance and sexual liberation. More overt expressions of public sexuality and the alternative commerce of men 'doing business' were not recognised in the contemporary Gay Village despite their historical significance and on-going occurrence. Public spectatorship made the village a widely recognisable place that attracted men who 'cruised' the village looking for sex with other men, and those who visited the village to 'do business'. The histories and continued use of the area as a place for cruising and business were less publicly known and evaded formal articulation in maps and written gay histories. The village known by the men I was working with was one of glances, repetitive patterns of walking and waiting. The lives of the lads 'doing business' were particularly beset with periods of depression, violence, drug and alchol use which were interwoven with their involvement in sex work. The details of their stories and the challenges and risks of their lives were not visible in the neatly packaged brochures and gay press that idealised the Gay Village as a prized jewel in Manchester's cosmopolitan crown.

I focus here on how certain kinds of images and stories were mobilised by communities, city administrators and marketers to form a totalising imaginary of 'city zones' such as Manchester's Gay Village. These images concealed the lived experiences of many and prevented an appreciation of the dangers and affective realities of such users of urban space.

Ethnographic approach

During twelve months of ethnographic fieldwork, I conducted a number of formal and semi-structured journey-based interviews with key informants. The purpose of these trips was to explore their patterns of movement, the things that they noticed about the areas we walked and to share memories and opinions. During our time together we made recordings, took photographs using my phone camera, sketched and made notes. The resulting photographs, drawings, testimony and ethnographic reflections were layered and ordered into narrative sequences that described memories, feelings and the rhythms that dominated their lives. The use of visual methods and particularly drawing allowed us to incorporate aspects of their visual worlds, interiority and memories into these ethnographic stories. Anthropologists have depended a great deal on conversational interviews to address the inaccessible aspects of culture, which presents a methodological paradox in trying to access and convey through spoken words that which can 'only be lived but never thought and [is] in principal incapable of verbalisation' (Schultz 1932: 52 in Throop 2005: 502). The visual negotiation of 'that certain look' described in cruising encounters (Teunis 2001) and by Turner (2003) in *Backward Glances* would suggest a more nuanced examination of the way men see and recognise one another's desire. Such unarticulated qualities of life require the use of more evocative, multi-dimensional and sensuous expressions than the realist documentary conventions of anthropology permit (Crapanzano 2004;

Edwards 1999: 54). The use of conventional anthropological photography and film presented a number of practical and ethical problems in the context of my research. Many of the lads were suspicious of photography, seeing it as a form of surveillance and fearing the potential social, legal and personal consequences of being publicly identified as 'doing business'. In the case of men cruising, the use of photography presented this and other challenges. Those men willing to consent to be photographed whilst cruising were usually wishing to indulge in fetishist exhibitionism, and few men were willing to be fully photographed; they were only willing to display their bodies or genitalia. This would have changed the focus of my research from those men who wanted to cruise discreetly to those who sought certain kinds of exposure as a form of sexual pleasure.

The combinations of images and text in these ethnographic stories contrasted with other combinations of image and text used in tourism literature, economic strategies and by the police to characterise and manage the Gay Village. In the following, I will describe how certain aspects of gay communities and spaces are mobilised to suit the objectives of particular social movements and economies of the city. I will then show a story of the village produced in collaboration with Peter, a nineteen-year-old man who 'did business'. By showing these two very different ways of imaging and imagining the Gay Village, I wish to demonstrate the potential of immersive anthropological fieldwork for revealing insights and stories which upset master narratives that dominate the way parts of the city are perceived.

A history of the 'Gay Village'

Prior to the 1990s there were a number of different bars frequented by gay men and women in locations all over the city centre (Binnie and Skeggs 2004). There was no 'Gay Village' or an equivalent; however, the area around Canal Street had a reputation as a place of sexual permissiveness. The decline of the cotton industry and the advent of more efficient ways of transporting goods at the turn of the century led to the disuse of industrial buildings and the canal network infrastructure. Many buildings along Canal Street were abandoned by the 1950s. Sackville Park was overgrown and the canal that stretched from the village in either direction was full of pitch-black turns, intersected with alleyways and patches of waste ground. The water channel had dried up and parts were built over. The dim gas-lit streets and the proximity to road and rail links made the area ideal for the clandestine activities of 'queers', prostitutes and their punters, and criminal gangs. Pubs in the area, where frosted glass and low lighting concealed their interiors, were not exclusively gay but frequented by all manner of colourful characters, outsiders and crooks.

Despite the legalisation of homosexuality in 1967, James Anderton, a Christian lay preacher and Manchester's chief constable between 1976 and 1991, targeted gay people as part of a moral crusade to 'clean up' the city, increasing patrols and raiding venues. He infamously described gay men, prostitutes and drug users with HIV as 'swirling in a cesspit of their own creation' (Clarity 1987). Anderton was frequently criticised for his heavy-handedness, religious moralising and open homophobia.[3] During this period, gay people increasingly focused on Canal Street, since prostitution and gang culture had reduced in the area. Ironically Anderton's crusade provided a soli-darity, safety and greater concentration of gay people, which was critical to the development of the Gay Village (Taylor, et al. 1996: 184).

At the same time, gay community groups were lobbying for greater rec-ognition by the City Council, which became the first UK Council with an advisory committee on LGBT issues, support for same-sex marriage, and opposition to the controversial 1988 section 28 laws, leading to their repeal in 2000. In 1990 'Manto', a shortening of the phrase 'Manchester tomorrow', was the first bar on Canal Street to have large glass windows – a self-conscious gesture by owners Carol Ainscow and Peter Dalton that openly advertised the sexuality of its patrons. As Binnie and Skeggs recount: 'The architectural design was a queer visual statement: 'We're here, we're queer ... so get used to it. It was a brick, glass and mortar refusal to hide anymore, to remain underground and invisible' (2004: 48).

In her study of Toronto's Gay Village, Nash (2006) argues that gay social spaces are subversions of societal norms through a visible collective habita-tion, appropriation and territorialisation of otherwise fluid urban spaces. She suggests that Gay Villages emerged globally from the 1960s to 1980s with 'collective enactments' of gender between otherwise diverse, queer individu-als who had been thrown into physical proximity due to the economic and social hardships they faced (Nash 2006). The clustering of gay venues and community groups in certain neighbourhoods provided an enclave, a physi-cal centre of safety from where gay men, lesbians and their allies were able to strengthen their political and economic position, foster a sense of community and work toward public acceptance through a combination of enhanced vis-ibility, entrepreneurship and political struggle (Myslik 1996; Nash 2006: 3). In Euro-American contexts, this assertion of particular streets or city districts as gay, artistic or bohemian was so successful that visually distinct, bounded gay urban zones have come to play an important part in regeneration strategies and tourism campaigns (Binnie and Valentine 1999: 175).

In Manchester, the success of the Gay Village is similarly attributed to a mixture of emerging gay rights, cultural territorialisation, entrepreneurship and gentrification. It is a powerful story that fitted with a broader vision of Manchester as a post-industrial centre of innovation and regeneration. In addition to this, the devastating impact of the IRA bomb on 15 June 1996 led to a massive injection of cash from the European Union in order to regenerate the city centre. Taylor, et al. (1996) identify how the notions of Mancunian cultural entrepreneurship transcended certain boundaries of social class:

> The dominant image of the Mancunian of the 1990s, of the street-wise 'scally' (scallywag) doing business across the world or profiting from local initiatives in the entertainment business (the pop groups of the 1980s 'Madchester' or the Olympic bid in 1992), we would argue is no overnight invention. (Taylor, et al. 1996: 183)

Mellor (1997) traces the influence of economic regeneration in the city to an idea of Mancunian culture best summed up by Peter Saville's phrase: 'original modern' (see Introduction above), describing Manchester's traditional spirit of innovation that drove both the Industrial Revolution and the cultural regenerations in music, television and art in the decades following industrial decline. This phrase was subsequently adopted by Marketing Manchester, a limited company funded by Greater Manchester's ten local authorities to co-ordinate tourism strategies and manage the city's public image on a national and international stage. It describes the city as a historically grounded but forward thinking, post-industrial, cosmopolitan and creative city (O'Connor 2007: 13).

Like many other post-industrial cities, Manchester lacked traditional iconic tourist attractions and therefore sought to promote other aspects of its 'cultural economy' to potential visitors (Binnie and Skeggs 2004; Hughes 2003; Taylor, et al. 1996). In 1999 Marketing Manchester capitalised on the city's association with gay lifestyles with the launch of the Manchester Gay Tourism campaign (see Hughes 2003). The village was strategically incorporated into the city's 'culture led' programme and has remained central to the marketing vision of Manchester in the twenty-first century (Haslop, et al. 1998; Quilley 1997, 1999). This led to grants for public beautification and a publicity drive promoting the area's 'gay credentials' through local businesses and in civic marketing and mainstream media. Nash writes in her historical study of Toronto's Gay Village that 'far from being a singular and well-orchestrated political strategy to control urban spaces for the benefit of a fixed and coherent gay and lesbian community, the formation of a Gay Village (in Toronto) was a messy and largely haphazard process with multiple players asserting contradictory strategies with largely unforeseen results' (Nash 2006: 4). In Manchester, there seemed to be an operational and strategic alliance of key stakeholders who shared information, circulated policy documents and strove towards shared goals of managing the economic and social concerns of the village. Figure 4.2 shows a diagram that illustrates my understanding of some of the ways that these organisations worked with one another.

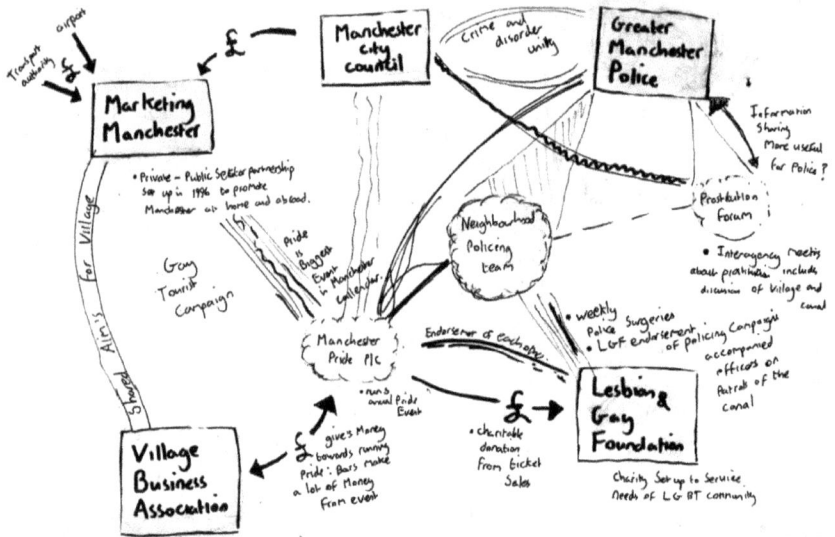

Figure 4.2 Relationship map of key agencies involved in Manchester's Gay Village

These surface images map out the village as a bordered, commercial and family friendly 'gay space' to be featured in tourist maps and gay literature (Skeggs 1999). In her book on window-shopping, Anne Friedberg (1993), considers looking at shop windows to be a mode of spectatorship that acknowledges the productive role of film, photography, print journalism, fashion and other everyday visual presentations as commodified cultural forms. The kinds of display found on and about 'Canal Street' conflate memories and lived experiences with fantasies and dreams that pass as revelations about social reality (Friedberg 1993: 1–7). Just as Walter Benjamin [1935] (1965) describes shop windows in the Arcade's project as 'thought images', so the windows of the pubs and bars in the Gay Village make visible the gay community in a way that represents a metaphorical 'coming out' in Manchester's urban imagination. Such 'imaginations', the combination of these images and stories of success and celebration at street level and in strategic policies, had a profound influence on the expectations of visitors to the village. David Harvey (2009) describes how such stories and images contribute to 'imaginations' that act as epistemological mediations of existing urban conditions that assist the development of a certain set of relationships between the self and the city. These imaginations shape otherwise limitless ways of experiencing the city. Doreen Massey in *For Space* (2005) describes how such master narratives dominate and conceal the multiple connections between imagination, space and politics that reveal space as primarily relational and made up of many simultaneous stories.

Haslam (1999) has shown how the cultural image of Manchester should be moderated by taking into account the levels of illiteracy, poverty and mental illness, particularly among young men, that emerged in the 'Madchester' period of the 1990s. The enclosure of these gay spaces as a kind of urban stronghold is particularly linked to a symbolic and literal male dominance of the 'villages' across the world (Green 1997; Nash 2006; Taylor, et al. 1996: 187). This male dominance was certainly evident in Manchester's Gay Village, where out of thirty venues only two were marketed toward lesbians, and none operated a women only door policy. Although many were 'mixed', most capitalised on the interests of gay men, who were perceived as the bigger spenders of the so-called 'pink pound' that drove the Village's night-time economy. Two venues actively turned women away at the door. Scratch the surface of the Gay Village and another much darker story emerges.

Mapping the village

Robins (1991 in Massey 1993: 68) argues that cartographic boundaries that mark parts of the city as distinct zones are the result of a tension between a desire to conceive of the city as a static physicality and the recognition of the diverse and multiple flows of people and materials that constitute urban experience. It is a tension drawn from the kind of Cartesian mapping critiqued by Doreen Massey who argues that space, rather than being composed solely of the physical plane, is best conceived of as relational in aspect. According to Massey, maps recreate and tame space as an ordered surface that presents a totality of connections (2005: 106). The enclosure of regions as zones, like the Gay Village, is a symbolic attempt to control the unruliness of space. As Rose argues, the city becomes no longer 'a complex of dangerous and compelling space of promises and gratifications, but a series of packaged zones of enjoyment, managed by an alliance of urban planners, entrepreneurs, local politicians and quasi-governmental regeneration agencies' (2000: 107 in Binnie and Skeggs 2004: 46). In the same vein, Borden, et al. (2000) contends that such cartographic enclosures are voids of meaning that become analytic categories or 'concepts without life'.

Bourdieu (1979) has argued that the political functions of certain symbolic systems are privileged over the logic-systems of those engaged in life in a way that serves particular interests, which are then presented as universal. The critical point here is that cartographic images work in collaboration with particular histories, other images and regulatory actions to create totalising imaginaries that characterise parts of the city and thus dominate other stories that might be told of urban spaces (Borden, et al. 2000: 8–12; Massey 2005). As Binnie and Skeggs describe, 'an image of imaginary cosmopolitanism' is built around the village's gay identity, emphasising characteristics that are particularly profitable to marketers (2004: 49–50). This denies the enactment and legitimacy of multiple queer subjectivities that subvert such rigid dichotomies (Hubbard 2008: 654) and/or occur outside of these zones, like cruising and business. Understood in this way, the contemporary map of the Gay Village is a metonym and an integrating, totalising tool for a number of other boundaries that define the gay community. The economic interests of maintaining these boundaries for businesses and other stakeholders required activities that fell outside of them to be strictly regulated and in some instances eradicated. Maintaining the village's reputation as a welcoming, hedonistic party zone that was also family friendly was a tightrope walk, especially given that the commercial activity which made the village a success contributed to some of the area's perceived problems. The area's reputation and the popularity of bars and clubs led to other private entrepreneurs and breweries opening up new venues. The increased competition encouraged a lowering of drinks prices and the extending of opening hours (some until 10am), leading to an increase in drinking-related crime, social disorder and complaints about noise (Hughes 2003; Moran, et al. 2003; Pritchard, et al. 2002; Skeggs 1999). Many representatives of the gay community claimed that the village no longer provided a safe, friendly space for the gay people it symbolically claimed. They also believed Canal Street had developed a zoo-like appeal for straight people (Binnie and Skeggs 2004; Visser 2003). Maps played an important part in managing the resources of policing these issues and determining in which zones they were particularly problematic.

The map shown in Figure 4.3 was provided through personal communication.[4] It shows how Greater Manchester was divided into twelve police divisions denoted A–Q. The city centre is the A Division and is further separated into 6 'neighbourhoods'. The Canal Street area is part of the A1 zone or the 'Village beat' as the police referred to it.

The village neighbourhood policing team met with residents, businesses, the Council and community groups through regular 'surgeries'. Although gay bars, clubs and community organisations were no longer subject to discriminatory police action, cruising and 'business' were still important concerns for the police. Anderton's moral campaign of the 1980s was replaced by concerns for public decency, violent crime, sexual health, the views of new residents and accidental deaths. The proximity of the Gay Village to Piccadilly Station, and the use of the canal as a route to the 2003 Commonwealth Games Sports City development made public sex a potentially international embarrassment. As a result, pubs and clubs operating 'dark rooms' (places where men could have sex with one another on premises) were warned by police and even raided. Lighting, CCTV and outdoor speakers were installed along the towpath and connected to a central CCTV office, and police patrols were increased

Figure 4.3 Police city centre 'beat' map

Alongside the normative control of sexual behaviour, regulatory actions by the police were also orientated around the movement of alcohol, illegal drugs, violence, the sound of late night revellers who left the bars and clubs in the early hours of the morning, and the activities of beggars and rough sleepers. While their efforts in these areas had limited success, public sex remained an easy target for police, as it did not involve risky operations or interfere with the city's taxable night-time economies.

The use of statistics based on the cartographic zoning had certain limitations. I observed this at first hand as an outreach worker. Between 2007 and 2010 I attended regular prostitution forum meetings between police, the local crime and disorder unit of the City Council and organisations working with men and women who sold sex. In 2009, the police presented statistics at this meeting which showed an increase in violence in the village area. This increase was used to justify a zero-tolerance approach by police towards public sex and sex work, even though there was no detailed examination of where such violence had occurred in the zone, the point of contact or whether it was related to cruising and 'business' at all. After this meeting I spoke with a gay-identifying police officer who explained to me how there was a desire to bring previously unruly homosexual encounters in line with normative ideas around sex and sexuality:

Well, obviously that sort of thing can't go on in the village anymore. Besides they have no need to do it like that. There are all the clubs and bars, and if they

want sex they can go in the sauna ... obviously we've got better things to do with
our time than chase people down there [the canal] but we have to respond to
complaints from the public!

Between 2007 and 2010, there were two police 'crackdowns', which involved
increased patrols and co-ordinated efforts with gay charities and press to warn
cruising men of potential prosecution. The LGBT Foundation ceased sexual
health outreach work into cruising grounds in case such activities were seen
as tacit acceptance of cruising. In fact, during my fieldwork, the Foundation,
which was the main organisation advocating for the rights and wellbeing of
the gay community in Manchester, accompanied police to warn men against
the dangers of cruising. This sharing of space and goals between the police and
representatives of the gay community meant that the acceptance of gay sexual
identity on a civic level was predicated on an expectation that the visibility of
sexual conduct could and should be managed (Valocchi 1999) by the community. As I made clear in my introduction, it is not my intention to advocate
that these should be less subject to regulation but to examine the impact this
targeting of certain kinds of sexuality has in what was recognised by many as
part of 'village life'.

Regulating public sex in the village played its part in creating a sense of unity
and order of experience through the capacity to identify dirty or polluting
activities in spatially symbolic terms – that which Mary Douglas characterises
as 'matter out of place' (1966: 41). This was done in the case of the Manchester
Gay Village with highly particular social, political and economic aims.

> The idea of society is a powerful image. It is potent in its own right to control or
> to stir men to action. This image has form; it has external boundaries, margins,
> internal structure. Its outlines contain power to reward conformity and repulse
> attack. There is energy in its margins and unstructured areas. For symbols of
> society, any human experience of structures, margins or boundaries is ready to
> hand. (Douglas 1966: 115)

What is at issue here are the particular modes of imaging and visibility by
which the activity of men seeking sex with other men in the Gay Village
was apprehended and therefore treated as anomalous and thus 'dirty'. Sex in
public was regulated using the offence of 'outraging public decency', which
rested on an indecent act being potentially witnessed by two or more people.
In short, although public sex wasn't itself illegal, the potential for being seen
was against the law. Although some men fetishised the danger of being seen,
or 'caught in the act', most concealed their activities from those not directly
involved, both in the sense of physical concealment and in the sense of how
they talked about their actions. The regeneration of the city centre since the
1990s had capitalised on former industrial architecture and waterfront as

prime real estate, meaning that places near the village where sex in public occurred had been thrown open to a potentially much larger spectatorship. It was the public form of its visibility that made cruising and doing business 'matter out of place'. This may also be seen to be formative of the kinds of visuality and visibility by which cruising and business persisted.

Cruising and business involved ways of knowing the village that were neither neat nor clearly understood – understandings that were formed in the rapid connection of eyes, patterns of long established flows of movement and in the flitting nature of the glance. It was the uncertainty of the ways they occurred that disrupted the established public images of the village as a successful economic entity and an ideologically and geographically bordered zone. They were activities that persisted and defied the physical and ideological boundaries of the village and gay identities that were deemed acceptable in open public discourses.

Gay spaces claim to provide certain protection and representation for members of the LGBT community (Hindle 1994; Hughes 2003; Quilley 1997). These works have tended to complicate the coherent image of the Gay Village as a safe and representative space for the LGBT community. Lesbian women, for example, often feel less represented, accepted and catered for in the village (Green 1997: 52; Pritchard, et al. 2002), an experience echoed by gay people of different racial minorities (Rushbrook 2002). This is an exclusionary sentiment shared by transsexual and bisexual men and women (Nash 2006). The men who I knew that did business often shifted how they defined their sexual orientation, sometimes they said they were straight, in other situations they said they were bisexual. More often they evaded suggestions of any fixed sense of sexual identity.

The spoken negotiations involved in doing business often involved a measure of ambiguity between what was said and what was implied. Partially due to the social, personal and legal implications of being involved but also because both business and cruising were part of other everyday activities, relationships and bodily practices like drinking in pubs, socialising with friends, wandering and waiting. Cruising encounters where money was not exchanged usually involved indirect conversation or no speaking at all which presented a number of challenges for carrying out ethnographic research on this subject.

Peter's village

The following pages contain a segment of graphic novel created in collaboration with Peter, a nineteen-year-old 'working lad' who came to the village primarily when he needed to earn a bit of money (which at this point was every day). Its production involved some consultation, yet the material was produced mostly from notes and ideas we worked out together sitting in one of the back street fast food restaurants of the village. There are increasing calls for recognition of the way graphic novels and cartoons are able to display culturally distinct aspects of people's lives (Alfonso 2004; Galman 2009; Ruby 1995: 81; Thompson 2012). These 'ethno-graphics' allowed me to combine the critically important facets of visuality, visibility and narrative that were essential to my informants' understanding of the city and their experiences.

I asked Peter how he knew about the village. He described it twice: the first description involved the publicised images and stories of the village, epitomised by the tourist map and reflecting a bordered, safe, cosmopolitan, 'European gay mecca' (Healthy Gay Manchester 1998 in Binnie and Skeggs 2004: 49). The second account is different, more personal, uncertain, often unpleasant, and, he felt, unrecognised by a great many of the people who visited the village. Peter said that 'everybody knows about the village! I guess I always knew what it was'. He told me that he had a frustrating day waiting for a punter. Then he contradicted his earlier statement by saying 'nobody really knows about the village; there's a dark side to it, dark stuff, like'.

His phrase 'the dark side' of the village came up repeatedly during my fieldwork. A filmic cliché from the Star Wars franchise, the term 'the dark-side' describes the literal darkness of the park at night and unlit places along the towpath where men would have sex and lads would go with punters. Darkness also operated less literally, to refer to the state of not being made aware of something that is, of being 'kept in the dark'. This sense of something being veiled or hidden was spoken about as being 'shady' and being about 'dark things' that were unpleasant to think and talk about. The literal and figurative senses of darkness were also synonymous with a sense of uncertainty, danger, fear and sexual freedoms (Freud 2003 [1919]; Levy 1975; Throop 2005).

Peter had rarely spoken to me directly about doing business. I had met him several years before while doing street outreach with 'working lads' for a local charity and applied arts organisation. At first, he described what he did as 'scamming' older men or 'robbing'. Over time and without an open declaration it became understood between us that when he referred to these activities he was really describing sex work.

Peter often persuaded me to buy him a box of chips, and we occasionally got the chance to sit down and chat away from the other lads and the punters. He had been in town all weekend. He had fallen out with his girlfriend who was pregnant with his child. He was tired and had been drinking and smoking weed. He told me that he had not had 'one' all day. I understood 'one' to mean a punter, but thought I would take the opportunity to clarify. He grunted an affirmation and seemed to consider this question permission to talk further about the way he saw the village.

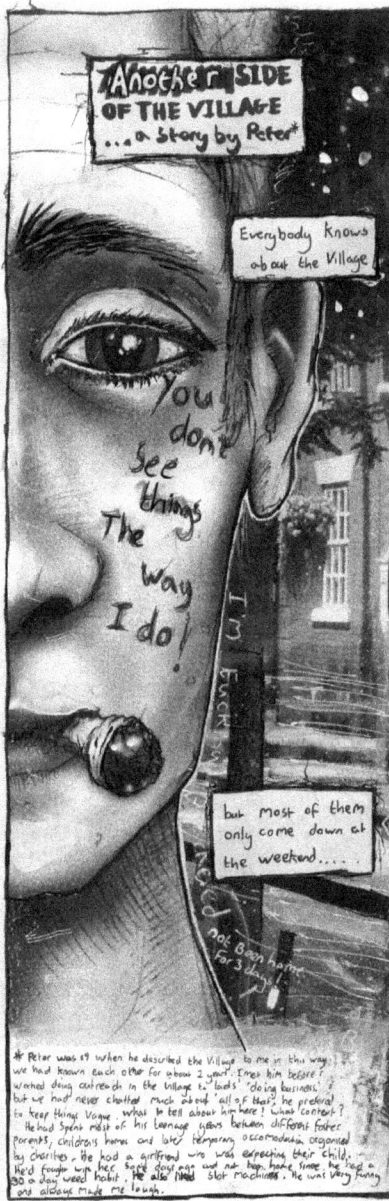

Figure 4.4 Exploring the Gay Village as a graphic novel

Figure 4.5 Exploring the Gay Village as a graphic novel

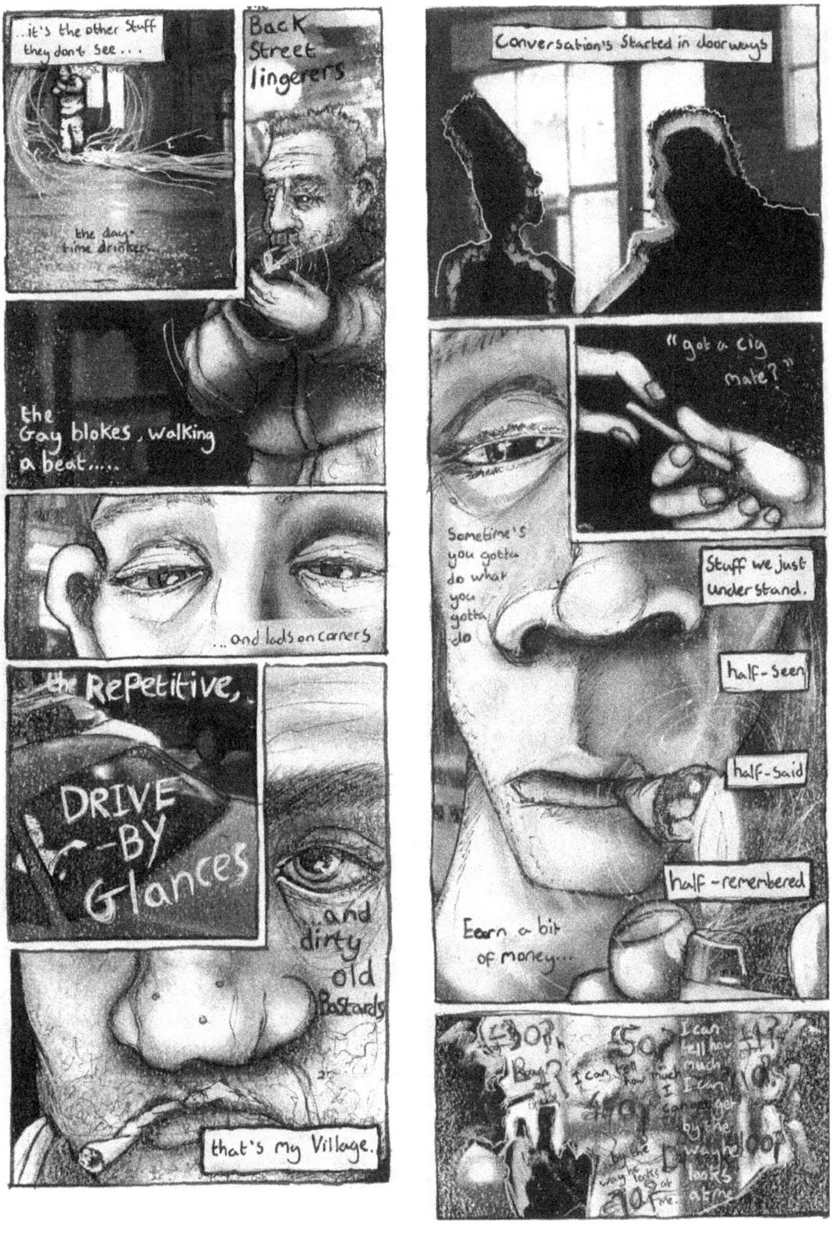

Figure 4.6 Exploring the Gay Village as a graphic novel

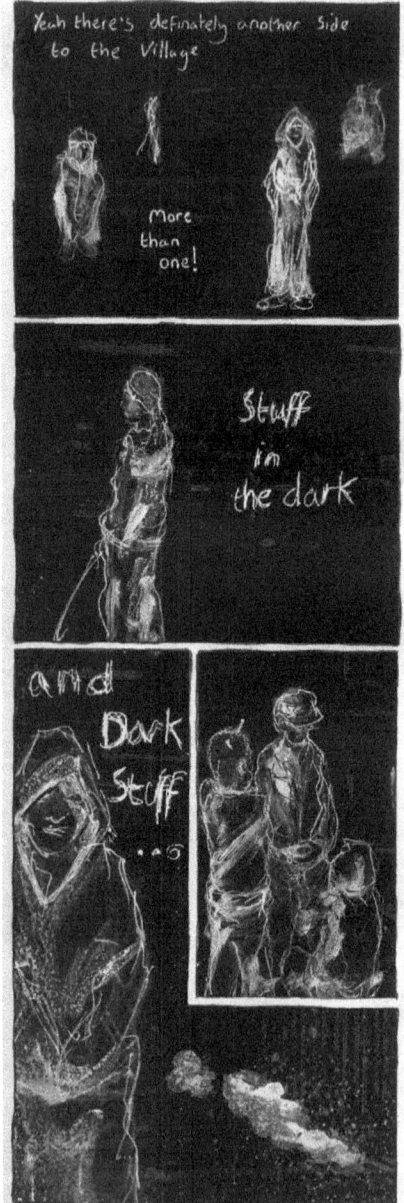

Figure 4.7 Exploring the Gay Village as a graphic novel

Conclusion

Dwight Conquergood (2002) draws upon Michel de Certeau who argues that 'what the map cuts up, the story cuts across' (1984: 129) making a distinction between the transgressive travel between two different ways of knowing: one official, objective and abstract, represented by the cartographic map; and the other practical and embodied, that can be told with the story (2002: 1). The sense of place described by Peter involves the recognition of forms that are fluid, incomplete and uncertain. They are suggestive of an openness to occurrences that differed from those offered in the official images of the village as a cosmopolitan, family friendly, safe party zone. Peter saw a more uncertain village, one which could contain multiple potential meanings, some of which were hidden by active concealment, and others that slipped beneath the public discourses of the Gay Village. Another useful way of thinking about this darkness is provided by De Certeau:

> When one examines this fleeting and permanent reality carefully one has the impression of exploring the night side of societies, a night longer than their day, a dark sea from which successive institutions emerge, a maritime immensity on which socioeconomic and political structures appear as ephemeral islands. (1984: 41)

Peter's dark side of the village was also the village in the light, envisaged in the windows of bars, the pages of magazines, maps, and the well-established history of Manchester's gay community. This was an urban vision that, as De Certeau describes, show us how 'the manageable city conceptually becomes the city itself' by offering ways that the city can be conceived and constructed as stable, isolated and interconnected (1984: 94). This official, bounded Gay Village furthered the concealment of already entrenched flows of cruising and business in order to benefit those able to capitalise on the image of a hedonistic yet safe gay utopia. De Certeau argued that subjective knowledge and collective understandings of community are the necessary stories from which the particularities of *real* cities must be revealed to resist totalising concepts (in Borden, et al. 2000). I would add that how such stories are revealed is also important.

As Massey claims, space is 'the simultaneity of stories so-far' (2005: 9). The story of Peter told in this chapter is just one such story. My use of graphic stories aims to collapse a gap between practical knowledge and propositional knowledge (Conquergood 2002: 153). Attempting to explore urban spaces through such material may disrupt the profitable calm image of the village perpetuated by marketers, and instead demand attention to ways of improving the wellbeing of men engaged in business and cruising.

Notes

1 Credited with cracking the enigma code used by Germany in World War II and with the birth of computing, Turing was convicted of homosexuality in 1952 and underwent chemical castration as part of his punishment. He is suspected of eating the cyanide impregnated apple to commit suicide in 1954.
2 *Queer as Folk* was a Channel 4 television series released in the UK in 1999, chronicling the lives of three gay men in Manchester. The series caused controversy for its risqué scenes of homosexual sex and drug use.
3 Despite this, he was knighted after remaining in office for fifteen years. www.telegraph.co.uk/news/uknews/law-and-order/8991935/Margaret-Thatcher-saved-career-of-police-chief-who-made-Aids-remarks.html. Accessed 15 June 2013.
4 Spurgeon, I.P. (2013) 1 August 2013. *RE: GMP maps.* Personal communication.

References

Alfonso, Ana Isabel. 2004. "New graphics for old stories: representation of local memories through drawings". In *Working Images: Visual Research and Representation in Ethnography.* A.I. Alfonso, L. Kurti, and S. Pink, eds. pp. 72–90. London: Routledge.

Benjamin, Walter. 1969 [1935]. "Paris, the capital of the nineteenth century". *Perspecta*, 12: 165–172.

Binnie, Jon and Beverley Skeggs. 2004. "Cosmopolitan knowledge and the production and consumption of sexualized space: Manchester's gay village". *The Sociological Review* 52 (1): 39–61.

Binnie, Jon and Gill Valentine. 1999. "Geographies of sexuality: a review of progress". *Progress in Human Geography* 23 (2): 175–187.

Borden, Iain, Joe Kerr, Jane Rendell, and Alicia Pivaro. 2001. *The Unknown City: Contesting Architecture and Social Space.* Cambridge, MA; London: MIT Press.

Bourdieu, Pierre. 1979. "Symbolic power". *Critique of Anthropology* 77 (4): 77–85.

Clarity, James F. 1987. "Britain begins crash campaign to educate public about the spread of AIDS". *New York Times.* Available at www.nytimes.com/1987/01/29/world/britain-begins-crash-campaign-to-educate-public-about-the-spread-of-aids.html.

Conquergood, Dwight. 2002. "Performance studies: interventions and radical research". *TDR/The Drama Review* 46 (2): 145–156.

Crapanzano, Vincent. 2004. *Imaginative Horizons: An Essay in Literary-Philosophical Anthropology.* Chicago; London: University of Chicago Press.

de Certeau, Michel. 1984. *The Practice of Everyday Life.* Berkeley: University of California Press.

Douglas, Mary. 1966. *Purity and Danger: An Analysis of Concepts of Pollution and Taboo.* London: Routledge.

Edwards, Elizabeth. 1999. "Beyond the boundary: a consideration of the expressive in photography and anthropology". In *Rethinking Visual Anthropology*. M. Banks and H. Morphy, eds. pp. 53–81. New Haven; London: Yale University Press.

Freud, Sigmund. 2003 [1919]. *The Uncanny*. London: Penguin.

Friedberg, Anne. 1993. *Window Shopping: Cinema and the Postmodern*. Berkeley; London: University of California Press.

Galman, Sally A.C. 2009. "The truthful messenger: visual methods and representation in qualitative research in education". *Qualitative Research* 9 (2): 197–217.

Green, Sarah F. 1997. *Urban Amazons: Lesbian Feminism and Beyond in the Gender, Sexuality, and Identity Battles of London*. Basingstoke: Macmillan.

Harvey, David. 2009. *Social Justice and the City*. Athens: University of Georgia Press.

Haslam, Dave. 1999. *Manchester, England: The Story of the Pop Cult City*. London: HarperCollins.

Haslop, Craig, Helene Hill, and Ruth A. Schmidt. 1998. "The gay lifestyle-spaces for a subculture of consumption". *Marketing Intelligence & Planning* 16 (5): 318–326.

Hindle, Paul. 1994. "Gay communities and gay space in the city". In *The Margins of the City: Gay Men's Urban Lives*. S. Whittle, ed., Vol. 6, pp. 7–25. Aldershot: Ashgate.

Holcomb, Briavel. 1999. "Marketing cities for tourism". In *The Tourist City*. D.R. Judd and S.S. Fainstein, eds. pp. 54–70. New Haven, CT: Yale University Press.

Hubbard, Phil. 2008. "Here, there, everywhere: the ubiquitous geographies of heteronormativity". *Geography Compass* 2 (3): 640–658.

Hughes, Howard L. 2003. "Marketing gay tourism in Manchester: new market for urban tourism or destruction of 'gay space'?" *Journal of Vacation Marketing* 9 (2): 152–163.

Levy, Robert I. 1975. *Tahitians: Mind and Experience in the Society Islands*. Chicago; London: University of Chicago Press.

Massey, Doreen. 1993. "Power-geometry and a progressive sense of place". In *Mapping the Futures*. J. Bird, B. Curtis, T. Putnam, G. Robertson, and L. Tickner, eds. pp. 59–70. London: Routledge.

— 2005. *For Space*. London: Sage.

Mellor, Rosemary. 1997. "Cool times for a changing city". In *Transforming Cities*. N. Jewson and S. MacGregor, eds. pp. 53–69. London: Routledge.

Moran, Leslie, Beverley Skeggs, Paul Tyrer, and Karen Corteen. 2003. "The formation of fear in gay space: the 'straights' story". *Capital & Class* 27 (2): 173–198.

Myslik, Wayne. 1996. "Renegotiating the 'heterosexual street': lesbian productions of space". In *BodySpace: Destabilizing Geographies of Gender and Sexuality*. N. Duncan, ed. pp. 156–170. London: Routledge.

Nash, Catherine Jean. 2006. "Toronto's gay village (1969–1982): plotting the politics of gay identity". *The Canadian Geographer/Le Géographe canadien* 50 (1): 1–16.

O'Connor, Justin. 2007. "Manchester: the original modern city". *The Yorkshire and Humber Regional Review*: 13–15.

Pritchard, Annette, Nigel Morgan, and Diane Sedgley. 2002. "In search of lesbian space? The experience of Manchester's gay village". *Leisure Studies* 21 (2): 105–123.

Quilley, Stephen. 1997. "Constructing Manchester's 'new urban village': gay space in the entrepreneurial city." In *Queers in Space: Communities/Public Places/Sites Of Resistance.* G.B. Ingram, A.-M. Bouthillette, and Y. Retter, eds. pp. 275–292. Seattle, WA: Bay Press.

— 1999. "Entrepreneurial Manchester: the genesis of elite consensus". *Antipode* 31 (2): 185–211.

Ruby, Jay. 1995. "The moral burden of authorship in ethnographic film". *Visual Anthropology Review* 11 (2): 77–82.

Rushbrook, Dereka. 2002. "Cities, queer space, and the cosmopolitan tourist". *GLQ: A Journal of Lesbian and Gay Studies* 8 (1): 183–206.

Skeggs, Beverley. 1999. "Matter out of place: visibility and sexualities in leisure spaces". *Leisure Studies* 18 (3): 213–232.

Taylor, Ian, Karen Evans, and Penny Fraser. 1996. *Global Change, Local Feeling and Everyday Life and the North of England: A Study in Manchester and Sheffield.* London: Routledge.

Teunis, Niels. 2001. "Same-sex sexuality in Africa: a case study from Senegal". *AIDS and Behavior* 5 (2): 173–182.

Thompson, Matt. 2012. "The Illustrated Man vs. Super-Graeber". Available at savage-minds.org/2012/10/30/the-illustrated-man-vs-super-graeber/.

Throop, C. Jason. 2005. "Hypocognition, a 'sense of the uncanny', and the anthropology of ambiguity: reflections on Robert I. Levy's contribution to theories of experience in anthropology". *Ethos* 33 (4): 499–511.

Turner, Mark W. 2003. *Backward Glances: Cruising the Queer Streets of New York and London.* London: Reaktion.

Valocchi, Steve. 1999. "The class-inflected nature of gay identity". *Social Problems* 46 (2): 207–224.

Visser, Gustav. 2003. "Gay men, tourism and urban space: reflections on Africa's gay capital". *Tourism Geographies* 5 (2): 168–189.

Figure 5.1 Fenced-off shelter in Cheetham Park

5

MAKING AND ENABLING THE COMMONS: SHARED URBAN SPACES AND CIVIC ENGAGEMENT IN NORTH MANCHESTER

Luciana Lang

Introduction

> You can take the girl out of Cheetham, but you will never take Cheetham out of the girl. (Ruth, a volunteer at the Jewish Museum)

Cheetham Park in North Manchester was one of many parks created in the early nineteenth century to address public concerns about rising levels of pollution from the industries in the city. At the time of its opening in 1885, Cheetham Park was described as: 'an important factor in maintaining and strengthening the health of a community, and they have done and are doing much to brighten life in narrow streets and in a damp and smoke-laden atmosphere' (Doyle 2013).[1] The infrastructure of parks reflected the commitment by local authorities towards fostering civic behaviour, education and entertainment through the provision of sports facilities, such as tennis and bowling, public galleries and music concerts. Parks were regarded as a place for physical activities and active citizenship, and for alleviating health problems related to the rapid industrialisation in the city. But the emergence of parks has also been interpreted as a reaction to the loss of public commons and the growing privatisation of land (Doyle 2013).

This chapter explores the concept of the 'commons' and the tensions brought about by changing attitudes regarding rights and obligations towards public land. The term will be deployed henceforth to refer to civic commons as opposed to ecological commons, such as air, rivers or oceans. The insights here are drawn from ethnographic material collected during a participatory art and research initiative to enhance community involvement with Cheetham Park, led by Manchester Jewish Museum and the University of Manchester. The spring newsletter issued by the Jewish Museum at the start of the project in April 2015 made references to how the value of the park had rapidly diminished over time: 'once a social hub', it is now 'in serious decline with a derelict bandstand and overgrown flowerbeds'. The leaflet explained the rationale for the project as rekindling the community's interest in the park. The project was to resume work that had been started in 2013 by the artist collective Public Works with the DIY Common initiative,[2] which ran a series of free craft workshops in the park supported by the National Heritage Fund. The premise that Cheetham Park was a commons was stated from the outset, hence my motivation to use the concept as a framing for this discussion.

The issue of management of public land, or lack of it, is at the heart of this discussion, not least after the noted transition from managerialism to entrepreneurialism in urban governance (Harvey 1989; Peck and Ward 2002). Vinay Gidwani and Amita Baviskar (2011) make a distinction between 'commons' and 'public spaces', whereby 'public' is a juridical category which stands in opposition to 'private', and the 'commons' are in the realm of custom, standing, at least in theory, outside the limits of law. However, for the purpose of this ethnography, the two terms of commons and public spaces will be used interchangeably. The concept of commons is helpful as it illuminates the interface between civic engagement and public authorities; between rights and obligations. The term refers to 'a property with no rights allocation and regulation' thus 'belonging to everybody and hence to nobody' (Eizenberg 2011: 765), and highlights the subversive potential that the 'commons thrive and survive by dancing in and out of the State's gaze, by escaping its notice' (Gidwani and Baviskar 2011: 42). These understandings invite us to question whether public parks could be described as a commons, given the amount of monitoring and regulation that such spaces are subject to. Thus, I have utilised the concept as an ideal model, in the Weberian sense, an abstract concept against which I evaluate the urban interventions I am analysing. I deploy the gerund form of the term to formulate my research question of what fosters and hinders 'commoning', here understood as practices that reconfigure public land based on horizontal organisation (Linebaugh 2009).

Ethnographic approach

I explore three spaces of potential and actual commoning that came to the fore while I was carrying out research on local memories. This excavation of the past (Benjamin 1932) took place during my residency as a researcher in Cheetham Hill, where I conducted around forty-five interviews with local residents and with volunteers at the Jewish Museum. I also had access to transcripts of the oral histories databank stored at the museum. Networking was a core part of my ethnographic approach: from grassroots, health, cultural and environmental organisations, such as Growing Manchester, Sow the City, Living Streets, Zest Healthy Living network, Manchester Local Record Centre and Rainbow Surprise, to stakeholders such as the Housing Association, a local primary school and the Council representative in charge of parks. I attended meetings, helped organise community events, created a website for the project, participated in craft workshops, parades and gardening endeavours and contributed to the Gazette started by the artist in residence. The analysis sheds light on the question of *why* local community and authorities no longer engage with the idea of the cultural and natural heritage of the park, while challenging the dominant discourse by stakeholders, such as local authority and Housing Association representatives, that people in Cheetham Hill are disengaged because the community is 'too ethnically diverse'. Such pluralism, in the eyes of some, would supposedly hinder the sense of community, an assumption I was urged to question.

The collections at the museum motivated me to include the historical and socio-economic background of Cheetham Hill as a backdrop to my research. The ethnography that unfolded gradually unveiled three spaces of urban intervention that, in light of the literature, could be interpreted as experiences of commoning. The park sets the backdrop to the narrative, the Wai Yin Welcome Centre gives us a glimpse of contemporary every day practices that reflect socio-economic adaptations in a post-industrial Manchester, and the adventure playground shows the passage into what could be described as a neo-liberal management of public land. Commoning is the guiding thread that sews together these different public spaces, against the backdrop of Cheetham Hill's streets, a necessary part of Cheetham Commons. These spaces relate to three distinct temporalities. First, the case of Cheetham Park offers a diachronic perspective, revealing how socio-economic changes affect the physical surroundings, infrastructure and practices of commoning in the park, against the backdrop of how the park features in old photographs and through oral histories. Second, the Welcome Centre gives a synchronic picture of the park under the current management model of public land, and third, the adventure playground offers a window into a model no longer in place. These different temporalities make salient both the rationale and the shortcomings of what has become the dominant model of managing public land in Britain today. The different scenarios point to three distinct models of managing public spaces.

The chapter argues that Cheetham commons are being made as people imagine and realise ways to adapt to new scenarios brought about by the collapse of work opportunities and the reduction of state support in a locality with pronounced economic disadvantages. Commoning initiatives reflect individual and collective efforts to be 'productive' in an area which is otherwise identified with high levels of unemployment. Similarly to the self-determination encouraged in the case of the civic parades analysed in this collection (ch 2, this volume), such initiatives are welcomed by the local authority, as long as they abide by the imperative of being economically sustainable in times of austerity. But these initiatives also involve a conversation between actors in different capacities; a relationship that is complicated by financial uncertainties (see also ch 9, this volume). Against this backdrop, commoning emerges as an attempt on the part of individuals to forge a sense of identity and cope with resulting challenges in post-industrial Manchester.

Setting the scene: the park and the moral economy in Cheetham Hill

In the accounts of interviewees born in the 1950s, the area surrounding the museum and the park was booming with life when they were growing up. The Jewish Hospital and the washhouse, a daily destination for many of

Figure 5.2 Boarded-up factory next to Cheetham Park

the interviewees, lay opposite Cheetham Park, and textile factories dominated the surrounding landscape. Cheetham Hill was once at the heart of the
thriving textiles and industrial landscape of Manchester. According to records
at the museum, the first Jews arrived in the area in 1780, offering services
as pawnbrokers, opticians and dentists, followed by traders from Germany
and Holland. Sephardi merchants of Spanish and Portuguese origin from the
Middle East and the Mediterranean arrived there from the 1830s onwards,
attracted by the textile trade and cotton mill industries. This ethnic group
was a substantial addition to the local population, foreshadowing the trend of
incoming migrants in search of work that characterised Cheetham Hill well
into the twentieth century. There were waves of migrants from the Russian
and Austro-Hungarian Empires fleeing poverty and violence, followed by
refugees from Nazism; then by Egyptians, Hungarians and Iranians after the
1950s.[3] According to an informant of Jewish origin, going to Manchester was
such a popular destiny that the expression 'May he live in Manchester' became
a commonplace blessing to new-born babies.

The moral economy (Thompson 1971)[4] in the Cheetham area in the early
twentieth century is evocatively told through photographs on display at the
Jewish Museum, shedding light on the histories and relations intertwined
with the area.

Figure 5.3 Hat maker's workshop

Figure 5.4 Diorama of tailoring workshop in Cheetham Hill

The dioramas in the museum complement the picture by providing a sensorial experience of life and work for local families through three-dimensional displays, highlighting the importance of the textile trade for the community. The fact that the onlooker can almost touch the objects, displayed in a way to convey the actions by the labourer, is enhanced by a hyper-real *mise en scène* of the craftsperson's tools and unfinished work, only a few lifetimes before. The crystallised scene, emphasised by the half-opened can of waterproofing rubber seal used in the manufacturing of raincoats that brought reputation to the area, is pregnant with meaning and semantic implications of what life must have been like at this early stage of capitalism when workers still handled their means of production. As for the voyeur, the diorama has kept its aura, since it is not a reproduced image but a life-size installation that oozes smells that cannot be felt, and simulates actions by people who cannot be seen.

Nowadays, the buildings around Cheetham Park are like simulacra (Baudrillard 1994). Originally referring to a map that simulates a territory, a simulacrum generates a hyperreal image no longer connected to reality. Material traces of landmarks shown in photographs in the museum can be found in and around the park in the form of boarded up factories isolated by barbed wire, empty spaces with broken windows, and fenced-off park shelters. However, the area surrounding the park also has examples of distinct phases of redevelopment since industrial times. The Jewish Hospital has been replaced by houses; a mosque has been built across the street from the park; some of the old manufacturing units are now distributers of goods manufactured elsewhere; and a children's nursery was built on park grounds. If a high percentage of the local community prior to the 1950s was of Jewish origin, the social landscape nowadays is much more diverse. Cheetham Hill was characterised as one of the most ethnically diverse areas in Britain according to the UK 2011 census, results disseminated in articles, documentaries and university reports (Crisp 2014; Crossley 2013; Garrett 2016; Jivraj 2013; Office for National Statistics 2011). The historical connections with the textile trade still attract people with related skills, who either have relatives living in the area or have heard of its reputation. Tailoring was a ubiquitous form of labour in the area until the 1970s, and many of the local people I interviewed had some connection with the trade.

> My mum would sit by the sewing machine and work all day. She would do any jobs going: bags, trousers, coats, you name it! She would also sew for the Muslim community. (Sandra, a volunteer at the Jewish Museum)

> We would help our neighbour who had a tailoring business. He would pay me and my brother to sew buttons on the garments. (Wania, a regular visitor to the Wai Yin Welcome Centre)

On my visits to the Wai Yin Centre I would often chat with Katie, a fifty-two-year-old local resident who always wore a head scarf and described herself as both a 'devout Muslim' and a 'Cheetham girl': her North Manchester accent attested to the latter claim. Katie was born in Pakistan but moved to Cheetham Hill at the age of two. She was proud of the industrial heritage of the area, and described how she had become a warehouse manager of a local clothing firm before the company shut down. Her dad had been a steel worker in Salford and her mum a machinist who worked from home for manufacturers and for the local community. In our discussion about her upbringing she reminisced about her textile heritage, while busily crocheting a cap:

> Even though she [her mother] didn't teach me, I learned from her and I could sew anything, no one knew how I did it!'

Another interviewee at the Way Yin, who had recently arrived from Syria where he used to work in the textile industry, told me how, after securing refugee status in Ireland, he had decided to come to Cheetham Hill because of the area's reputation in the textile trade. However, amongst other problems related to starting a new life in a new place without his family, he came to the realisation that the local trade is not quite what he had expected. While local businesses continue to focus on textile-related merchandise, the nature of the trade has changed significantly. The products no longer consist of locally

Figure 5.5 Wholesale stores in Cheetham Hill and opposite the park

manufactured goods. Instead, retail stores display in their windows merchandise from China and Taiwan. For example, a company across the road from Cheetham Park stores imported goods in its warehouse for companies without storage facilities that cannot afford to wait for goods to be dispatched by manufacturers in distant places of the globe. The textile trade has also shifted geographically, taking over old buildings on Cheetham Hill road and signalling changes in capitalist practices.

It is impossible to talk about the welfare of Cheetham Park without taking into consideration the area where it is located and its socio-economic transformations over the years. These changes were experienced in a walk designed by DIY Commons with a group of visitors from the European Association of Cultural Centres, who were interested in the art-research residency at the Jewish Museum, and in particular in how we were promoting community engagement with Cheetham Park. The purpose of the walk was to guide the visitors through different experiences of public spaces in Cheetham Hill, starting from the museum and its collection of representations of the area, then going through the back streets, then up the road to the park, and finishing at the Wai Yin Centre. As we walked from the museum towards the park, through the hub of wholesale shop units scattered along the back streets, one of the visitors who was familiar with the city described the area as 'a very grim part of Manchester', while another visitor remarked on how deserted the streets were. As we turned the corner and caught sight of the panoptical tower of Strangeways Prison, an infamous landmark in Manchester, a visitor from Denmark asked if people actually lived in that area. A French participant compared one of the shop windows we passed, displaying a variety of wigs, fancy hats and costumes, to the dioramas and old photographs at the museum prior to the walk. She remarked on the two apparently different types of processes and products: the manual labour involved in making hats and raincoats as seen in the dioramas, and the manufactured wares produced miles away on display in the shop windows of Cheetham Hill.

Marx describes commodities as the process through which 'labour-power' is taken to the market. The types of commodities present in Cheetham Hill's past and present could be seen as distinct 'congealed quantities of homogeneous human labour' (Marx 1976 [1867]: 128). This part of Manchester, with its focus on the wholesale aspect of the global market, is just as telling of the current stage of capitalism and its subsequent effects as it was in the 1800s when Marx was writing *Capital* sitting in the Chetham's Library ten minutes down the road. Back then, the initiative to create parks was to offset the health hazard produced by the polluting effects of industrialisation. The image of the fenced-off shelter in the park that opens this chapter reflects the recent decline in the local economy, even if the wholesale trade in Cheetham's backstreets connect the area with the global circulation of goods.

By the time the walking group reached the park, people's curiosity had turned into puzzlement as they looked at the fenced-off heritage band stand and shelter, and the empty park. One of the participants asked in dismay: 'Don't the local authorities in this country look after the parks?' This question highlighted the issue relating to commoning in Cheetham Hill, namely the reputation and administration of 'the public good'. Between people's conflicting views and different ways of engaging with public land, the big enigma was how to negotiate rights and obligations towards the commons in a locality with so little investment from public bodies.

Commoning in Cheetham Park

The issue of obligations and people's rights to public parks presents us with a riddle. If we say the park is a commons and people can claim their right to it, would that imply that its responsibility should be on the public? Or inversely, if the park is the responsibility of the City Council, does that imply it is not a commons? Since the publication of *Tragedy of the Commons* by Garrett Hardin (1968), discussions on the commons have always been intertwined with the conundrum of how to manage something that by definition belongs to all. Hardin's thesis, that self-interest would end up jeopardising collective resources because of people's tendency to take more than their fair share, provides an important strand of the debate and must be addressed, even if to be criticised. Hardin's critics claim that by focusing on self-interest and undermining the experience of mutuality engendered in the commoning process the author drives the analysis away from where the real problem actually lies: the demise of the commons as part of a process that created a landless class through land privatisation and commodification. Eizenberg (2011) sees Hardin's thesis as an extension of the reasoning that saw the commons as an obstacle to productive agriculture in the fourteenth century. Furthermore, because Hardin's argument is associated with Malthusian thought and social Darwinism, it was hijacked by Neo-Conservatives to justify political agendas set to protect individual and property rights. In other words, Hardin's argument is mostly dismissed because of its conservative underpinnings, and his pragmatic concerns with the issue of regulating rights and obligations with regards to the commons are also undermined.

Yet many would agree with Hardin's conclusion that the commons need to be regulated (1968), and that the problem with Cheetham Park is that it lacks monitoring. Judie, a volunteer at the Jewish Museum, who was raised in Cheetham, said she wouldn't take her grandchildren there: 'The park is very different now, I don't go there anymore'. Jackie, whose parents came from the West Indies, had lived all her life next to the park. She believed the whole area had deteriorated: 'They really need to do something about this park'. Such views were expressed by those who had seen the park in different days. Many interviewees remarked on how the park was like an oasis amidst a very grey industrial Manchester:

> I used to love that park. Back then it was the only green place in the area. (Jo, a local resident born in 1929)

Judging from the records kept by the Jewish Museum about the park, such as photographs and the attendance book for the bowling green, Cheetham Park, popularly known as Elizabeth Street Park, was an integral part of the local community. People fondly remember passing the park on the way to the old washhouse, drinking from its water fountain, and listening to the Salvation Army brass band. The park was a place where children would play hide-and-seek around the bushes, practice singing in the bandstand, or go on dates in the evenings under the strict watch of the park keeper. Many regret the demolition of the park lodge and of the bowling green, where so many of the older generation played on a regular basis:

> There was a quirky park keeper's lodge. Our imagination ran wild with that house. I was quite sad when they pulled it down. (Denise, a local resident)

Denise was, in her words, 'born and bred' in Cheetham, and is now a Born Again Christian. Her dad was a window cleaner, and her mum a typist. She remembers the park in the 1960s and 1970s:

> Lots of children would play there but there used to be quite a lot of broken glass in it because vagrants would sleep in the bandstand in the park and drink Strong Bow cider. But Cheetham Park was the prettiest park because there was [sic] lots of flowers, and a tennis court, and a bowling green.

The structures in and around the park also informed Denise's dreams and ambitions:

> Opposite the swings, there was the Jewish Hospital. I would swing in there and I would think 'one day I want to be a nurse, and I want to work there and I want to help people'.

Denise did in fact become a nurse, and joined the church choir after years of practising in the bandstand because of its acoustics. But not all accounts follow a positive nostalgic tone. For Katie, the park is associated with danger. She explained how she enjoyed going to the park with her family but her mother did not let her go there alone:

> I used to take my recorder with me and play it in the bandstand; sometimes we would get wild flowers and decorate the band stand. People in the bowling green didn't let us watch them. In them days there was racism, especially from the older men.

These accounts of the park reveal how there was significant commitment from the authorities to keep the bowling green, the bandstands, the flower beds and the park keeper, along with his lodge, until the 1960s. It was a place for leisure pursuits and freedom for children to play, even if it was also seen as a place of risk and discrimination in the form of racism. With the change in socio-economic conditions, came changes to the relationships between residents and the local authority's relationship with Cheetham Park. The Jewish community that had populated the area for most of its history moved north to Prestwich, other ethnic groups arrived, and the funding dwindled.

While the park's intangible cultural heritage lives on in people's memories and in photographs at the museum, its natural heritage is still tangible. I invited Steve, a bird specialist from the Greater Manchester Record Centre, an organisation that has a wildlife databank for the Manchester region, to a birdsong workshop at Cheetham Park. He identified eleven species of birds amongst the oak trees and red apple heritage tree, which delighted the school children who came for a historic tour of the park as part of my attempts at engaging the public with commoning. On the far side, there were surviving herbs that were planted two years ago by the DIY Common Project, people arriving to attend prayers at the mosque, and driving instructors taking advantage of the deserted streets to teach their students. But what was missing, compared to the narratives of those who remembered the park in its days of glory, was the enabler, invisible to most, who kept the shelter and bandstand secure, the flower beds neat, the bowling green usable and the park keeper's lodge tidy. These features and facilities created for the park are 'resources' in public land. They have to be monitored and looked after for commoning to be sustained. But in the current scenario of severe cuts to services, there was no one there to perform this role.

As for the local authorities, it became clear that Cheetham Park was not receiving attention because it was not seen as being sustainable in economic terms. The rationale for park management in times of austerity politics is predicated on how economically sustainable a park can be. Thus, if a park happens to have an active 'Friends of' group, which invests in the upkeep of their piece of public land and runs fund-raising activities to support renovation work, the park then becomes economically viable. This willingness by local residents to take on some of the responsibilities can influence local Councils' decisions with regards to investment in a green space. In our brief discussions with Council officers, it emerged that they do not trust that the community would be willing to share some of the responsibilities, precisely because they see the area as being constituted by communities in the plural rather than by a 'community'. The Housing Association had tried to set up a tenants' association without success. Two members of staff explained their views to me:

> People in Cheetham Hill are very territorial and tend to stay within the boundaries of their separate areas.
> The area is too culturally diverse so people keep to themselves.

The Housing Association was keen to collaborate with our project because they 'found it really difficult to network in Cheetham'. It is as though, in their view, only a community in the singular could effectively assume a protagonist role. There never was, of course, such a homogeneous community here, but there used to be a much greater sense of obligation from the local authorities. Facing frustration on our attempts to call the attention of the authorities, we resorted to commoning by reconfiguring the landscape through horizontal organisation (Linebaugh 2009): we organised craft workshops in the park; set up tables with food, drinks and a wood-burning stove; we wandered through the park collecting litter; and we invited the Sacred Sounds Women Choir to sing outside the fenced-off bandstand. Although we felt as though we were 'commoning', most of the people who were involved were not local residents and very few locals joined us. I was beginning to lose faith that we would ever see any commoning in Cheetham Hill when, by tracing the connections of the now extensive network we had formed in the area I came across the Wai Yin Welcome Centre, three streets away from the park.

Commoning at the Welcome Centre

We call ourselves the soul food bank. (Barbara, one of the permanent staff at the Wai Yin Centre)

The Wai Yin started as an organisation by and for Chinese women in 1988, and now has three centres in Manchester catering for different groups of people. In 2012, Wai Yin was approached by Cheetham Community Together and asked to start a centre in Cheetham Hill under the name Active Citizenship. After acquiring the current building from Manchester City Council, the centre started to distribute food and give advice and support on employment, domestic violence, and youth and mental health. They offer free lunch three times a week, catering for around one hundred people and more than sixty-three nationalities. The centre has over thirty volunteers and three members of staff. The head of the centre explained how he was inspired by the way the Chinese structure their understanding of the world, which is connected with health and wellbeing, around the five elements that make up the universe: fire, metal, water, wood and earth:

We decided to structure the garden around these five elements, so when we built a barbecue, we included a non-sloping roof made of metal. I read about an urban fish farm in New York and we decided to create a carp pond. The idea is to collect the water of the roof in big bins for the fish pond, and then re-use that for the garden. The water is very rich in nitrogen because of the fish waste. The airport is going to fund the pond through the green city fund. The dream is eventually to create an Incredible Edible vegetable patch and an orchard over in that other patch of Council land. The Council around here is really good with that kind of thing and they already gave us permission to use the land. The Poles, Lithuanians and Latvians who come here are used to going out and collecting food. This lot here knows about things like mushrooms and other foods, so they can help us.

I started volunteering in the Wai Yin community garden in June 2015 in order to meet people locally and participate in the everyday life at the centre. I got involved in weeding, planting, watering, whilst having conversations with visitors working on the garden. Smokers from the centre would also spend time outside and children were drawn to the strawberries, marrows and pumpkins. People from different countries compared gardening practices 'back home' in Pakistan, Poland, Eritrea, India, Cape Verde or China, and the best ways to grow vegetables. Herbs and their aroma prompted conversations about the medicinal qualities of particular plants, and exchange of cooking recipes, while the running chickens fostered a heated debate on the difference between Halal and Kosher meat, and related religious practices.

Contrary to the assumption others had voiced that cultural diversity thwarts engagement and forecloses collaboration, the collective garden at Wai Yin was evidence that complex collectives can instead generate new spaces of mutuality. Simone describes such complex collectives of urban centres, assemblages of 'bodies, landscapes, objects, and technologies' as 'a thickening of fields' (2004: 497). In a place where as many as thirty different languages can be heard in the space of one hour the common language of gardening makes this urban space legible, enabling other means of interaction that overcome barriers of culture and language. This perhaps explains why urban commoning is so often about 'planting rhubarb' (McGuirk 2015): the practice of growing food grants people a sense of accomplishment by working towards a common purpose in a scenario where their capacity for a productive life is undermined elsewhere.

Linebaugh described the commons as 'a subsistence regime' prior to capitalism (2012), and many around Wai Yin felt drawn to the potential for being self-sufficient and contributing towards, for example, the ingredients of the food that would be shared at the centre at lunch time. People found in the gardening activities an opportunity to reassert themselves through a skill they possessed and which was otherwise untapped. They often commented on how that space was reminiscent of life back in their hometowns, and how their relationship with plants was embedded in the history of their own lives (Bennett 2014). Geordie, the most experienced gardener, would offer advice on vegetable-growing techniques or help people identify the seedlings. Like most users of the centre, Geordie was unemployed, but volunteered in the garden three times a week. As a child in Newcastle he helped his father with the rose garden, 'the best roses in Newcastle my dad had!', and grounds his gardening skills in his life trajectory:

> I didn't do well at school but when I was doing this horticultural course I could
> do all the maths when it came to plants and planting days.

The potential pitfalls surrounding free access to resources belonging to the commons emerged on a number of occasions, when disputes arose around the permission to pick the ripening vegetables. The first time, the contention was related to the strawberries, then to the marrows, the pumpkins, the leeks and even the herbs. On a couple of occasions some people were emotionally distressed to discover that a much awaited vegetable had been taken from the garden without proper consent. It was decided that there ought to be a

Figure 5.6 Geordie with freshly picked courgettes next to the carp pond, and the chickens

hierarchical ordering of who could pick the ripe produce. Geordie was left in charge of the vegetables, and I was given responsibility for the herb garden. Any picking would henceforth have to get Geordie's consent, but all agreed that 'strawberries are there to be eaten', a telling example of Linebaugh's horizontal organisation (2009) and commoning in the making. But would such horizontality work in the commoning of a public park? I asked Katie what her views were on the current state of the park:

> I don't like it. It's just completely changed. The playground has changed, it's all about health and safety now, they are just wrapping everyone in cotton wool. But you know, we used to have an adventure playground here. It was right here [she was pointing to the empty plot of land opposite the Wai Yin]. We used to like a bit of rough and tumble. We were always scratching and scraping and ripping our clothes, but we had a jolly good time.

Commoning in the 1970s

The adventure playground Katie talked about was on a plot of common land just outside the building where the Wai Yin is. It was started in 1975 by Jack, who used to travel frequently to London as a truck driver. On one of his trips he found out that some people had started an adventure playground in Islington, north London, and he thought Cheetham could really do with something similar:

> There was nothing for the kids in the estate and they were wandering about causing trouble. At that time, the Council had started these play schemes. You didn't have to be a play leader, as long as you were a parent and accounted for the money, you were ok. So, we applied for a grant and got 150 quid for it, so we started a play scheme.

He saw some empty land just three streets away from Cheetham Park where Council terrace houses had been pulled down. A couple of houses still had doors on them:

> We got a group of kids together and they said 'we can strip those houses down', and they did. We used old doors, and stuff taken from the houses. In those days there was none of this health and safety business. We got this telegraph pole that had been pulled down and planted it at an angle, put a rope on it, and there we had a swing for the kids. With the doors, we built a slide eight foot wide and thirty-two feet tall. Fifty kids came on the first day, the next day 150 came.

Jack heard that some grants were being made available for adventure playgrounds and told a local Councillor about his plans. He was invited to a meeting at the Town Hall where the discussion focused on whether the land belonged to the Council or to the Housing Association, and neither the Council nor the Housing Association wanted to assume responsibility for it. It was then that Jack intervened:

> I don't have time to mess about, I'm a bloody truck driver! If the land doesn't belong to the parks and doesn't belong to the Housing Association, it belongs to the people of Manchester, and the people of Cheetham Hill want to make use of it!' So they told me to just get on with it and I got out of there with a cheque for 12 thousand pounds, this in the seventies, which was to cover the start-up and a year's expenses. So we set up a bank account at the Co-op and a committee, my wife became the treasurer and four other neighbours took on different roles. There was this kid in the estate who was a bit wild and didn't have a job, but he knew the other kids, so we got him to look after the adventure playground.

The assertiveness that Jack showed over his right to the plot relates to a longer history of the working class claiming rights to land. In the seminal work *Customs in Common*, E.P. Thompson (1993) notes that 'custom lies upon the land' and gives evocative accounts, going back as far as thirteenth-century England, of disputes over common rights regarding access to resources such as timber and peat. He also observes how the commons are often the locus of class conflict and remarks that 'victories, of the humble citizen over the great or the royal, were decidedly infrequent' (Thompson 1993: 113) but did occasionally happen. Jack is fully aware of his achievement but concludes his story by saying:

> There's no way something like that could be built now. Margaret Thatcher pulled them all down and now there's no money for such things.

The political era Jack refers to was about more than pulling down makeshift adventure playgrounds. The sense of working-class pride, which explains at least in part Jack's assertiveness in demanding his right to the common land, was gradually erased over the three decades that followed with the increasing difficulty faced by the low-skilled labour force to find work. Back then, something else united the kids that played in the adventure playground, and their families and neighbours. Katie, Jack, Denise and others who I met at the Wai Yin, and who remember the playground, shared something with Jack, the truck driver who did something for the kids in the estate in his spare time. Between them, there were 'socio-economic commonalities of a multiracial British working class' (Edwards, et al. 2012: 5). Being part of the contingent of low-paid workers who lived in a housing estate was a collective identity that overrode cultural differences, providing a sense of belonging prior to the shift in subsequent years that focused on cultural distinctiveness.

According to Graham, the head of staff at the Wai Yin, one of the reasons the centre is a thriving social space is because people congregate in spite of different religious affiliations:

> Normally, people socialise at the mosque or at the church, but Wai Yin offers this unique opportunity of bringing together people from different cultural backgrounds who hardly ever socialise.

In sum, both the adventure playground and the Wai Yin managed to mobilise a highly multicultural community around collective commoning, thereby debunking the dominant discourse this study had questioned from the outset, that the community does not engage with the park because it is 'too culturally diverse'.

Conclusion: active citizenship through the commons

The three spaces of commoning analysed in this chapter were initiated by different individuals and groups, and motivated by distinctive interests. But it becomes clear that as public space gets appropriated by different groups, the process of commoning makes different collectives tangible. In the case of current attempts at commoning in Cheetham Park, the initiative is driven by people outside the community who want to make the historical heritage of the place more tangible. In the case of the Welcome Centre, commoning is conjunctural: there is a vision, available land through an enabling Council, and collective participation in the production of food. As for the adventure playground, the motivation was, in Jack's words, to 'keep kids out of trouble', but commoning would not have been possible without the help from the Council.

The case of the adventure playground could be described as a form of bottom-up initiative and perhaps more akin to Eizenberg's counter-hegemonic characterisation (2011). It had considerable impact on local life and it was funded by the Council. The impact of the Wai Yin was significant, and here the Council appears again as an enabler through funding and support. As for Cheetham Park, local concern lies in the possibility that the State's gaze will vanish for good after 130 years. Discussions with authorities have focused on strategies such as listing the band stand as a heritage site to secure the space. By focusing on those three instances of commoning in Cheetham Hill, one can better evaluate what went missing from the park, since it was at the heart of community life, and the analysis suggests that it is a matter of balancing out rights and obligations. In times of austerity, the biggest threat to the commons is the imperative for it to be financially sustainable without becoming a burden to the Council. Without financial backing, the Council can no longer be an enabler in the case of the park, but in the example of the Wai Yin, others take on the role of enablers, with the Council facilitating commoning through the lease of land.

The ethnography reveals a common-sense notion that the management of public land requires rules, a point that has been remarked upon in the literature (Ostrom 1990; Wall 2014) and which is not completely at odds with Hardin's (1968) premise that individual freedom may be detrimental to the collective. While a sense of autonomy is paramount for people's motivation towards commoning, without proper management there arise disruptions which can take varying forms. Commoners may be denied access to common resources or structures (such as the bandstand). Or commoners may act in such a way as to threaten the commons (for example, by littering) or using the space in ways that do not benefit the collective. In other words, the problem is not the plurality of communities, and this is made clear with the commoning example at Wai Yin.

In conclusion, this ethnography has demonstrated the complexity of defining the concept, showing how the commons is 'made' (Gidwani and Baviskar 2011) by the hands and affects of a multitude of actors, within particular temporal and spatial configurations, and informed by specific economic and political agendas and restrictions. Over the years, the commons as a topic has attracted a great deal of political attention. The culprit for some is the process that created a landless class through land privatisation, a problem that has only been aggravated by the crude reality that this landless class is now also a workless class, which explains the commonality experienced by those commoning at the Welcome Centre, and in other cities the world over.

It is the potential of involving people in a common pursuit of being productive, be it by growing a vegetable garden or building an adventure playground, that makes commoning appear as a solution, and one that goes beyond cultural specificities. Thus, commoning is better understood as a process, and in the progressive tense, hence the emphasis on the gerund form of the verb. That said, the analysis demonstrates the importance of organisations to support local residents for the commons to thrive. While austerity measures should not exempt local Councils from the need to enable the commoning process, the current scenario demands that civil society take on the burden of obligations in order to secure their rights to participate in and realise collective city spaces. Furthermore, the analysis above has shown that people have to make demands and devise strategies in other to retrieve their right to the commons and practise their imagined versions of the city.

Acknowledgements

I am grateful to the Jewish Museum for opening the door to past and present perceptions of Cheetham Hill, and to Abigail Gilmore, Torange Khonsari and Jennifer Allison, who had key roles in the 'commoning experience' in Cheetham Park. I would also like to give a special thank you to Jessica Symons and Camilla Lewis for inviting me to contribute to this volume, and for offering valuable feedback on the earlier versions of this chapter. Finally my heartfelt gratitude to the local people of Cheetham Hill.

Notes

1 Extract from the *Handbook of the Manchester City Parks and Recreation Grounds*, 1915, in Doyle (2013).
2 The DIY Common project, which included planting a herb garden, making natural dye from plants in the park, and weaving from naturally dyed yarn, set out to promote productive ways of using Cheetham Park's natural resources and 'community making'.
3 www.manchesterjewishmuseum.com/collections/. Accessed 9 February 2017.
4 I am here employing E.P. Thompson's definition of the term as 'the traditional view of social norms and obligations, of the proper economic functions of several parties within the community, which, taken together, can be said to constitute the moral economy of the poor' (1971: 79).

References

Baudrillard, Jean. 1994. *Simulacra and Simulation*. Ann Arbor: University of Michigan Press.

Benjamin, Walter. 1932. "Excavation and Memory". In *Selected Writings Volume Two, Part Two: 1931–1934*. H.S. Eiland and M.W. Jennings, eds. London: Belknap Press of Harvard University.

Bennett, Julia. 2014. "Gifted places: the inalienable nature of belonging in place". *Environment and Planning D: Society and Space* 32 (4): 658–671.

Crisp, John (director). 2014. "No foreigners here: 100% British". Channel 5.

Crossley, Lucy. 2013. "Welcome to Britain's most diverse street! Road where half of residents speak English as a second language is home to migrants from across the globe". *Daily Mail Online*, 2 February 2013. Available at www.dailymail.co.uk/news/article-2272308/Welcome-Britains-diverse-street-Road-half-residents-speak-English-second-language-home-migrants-globe.html.

Doyle, Patrick. 2013. *History of Parks in Cheetham, Broughton and Salford*. Report for the Understanding Everyday Participation project.

Edwards, Jeanette, Gillian Evans, and Katherine Smith. 2012. "The middle classification of Britain". *Focaal – Journal of Global and Historical Anthropology* 62: 3–16.

Eizenberg, Efrat. 2011. "Actually existing commons: three moments of space of community gardens in New York city". *Antipode* 44 (3): 764–782.

Garrett, Bradley L. 2016. "What the battle for Freeman's Wood says about the future of our common land". *Guardian*, 10 February 2016. https://www.theguardian.com/cities/2016/feb/10/battle-for-freemans-wood-lancaster-common-land-locals-property-development. Accessed 26 May 2017.

Gidwani, Vinay and Amita Baviskar. 2011. "Urban commons". *Economic & Political Weekly* 46 (50): 42–43.

Hardin, Garrett. 1968. "The tragedy of the commons". *Science* 162 (3859): 1243–1248.

Harvey, David. 1989. *The Condition of Postmodernity: An Enquiry into the Origins of Cultural Change*. Oxford: Basil Blackwell.

Jivraj, Stephen. 2013. "Local dynamics of diversity: evidence from the 2011 census". University of Manchester/CoDE.

Linebaugh, Peter. 2009. *The Magna Carta Manifesto: Liberties and Commons for All*. California: University of California Press.

— 2012. *Ypsilanti Vampire May Day*. In Counterpunch. Available at www.counterpunch.org/2012/04/27/ypsilanti-vampire-may-day/Marx, Karl. Accessed 14 April 2016.

Marx, Karl. 1976 [1867]. *Capital: A Critique of Political Economy*. London: Penguin.

McGuirk, Justin. 2015. "Urban commons have radical potential – it's not just about community gardens". *Guardian*, 2015. https://www.theguardian.com/cities/2015/jun/15/urban-common-radical-community-gardens. Accessed 26 May 2107.

Office for National Statistics. 2011. UK 2011 Census. Available at www.ons.gov.uk/census/2011census. Accessed 14 April 2016.

Ostrom, Elinor. 1990. *Governing the Commons: The Evolution of Institutions for Collective Action*. Cambridge: Cambridge University Press.

Peck, Jamie and Kevin Ward. 2002. *City of Revolution: Restructuring Manchester*. Manchester: Manchester University Press.

Simone, AbdouMaliq. 2004. 'People as infrastructure: intersecting fragments in Johannesburg'. *Public Culture* 16 (3): 407–429.

Thompson, Edward P. 1971. "The moral economy of the English crowd in the eighteenth century". *Past & Present* 50: 76–136.

— 1993. *Customs in Common: Studies in Traditional Popular Culture*. New York: The New Press.

Wall, Derek. 2014. *The Commons in History: Culture, Conflict and Ecology*. Cambridge, MA: MIT Press.

Figure 6.1 Imagining Manchester

6

Urban futures and competing trajectories for Manchester city centre

Elisa Pieri

Introduction

In this chapter I argue that engaging urban futures as a heuristic reveals not only important tensions connected to future developments and imagined uses of the city centre, but also opens up to scrutiny the present experiences and uses of the city centre, and the competing interests that a range of actors currently have.

Governance in Manchester is often described as resulting from a successful and harmonious deployment of public–private partnerships (Kellie 2010; Peck and Ward 2002), one that other cities in the UK strive towards (Taylor, et al. 1996). In this chapter I take Manchester city centre as the focus of my research and argue that exploring the priorities of a variety of stakeholders reveals the existence of tensions, otherwise easily glossed over. Critically engaging with urban futures as they are mobilised by institutional stakeholders, and eliciting those that other actors may envisage, highlights whose interests are currently being prioritised and whose are being traded off.

This chapter is based on empirical research conducted between 2011 and 2014 on Manchester city centre, which included an analysis of media and policy documents, participant observation of public events in the city centre, and interviews and focus groups with city centre users, workers and residents. While calling for a careful appraisal of the underlying values inbuilt in any urban vision, the chapter centrally and critically engages with future trajectories pursued in Manchester.

Drawing on Science and Technologies Studies (STS), and specifically on the sociology of expectation, I provide a theorisation of the processes of visioning, with a view to increasing democratic scrutiny and contributing to more socially resilient policy making. What I aim to demonstrate, through the findings of my Manchester-based fieldwork, is that approaching *futuring* processes in this fashion (developed as an STS approach to emergent innovations in the biosciences) is also relevant to our understanding of the urban domain, and applicable beyond the case study of Manchester city centre.

The importance of urban futures

With more than half of the world population currently living in urban areas (United Nations 2014), and a projected and sustained growth in this number in the near future, the debate over urban futures is extremely lively and only likely to intensify. Cities remain highly differentiated, not least in respect to how governance is exercised, but also in their response to growing populations and infrastructural needs (Parnell 2012). However heterogeneous, the futures of cities occupy a central role in policy making today, and many of the challenges we face, and the solutions we seek, are framed at the scale of the city – for instance, under the paradigms of the sustainable city (Guy and Marvin 2001; Hammer, et al. 2011), the smart city (Batty 2012),[1] the resilient city (Coaffee, et al. 2009),[2] and the multi-cultural city (Amin 2002; Wood and Landry 2008).[3] Imagining cities in the future can engender discussions about urban ideals[4] or about the transformation and adaptation of existing settlements (Amin 2013) in response to pressing challenges.[5] These processes are accompanied by the resurgence of lively debates about the infrastructure of cities, the nature of city living, the public realm, risk, urban sociability and cosmopolitanism.

Futures are often mobilised through powerful visuals that give them a three-dimensional solidity and contextualise them within discursive narratives. The relationship between visual and discursive practices is far from straightforward. As debated within semiotics, the visual and the discursive can reinforce the meaning of each other – anchoring or giving salience to some meanings amongst other possible ones – but they can also open up new interpretations (Barthes 1957, 1977). In works of fiction and art,[6] renditions of utopias, dystopias or parallel worlds are routinely engaged and relatively common. Similar practices, however, are habitually deployed to facilitate decision making and policy in the urban by various professionals. Architects, designers, property developers and regeneration teams of policy makers make extensive use of 3-D modelling (for an interesting account of the changes in visualisations as a result of iteration and changing investment circumstances, see Yaneva 2012). In planning and development, the extensive use of 3-D modelling is also the norm (see also Harvey 2009). Visualisations are an important pre-requisite for the commitment of investment and the shaping of any project under discussion or at various stages of actualisation. A selection of visualisations is also disseminated more widely to the general public through various media, as illustrated by the many promotional videos available online on any major urban development and impactful project. Examples range from the most renowned projects, such as the creation of a new city (such as Masdar City in Abu Dhabi, the first eco city)[7] to smaller regeneration sites. An illustration of the latter in Manchester is provided by the NOMA development on the edges of the city centre. This was visualised in an online video, entitled *NOMA A Pioneering Development*, which simulates the traversing (sometimes as a pedestrian, sometimes at bird's-eye view)[8] of the regenerated built up area ahead of its redevelopment.

The built environment also provides a powerful material and visual conduit for futures envisaged for such spaces (Degen 2009; Flusty 2001, 2006; Smith 1996), promoting certain activities and uses of space and discouraging others from taking place. Whereas in a 3-D modelling video animation, a running commentary may explicitly convey future aspirations, the latter are indirectly evoked in the physical environment. For example, the built environment of the new Media City, just outside central Manchester, conveys many meanings and aspirations about the regeneration of this area of Salford. It visually replaces[9] the dereliction associated with deindustrialisation (Taylor, et al. 1996) and strongly suggests the presence of creative industries and of the kind of economic and media activity that would connect this area with other global media circuits (Short 2004). It thus signals the status of Media City as an entrepreneurial site (Haider 1992; Harvey 1989; Kotler, et al. 1993) open for further investment. It is in this sense that the built environment can also be taken to perform aspirations about specific futures.

The research I present here focuses on the *discursive* practices of futuring, showing how they play a significant role in mobilising urban futures, especially in policy-making arenas. Reviewing the policy and strategy documents on Manchester city centre, I found many explicit articulations of the institutional visions for the future of Manchester city centre. The visions thus gathered were used in various other phases of my fieldwork, and enabled me to probe further into the views of institutional stakeholders.[10] The institutional visions of the future of the city centre included the following:

> The wider vision for Manchester is clear ... to ensure that the city is: a major European regional capital, a centre for investment growth.
>
> Manchester and its city centre are competing internationally ... External views of Manchester's quality of life as a whole are strongly determined by perceptions of the city centre ... Achievement of our vision for the city centre will ensure positive perceptions of Manchester, for both investors and residents.
>
> The city centre will reflect Manchester's ambition to be in the front rank of cities in Europe and the world. (MCC 2009: 6, 3, 7)

These aspirations, unequivocally linked to enhancing Manchester's global positioning and its attractiveness to flows of tourism and investment, reflect the deeply entrepreneurial turn (Harvey 1989; MacLeod 2002; Savage, et al. 2003) which the city's governance has embraced. This shift to entrepreneurial forms of governance (see also chs 1, 2 and 3, this volume) has been theorised across urban sociological literature on Manchester since the 1990s (see especially Cochrane, et al. 2002; Peck and Ward 2002). What the literature does not sufficiently address, and therefore what I seek to investigate, is whether there is the support for these visions across a wide range of stakeholders.

My fieldwork also explored local media coverage to tease out whether these futures were mobilised through local media too. These institutionally promoted visions were not only echoed in the press, but were strongly emphasised. Consider, for example, how the following local news article clearly articulates a key city aspiration – that of attracting event tourism and investment to Manchester and transforming it into the most prominent conference hosting site nationally:

> Manchester has gone from also-ran to conference capital of Britain … the Tory conference will generate £27m for the local economy a massive shot in the arm in difficult times … So-called business tourism in Manchester is now worth an astonishing £573m per annum … Last year, Manchester was voted third best conference destination in the world by a leading trade magazine … city leaders won't be happy until they are number one. (*Manchester Evening News*, 26 September 2011: 10)

Despite the prevalence of these narratives, theoretical and empirical work looking at whether these imagined futures are shared by a variety of actors beyond the main institutional stakeholders still remains scarce. To appreciate the significance and impact of these visions for a wider range of stakeholders (beyond city branders, policy makers and marketers), these processes of *futuring* need to be opened up and scrutinised further. I argue that this can be done through a theorisation of *futuring* advanced in other areas of the social sciences, namely within the field of STS. The next section will take a closer look at this body of work, highlighting the distinctive contribution it can make to our understanding of urban governance.

Methodology: theorising processes of visioning and futuring through an STS approach

The core argument I advance in this section, and in the chapter at large, is that the theoretical stance towards *futuring* elaborated in STS ought to be applied to the study of governance in the urban. As it renders explicit key value judgments that stakeholders hold, it highlights those that are currently prioritised (and reveals by whom), and those that are trade-offs. This approach can contribute to greater transparency, democratic challenge of policy and may encourage more socially robust policy making.

Even as I emphasise the relevance of an understanding developed within STS, it must be acknowledged that the preoccupation with governing futures can be approached from different angles within the social sciences. On one hand we can think of how attempting to govern futures has generated a theorisation of risk (Giddens 1999) and the Risk Society (Beck 1992), as a society increasingly concerned with images of the future and ideas of what it will bring, and engrossed in risk assessments and risk-benefit analyses. If we take a longer historical perspective on futuring, we can trace, through the work of Andersson (Andersson 2006; Andersson and Rindzeviciute 2012) for instance, the birth of futurology and geopolitical forecasting as a separate discipline since the Cold War era, and theorise the practices of scenario building, horizon scanning and other foresight exercises still prevalent in policy today. Another very fruitful approach is offered by scholars who highlight the types of precautionary, pre-emptive and preparedness strategies that ensue from the process of *futuring*. This work, varied as it remains, was spearheaded by the governmentality school (Castel 1990; Rose 1989; Rose, et al. 2006) in sociology, and is also pursued in geography (Amoore 2011, 2012; Anderson 2010) and philosophy (Agamben 2002; Massumi 2005, 2009). All useful on their own account, these approaches can complement each other and the STS approach I present below.

STS's understanding of futures has been developed through a large body of work on genomics that closely followed the mapping of the Human Genome in 2003. As such, it critically engaged with images, discourses and aspirations about genomic futures that at the time were seen to be just about to materialise. STS scholars have closely critiqued the promotion of technological innovations, in the fields of biotechnology and genomics, but also nanotechnologies and grid computing, on the basis of these promissory discourses and expectations of their applications (for instance Brown and Michael 2003; Brown, et al. 2000; Hedgecoe and Martin 2003, 2007; Pieri 2010). These discourses of hope and expectations integrate the emergent technologies within specific future scenarios and representations of the everyday – for instance that of personalised medicine, or of the smart home responsive to its user and the environment via nano-sensors and biometrics.

The initial focus on demystifying technological futures by revealing them to be hyped led to further theorisation in STS. Known as 'sociology of expectation' (Hedgecoe and Martin 2003), this later work highlighted that the future is not a neutral temporal space, but rather the catalyst of very real and very present trade-offs, for instance in terms of present investments, R&D and allocation of resources (Borup, et al. 2006; Brown and Michael 2003; Brown, et al. 2000; Pieri 2009).

What is significant about the STS approach to futures, therefore, is that it moves attention away from debates over the likelihood that a given scenario might materialise, and from its possible benefits (and risks), which are not yet achieved (or perhaps will never materialise). Instead, it redirects attention towards the very real trade-offs being made today, on the basis of some of the promises and the futures mobilised (Pieri 2009).

As Brown and Michael have noted (when looking at the life sciences and innovation in health domains), the future is more fruitfully engaged heuristi-cally, and there is an urgent need 'to shift the analytical angle from looking into the future to looking at the future, or how the future is mobilised in real time to marshal resources, co-ordinate activities and manage uncertainty' (2003: 2). A major implication of conceiving of futures in this way is that the tensions which lie within them can be explored. The futures, as political con-structs, can then be opened up to contestation.

In this chapter I show that the process of eliciting visions and imaginary of the future of Manchester city centre renders explicit some of the value judg-ments and priorities that different stakeholders may pursue. These priorities are embedded in specific future projections and discourses of what the city centre will be like and ought to be like in the future. Rendering these priorities and embedded values explicit allows us to open them up to greater scrutiny and accountability. As I will illustrate below, mobilising the population pro-jections for Manchester city centre and the findings of my ethnographic field-work, this approach allowed me to unpack the ways in which certain priorities may be shared across various stakeholders or be held by some stakeholders only (Pieri 2009). Before discussing the findings of my ethnography, the fol-lowing section briefly sums up its methods and the data collected.

Methods and data collection

In this chapter I draw on research conducted on Manchester city centre between 2011 and 2014, using qualitative mixed-methods (Mason 2006). This work directly elicited the views and priorities held by various stakeholders for the city centre. Through in-depth discussions about the future(s) of the city centre, the fieldwork uncovered both those futures which stakeholders identify as likely or inevitable, and those that they identify as desirable and to be prioritised.

The fieldwork included multi-stakeholder interviews and focus groups, doc-umentary and media analysis, and ethnographic observation of Manchester city centre, including participant observation of its many events.[11] The work aimed to provide a metaphoric 360-degree view of the city centre, offering multiple analytical entry points, and allowing a 'thick sociological description' (Atkinson 2005).

In 2012 thirty-nine participants were accessed in the research, twenty-eight via semi-structured interviews and eleven via focus groups. Interviews and focus groups were recorded, transcribed in full and thematically coded for the purpose of discourse analysis (Fairclough 2010) and frame analysis (Entman

1993; Kitzinger 2007) with the assistance of Atlas.ti software (Lewins and Silver 2007). Participants included institutional stakeholders and property developers actively involved in shaping the city centre, security experts, city centre workers and users, and city centre residents. The focus groups lasted two hours each and involved city centre residents only. The interviews with the other stakeholders generally lasted one hour.

Two media datasets were collected, providing a snapshot view of how Manchester city centre was discussed and portrayed in the local printed media in a daily newspaper (*Manchester Evening News*, August to October 2011), and a weekly city centre magazine (*Urban Life*, mid-July to mid-October 2011). A further database was compiled by collecting national daily printed media coverage about Manchester (in both national tabloid and quality papers) over a period of one month (August 2011), and used as a reference database when investigating the local coverage of specific events. Key policy documents were also investigated as they were considered a catalyst for further policy development. This media and policy material fed into various stages of the fieldwork, and excerpts were used to further explore participants' aspirations and imaginaries over Manchester city centre.

The aim of my research was to investigate security and cosmopolitanism, their relationship and impact on shaping the city centre.[12] A key research objective was to elicit the views and priorities of different stakeholders (including City Councillors, developers, businesses, citizens) about the future of the city centre at large (i.e. beyond issues of security and cosmopolitanism), to identify overlaps and divergences. I explored multiple stakeholders' priorities to tease out existing overlaps, tensions and trade-offs. This chapter draws on the data generated by this strand of the research (for an example of the work on security, see Pieri 2014).

The working boundaries of the city centre adopted in my research are those of the map produced by Visit Manchester.[13] Manchester city centre is relatively compact and is roughly enclosed within the Irwell River (to the West and North West), Whitworth Street West and Whitworth Street (to the South), Great Ancoats Street and Swan Street (to the North, North East). In the following section I describe some of its salient features before presenting and discussing my findings about its future trajectories and its resident population.

Manchester city centre

Manchester city centre is often portrayed as having undergone a very positive revolution since the late 1980s and early 1990s – an 'epic' transformation in the words of the City Council Chief Executive, Sir Howard Bernstein (in Kellie 2010: 10). Its regeneration was spearheaded by bidding for the Olympics and Commonwealth Games (Cochrane, et al. 2002; Holden 2002; Quilley 2002;

Robson 2002; Taylor, et al. 1996) and largely achieved through property development (Kellie 2010), including through the creation of new spaces of leisure
and consumption (see Bell and Binnie 2004, 2005 on the creation of the Gay
Village and new spaces of gastronomy, or consider the recent redevelopment
of Spinningfield, for example; Binnie and Skeggs 2004). The regeneration was
closely intertwined with a growing resident population, which in the 1960s
had dwindled to about 4,000 inhabitants and in the 1970s had reached an
all-time-low figure of 200 (Kellie 2010: 121). In the early 1990s the empty and
dilapidated warehouses, a visual reminder of the economic downturn and
post-industrialisation which marred the city through most of the 1980s, were
converted into residential property. The conversions became pivotal, along
with the changes discussed, in catalysing city centre resident growth (Kellie
2010; Taylor, et al. 1996).

The partnership mode of governance (Allen 2007; Peck and Ward 2002;
Taylor, et al. 1996) and the accompanying rhetoric of a harmonious marriage
of interests between public and private sector (Cochrane, et al. 2002; Holden
2002; Quilley 2002; Robson 2002; Taylor, et al. 1996) strongly enabled this
type of regeneration and continues to shape the city's politics today (Kellie
2010; see also other contributions to this collections, e.g. ch 1 by Knox). The
city centre continues to showcase the wider aspirations that institutional
actors hold for the city of Manchester as a whole, as evidenced in the city
centre Strategic Plan 2009–2012 (2009). These factors contributed to making
it a particularly salient site for my fieldwork.

By 2011 the city centre ward counted approximately 18,000 residents (Office
for National Statistics 2011a, 2011b), a number expected to have increased
already. The 2011 census data (Office for National Statistics 2011c: 2, Table
KS201, ethnicity of residents) reported resident ethnic composition to be
largely white,[14] with a lower number of residents of mixed ethnicity (a much
lower number of black or black British residents than the rest of Manchester,[15]
but with higher numbers of Asian or Asian British residents and of residents
of other ethnicities). The vast majority of residents were aged between 18 and
29 years[16] and the city centre had a population mean age of 27, considerably
lower than that of the city at large (Office for National Statistics 2011a, 2011b).

The area has striking features that set it apart from the rest of Greater
Manchester, such as a higher population density and smaller household size[17]
(Manchester City Council and NHS Manchester 2011: 4–5). When not living
on their own, residents share flats, and very few households count children
amongst their occupants (Manchester City Council and NHS Manchester
2011: 8).[18]

This ward is characterised by high household incomes and low deprivation
levels, particularly when compared to other areas of Manchester (Manchester
City Council and NHS Manchester 2011: 14). Almost all city centre residents

(96.6 per cent) live in private accommodation, mostly privately rented, but also privately owned (Manchester City Council and NHS Manchester 2011: 14). The most prevalent type of property is flats, whose value remains much higher than that of the average cost of property in Manchester (Manchester City Council and NHS Manchester 2011: 14).[19]

In terms of quality of life measurements, such as sense of place and sense of belonging, a pre-2011 study reveals that residents report high levels of satisfaction in their local area, but that fewer of them, when contrasted to the average for Manchester, feel able to affect decision making in their local area, and fewer when compared to the average but also to any other area of Manchester report a feeling of belonging to the area (Manchester City Council and NHS Manchester 2011: 26).

Competing interests and trajectories: the city centre resident population

In this section I mobilise the insights generated by my focus groups and interviews with a range of stakeholders[20] conducted in 2012 to argue that the aspirations of many stakeholders are being neglected and frustrated.

Even where superficial convergence over aspirations might at first sight be apparent, closer analysis of stakeholders' aspirations revealed deeper tensions and irreconcilable aims. For example most of the stakeholders accessed saw the city centre population as continuing to rise in the future and shared an understanding of its current composition. They identified changes to this composition as a key priority for the future. Stakeholders also tended to agree on the need to bring in more families.

Nonetheless, eliciting urban futures and analysing them carefully disclosed areas of tensions. The modalities of achieving the change in sociodemographics varied greatly. Residents' priority of introducing much greater demographic mix (not simply across a wider age range, but also through a much more radical socio-economic transformation) was not endorsed by institutional and business participants. The very means envisaged for bringing about residential transformation were widely divergent.

Many actors advocate the presence of more families and young children in the city centre. However, closer attention to the futures mobilised revealed only limited overlap. Institutional stakeholders (from Councillors to city branders within the tourist board) believed this change could be achieved through prioritising an expansion of the property stock:

> there is demand for at least another 1,000 apartments a year I think, to be delivered in the city centre over the next kind of five year or so. (Interview with Director of Marketing Strategy, Marketing Manchester)

what we need is high value aspirational family housing. (Interview with Chief
Executive, Manchester City Council)

Visit Manchester (the tourist board) and CityCo[21] auspicated a more family
friendly environment in the city centre – although, importantly, what they
envisaged was more oriented towards (families as) visitors rather than (families as) city centre residents. They considered change to be achievable through
a relatively small scale rebalancing of the events on offer. Other stakeholders,
however, prioritised changes in activity programming beyond a simple extension of the kind of activities on offer, towards partially reducing some of the
existing night-time economy, which they saw as in direct competition with
the one they were promoting.

More importantly perhaps, residents noted that in order to attract families
to the city centre a number of key services would need to be provided, such as
schools or doctors' surgeries, as well as the opening of more spaces like parks
and canal embankments:

> B: They built a lot of apartments ... the population is growing, but your
> prescription? You know, where's a dentist?
> G: Yeah, dentists, doctors, you know, there, there are no schools, that's why ...
> families that have children, when they get to 3 or 4 they kind of have to move
> out (Residents focus group 1)

> In the long term you'd want a mixture of people to live in the city centre, you'd
> want schools and facilities and doctors. (Interview with resident 2)

These discussions were revealing of the shortcomings that current residents
experienced in the city centre today. Furthermore, while attracting new
residents may require certain facilities, retaining them would also require
improvements to the current living conditions – by reducing certain types of
noise pollution, and better maintaining and cleaning the space and streets. As
noted by residents what would need prioritising is:

> liveability so that you don't then get ... a night club opening next door to you,
> that it can mean that you can't sleep. (Interview with resident 2)

The transience of the resident population was a recurrent issue brought up
by a variety of stakeholders and particularly by current residents, and not
simply linked to life stages (professionals starting a family in the suburbs,
older citizen moving to leafy areas to retire, and students leaving after completing university), but also connected to affordability (from the inflated costs
of food shopping in 'Local' and 'Metro' branches of supermarkets aimed at
visitors or office workers, to the high costs of city centre accommodation). The
analysis of stakeholders' priorities highlighted a view of the current city centre
property market as exclusionary and targeted towards the affluent, the young,

the childless, disclosing current concerns over social justice that would need redressing in order to create a city centre for all:

> a fair amount of people couldn't afford to live in the city centre now. Rents are higher … You don't want to create a community of just one kind of people in the city centre. (Interview with artistic lead, art venue, 2012)

> the rental market is up through the roof … it's getting ridiculous. (Resident focus group 1)

> J: more accessible accommodation for people. Affordable accommodation … [the city centre is] too expensive … it's targeted for the wealthy, the very rich. (Interview with Big Issue vendor)

> B: you might get … food tourists, … bars and restaurants … we all like to go to from time to time, but that's not necessarily, what they call the sustainable way of living for residents, and you know, the choice of supermarkets is limited.
> M: Yeah.
> B: To Metro stores effectively in the city centre.
> G: Yeah.
> M: They cost more. (Resident focus group 1)

Some of the stakeholders saw the introduction of (a measure) of affordable homes and social housing as a priority:

> the city needs to … think of providing stuff for everybody. You know I probably like to see a bit more social housing in the city centre as well … they have difficulty forcing developers to put in a proportion. (Resident focus group 1)

The institutional position, however, is one of absolute opposition to increasing the social housing stock in the city centre, epitomised in the following statement by the Council CEO, who claimed that:

> we need more social housing in Manchester [city centre] like we need a hole in our head. What we need is high value aspirational family housing. (Interview with Chief Executive, Manchester City Council)

Despite the recent recession and the booming rental market, the Council and property developers were still envisaging building property to sell. No references were made to improvements to the rental market, which contrasted with the current concerns of many other stakeholders, primarily current residents and their wish to prioritise security of tenancy.

The increased presence of students, which many considered would form a greater ratio of the city centre population in the future, was also seen by current residents as unlikely to stimulate demand for the services that they currently needed, and which most of the future population was also likely to need:

B: It might depend on the permanency of the city centre residents.
M: Yeah!
B: If it becomes a transit for finishing uni, young professionals, and then if
they move to have families let's say … the pressure, it might not be maintained
to improve the services.
M: I think, yeah, from a student point of view … they give you a sort of
induction sheet saying 'oh register with a GP' … everyone of my friends from
home never bothered with that. (Resident focus group 1)

The effects of transience were also perceived as disempowering and limiting
one's ability to participate in decision making about one's environment:

you need short term, as new people need to move in and out … but you also
need a cohort of people who are there for the long run, because then they get
involved in the community and they turn up for meetings and they talk to the
Councillors and they feel like … they *have* got an investment, they have got a
long term view. (Interview with resident 2)

City centre residents were adamant that the city centre needed to embrace
greater diversity and variety and cater for all. Moreover, some of the older residents indicated that they would like more mature residents to come and live
in the city centre, or highlighted some of the positive implications of having a
more varied age range base, when discussing their priorities:

as a person with grey hair, I'd like to see one or two more grey haired people
taking advantage of the life … wanting to settle in the city centre. (Resident
focus group 1)

There's not really an older crowd, … if there were things to encourage it … it's
something that could work. (Resident focus group 1)

I'd like to see more people living in town, and in a mixed community with families and older people, but people having facilities near them, and walking and
cycling, and getting the bus … you still want it to be a city, but a liveable city.
(Interview with resident 2)

I think there's a lot of people who complain about rowdiness; they complain
about drunkenness; they complain about litter … things of that nature and I
think if you change the age range of the people living in the city I think a lot of
those problems will sort of sort themselves out. (Resident focus group 2)

To sum up, there was apparent convergence over an aspiration to increase
the residential mix in the city centre, and this was (on the surface)
endorsed by all respondents. Property developers and institutional players
and branders favoured aspirational homes (as well as activity planning).
However, even if successful, the institutional response would only be very

marginally extending the demographic mix of the resident population along one dimension – that of the age range, bringing children together with their parents to the city centre. But it would not extend further the economic composition of the current city centre population, nor the age mix more widely understood. As such it is unlikely to meet the aspirations of the residents and other stakeholders accessed. Residents called for affordable accommodation (including a measure of social housing and improvements to the rental market, as well as envisaging other solutions[22]) and strongly advocated basic service provision and a resident-friendly economy (such as food shops) not principally geared towards the needs of visitors and commuters. Their priorities are neglected.

Eliciting and mapping different stakeholders' priorities about urban futures revealed many areas of divergence, along with some areas of convergence. The discourse of partnership, which emerged as a dominant narrative embedded in various stakeholders' accounts, as well as resulting in configurations easily observable ethnographically,[23] was also problematised as a result. By reflecting on aspirations and futures, drawing out their present implications, embedded values and inherent trade-offs, important contradictions began to emerge. Many of the accounts I have gathered open up scrutiny over the objectives currently pursued though public–private partnerships and call into question their priorities and aspirations.

Conclusion

The futures of cities occupy a central role in policy making today, and many of the challenges we face, and the solutions we seek, are often framed at the scale of the city. These processes are accompanied by the resurgence of lively debates about the infrastructure of cities, the nature of city living, the public realm, risk and urban sociability.

Futures are often mobilised through powerful visuals and discursive narrative, as well as through the built environment itself, which also provides a powerful conduit for such aspirations. In this chapter I focused primarily on the *discursive* practices of futuring. Reviewing the policy and strategy documents on Manchester city centre over the last ten years and the local media coverage, I showed that the institutionally promoted visions were strongly emphasised in the press too. Yet to appreciate the significance and impact of these visions for a wider range of stakeholders (beyond city branders, policy makers and marketers), the processes of *futuring* need to be opened up and scrutinised further. I argued that this can be done through a multi-stakeholder engagement theoretically grounded in STS, and have highlighted the distinctive contribution that taking this approach to *futuring* can make to our understanding of urban governance, beyond the case study of Manchester.

Involving a multiplicity of actors and engaging them in reflection about the future(s) of the city centre revealed limitations in the current use and management of city centre space. It showed how current practices impinge on the everyday life of residents and their aspirations for the future. This analysis highlighted the extent to which partnerships are believed to be operating with shared aims and interests, and cast doubts on the ability and willingness of private partners to take up roles that otherwise (traditionally or simply by default) fall onto the public sector. It also questioned the commitment of the public sector to meet some of the key needs and aspirations of current residents, illustrating whose priorities are currently traded off.

In this case study, competing objectives have been revealed through a discussion on the city centre population and its potential future trajectories. Other dimensions of my research echo these findings – similar tensions and contradictions emerged when actors discussed other aspects of the future of the city centre – namely public space, and its intended uses and users; security arrangements; leisure, activity planning and the economy of the city centre.

This novel approach, which applies to the urban domain a theorisation of futures derived from STS, allowed me to mobilise futures reflexively, as political objects, and as a heuristic. I was able to shed light on the present commitments and trade-offs that they engender. I have shown that this is an efficacious, interdisciplinary and mixed-methodology, pursued through multi-stakeholder involvement, to explore present priorities and practices in the urban. This approach highlighted the contested nature of current practices and trajectories, and the competing interests at play. It could, thus, be deployed to stir local governance towards more socially robust decision making. It grounds a move away from a discourse of partnership that glosses over whose interests are being currently pursued, towards greater accountability (Burgess, et al. 2007; Stirling 2010) and social agonism (Amin 2002, 2008; Watson 2006).

Acknowledgements

The support of Pathways to Cosmopolitanism, a collaborative research initiative linking the University of Manchester and the National University of Singapore, is gratefully acknowledged (2011–2013).

Notes

1 E.g. the European Commission's initiative on Smart Cities. Available at ec.europa. eu/eip/smartcities/index_en.htm. Accessed 19 December 2015.

2 E.g. the UN campaign on Making Cities Resilient. Available at www.unisdr.org/ campaign/resilientcities/about. Accessed 19 December 2015.

3 E.g. UN-Habitat 2004 Migrants and Multicultural Cities: Problem or Possibility? UN-Habitat Report Celebrates Multiculturalism: UN-Habitat Features. Available at cn.unhabitat.org/documents/media_centre/sowc/Featuremigrants.pdf. Accessed 23 May 2014.

4 E.g. the new cities or neighbourhoods under construction in the Middle East, such as Masdar City masdarcity.ae/en/ (accessed 19 November 2015), or in other eco cities in China (for example Dongtan).

5 From climate change to the pursuit of the knowledge economy.

6 E.g. *Our Life in the Future* by Graves and Madoc-Jones (2009), based on an aerial shot of London by J. Hawkes, www.london-futures.com/page/2/. Accessed 19 December 2015). Or the post-apocalyptic Manchester city centre images of James Chadderton www.urbanghostsmedia.com/2013/02/manchester-post-apocalyptic-visions-artist-james-chadderton-future-dystopia/. Accessed 25 February 2016.

7 www.youtube.com/watch?v=Llzq9YMsPP8 and www.youtube.com/watch?v=Fygh Lnbp2oU. Accessed 19 December 2015.

8 www.youtube.com/watch?v=gqW8qaoD9Sc. Accessed 23 February 2016.

9 Whether this means appropriately tackling or merely glossing over issues remains open to debate.

10 They also assisted in the identification of key institutional and business actors to interview. As prompts, instead, they were complemented by photos of city centre events taken during my ethnography. More on methods in the methods section below.

11 Including Chinese New Year celebrations and other festivals, Gay Pride Parades, political party conferences, as well as impromptu rallies after the 2011 riots. Observing these events involved noticing and interpreting the events that were unfolding, the setting and interactions, taking notes, talking to participants, taking photos, collecting material and objects that were being handed out.

12 See www.socialsciences.manchester.ac.uk/sociology/research/postgraduate-resear ch/post-phd-students/elisa-pieri/. Accessed 27 July 2016.

13 www.visitmanchester.com/media/115401/pocketpercent20mappercent202011_201 0.pdf. Accessed 1 June 2014.

14 68 per cent (Office for National Statistics 2011c: 2).

15 Only 2.4 per cent versus the 8.6 per cent average for the city (Office for National Statistics 2011c: 2).

16 The 20–24 age group alone accounted for 6,160 residents; there were less than 400 people aged 0–17, and only 1,358 adults and older citizens between the ages of 45 and 90+.

17 1.79 per household.

18 A mere 2.7 per cent compared to the 36.3 per cent city average.

19 One third of property are within Council Tax band D (the city average is 6.6 per cent), followed by a very significant number of band C and band E properties (Office for National Statistics 2011c: 10).

20 See data collection section for participants' details.

21 The city centre management company, a public–private partnership, cityco.com/. Accessed 23 December 2015.
22 Such as the retrofitting of historic buildings.
23 E.g. the same people sat on the boards of various organisation and public–private partnerships.

References

Agamben, Giorgio. 2002. "On security and terror". *Theory and Event* 5 (4). Available at http://muse.jhu.edu/journals/theory_and_event/v005/5.4agamben.html. Accessed 12 April 2014.
Allen, Chris. 2007. "Of urban entrepreneurs or 24-hour party people? City-centre living in Manchester, England". *Environment and Planning* A 39: 666–683.
Amin, Ash. 2002. "Ethnicity and the multicultural city: living with diversity". *Environment and Planning* A 34: 959–980.
— 2008. "Collective culture and urban public space". *City* 12 (1): 5–24.
— 2013. "Telescopic urbanism and the poor". *City* 17 (4): 476–492.
Amoore, Louise. 2011. "Data derivatives: on the emergence of a security risk calculus for our times". *Theory, Culture & Society* 28: 24–43.
— 2012. "Politics of possibility". Seminar delivered on 14 November 2012 at the University of Manchester.
Anderson, Ben. 2010. "Preemption, precaution, preparedness: anticipatory action and future geographies". *Progress in Human Geography* 34 (6): 777–798.
Andersson, Jenny. 2006. "Choosing futures: Alva Myrdal and the construction of Swedish Futures Studies, 1967–1972". *Internationaal Instituut voor Sociale Geschiedenis* 51 (2): pp. 277–295.
Andersson, Jenny and Egle Rindzeviciute. 2012. "The political life of prediction: the future as a space of scientific world governance in the Cold War era". In CRESC Annual Conference 2012 'Promises: Crisis and Socio-Cultural Change'. Manchester, 5–7 September 2012.
Atkinson, Paul. 2005. "Qualitative research: unity and diversity". Forum: *Qualitative Social Research* 6 (3): Art 26. Available at www.qualitative-research.net/index.php/fqs/article/view/4/10. Accessed 4 March 2014.
Barthes, Roland. 1957. *Mythologies*. Paris: Editions du Seuil.
— 1977. *Image, Music, Text*. London: HarperCollins.
Batty, Michael. 2012. "Smart cities, big data". *Environment and Planning B: Planning and Design* (39): 191–193.
Beck, Ulrich. 1992. *Risk Society: Towards a New Modernity*. London: Sage.
Bell, David and Jon Binnie. 2004. "Authenticating queer space: citizenship, urbanism and governance". *Urban Studies* 41 (9): 1807–1820.
— 2005. "What's eating Manchester? Gastro-culture and urban regeneration". *Architectural Design* 75 (3): 78–85.

Binnie, Jon and Beverly Skeggs. 2004. "Cosmopolitan knowledge and the production and consumption of sexualised space: Manchester's gay village". *The Sociological Review* 52 (1): 39–61.

Borup, Mads, Nik Brown, Kornelia Konrad, and Harro Van Lente. 2006. "The sociology of expectations in science and technology". *Technology Analysis & Strategic Management* 18 (3/4): 285–298.

Brown, Nik and Mike Michael. 2003. "A sociology of expectations: retrospecting prospects and prospecting retrospects". *Technology Analysis and Strategic Management* 15 (1): 3–18.

Brown, Nik, Brian Rappert, and Andrew Webster, eds. 2000. *Contested Futures: A Sociology of Prospective Techno-Science*. Aldershot: Ashgate.

Burgess, Jacquelin, Andy Stirling, Judy Clark, Gail Davies, Malcolm Eames, Kristina Staley, and Suzanne Williamson. 2007. "Deliberative mapping: a novel analytic-deliberative methodology to support contested science-policy decisions". *Public Understanding of Science* 16: 299–322.

Castel, Robert. 1990. "From dangerousness to risk". In *The Foucault Effect: Studies in Governmentality with Two Lectures by and an Interview with Michel Foucault*. G. Burchell, C. Gordon, and P. Miller, eds. pp. 281–298. London: Harvester Wheatsheaf Publishing.

Coaffee, Jon, David Murakami Wood, and Peter Rogers. 2009. *The Everyday Resilience of the City*. London: Palgrave Macmillan.

Cochrane, Allan, Jamie Peck, and Adam Tickell. 2002. "Olympic dreams: visions of partnership". In *City of Revolution: Restructuring Manchester*. J. Peck and K. Ward, eds. pp. 95–115. Manchester: Manchester University Press.

Degen, Monica. 2009. *Sensing Cities: Regenerating Public Life in Barcelona and Manchester*. London: Routledge.

Entman, Robert M. 1993. "Framing: toward clarification of a fractured paradigm". *Journal of Communication* 43 (4): 51–8.

Fairclough, Norman. 2010. *Critical Discourse Analysis: The Critical Study of Language*. (2nd ed.) Harlow: Longman.

Flusty, Steven. 2001. "The banality of interdiction: surveillance, control and the displacement of diversity". *International Journal of Urban and Regional Research* 25 (3): 658–664.

— 2006. "Culturing the world city: an exhibition of the global present". In *The Global City Reader*. N. Brenner and R. Keil, eds. Abington (Oxon): Routledge.

Giddens, Anthony. 1999. "Risk and responsibility". *The Modern Law Review* 62 (1): 1–10.

Guy, Simon and Simon Marvin. 2001. "Constructing sustainable urban futures: from models to competing pathways". *Impact Assessment and Project Appraisal* 19 (2): 131–139.

Haider, Donald. 1992. "Place wars: new realities of the 1990s". *Economic Development Quarterly* 6 (2): 127–134.

Hammer, Stephen, Lamia Kamal-Chaoui, Alexis Robert, and Marissa Plouin. 2011. "Cities and green growth: a conceptual framework". OECD Regional Development Working Papers 2011/08 OECD Publishing. Available at http://dx.doi.org/10.1787/5kgotflmzx34-en. Accessed 23 May 2014.

Harvey, David. 1989. "From managerialism to entrepreneurialism: the transformation in urban governance in late capitalism". *Geografiska Annaler* 71 (1): 3–17.

Harvey, Penelope. 2009. "Between narrative and number: the case of ARUP's 3D Digital City Model". *Cultural Sociology* 3 (2): 257–276.

Hedgecoe, Adam and Paul Martin. 2003. "The drugs don't work: expectations and the shaping of pharmacogenetics". *Social Studies of Science* 33 (3): 327–364.

— 2007. "Genomics, STS and the making of sociotechnical futures". In *The Handbook of Science and Technology Studies*. E. Hackett, O. Amsterdamska, M. Lynch, and J. Wajecman, eds. (3rd ed.) pp. 817–839. Cambridge, MA: MIT Press.

Holden, Adam. 2002. "Bomb sites: the politics of opportunity". In *City of Revolution: Restructuring Manchester*. J. Peck and K. Ward, eds. pp. 131–155. Manchester: Manchester University Press.

Kellie, E. 2010. *Rebuilding Manchester*. Derby: The Derby Group Publishing Company.

Kitzinger, Jenny. 2007. "Framing and frame analysis". In *Media Studies: Key Issues and Debates*. E. Devereux, ed. pp. 134–162. London: Sage.

Kotler, Philip, Donald Haider, and Iriving Rein. 1993. *Marketing Places: Attracting Investment, Industry And Tourism To Cities, States And Nations*. New York: Free Press.

Lewins, Ann and Christina Silver. 2007. *Using Software in Qualitative Research: A Step-by-Step Guide*. London: Sage.

MacLeod, Gordon. 2002. "From urban enterpreneurialism to a 'revanchist city'? On the spacial injustices of Glasgow's renaissance". *Antipode* 34: 602–624.

Mason, Jennifer. 2006. "Mixing methods in a qualitatively driven way". *Qualitative Research* 6 (1): 9–25.

Massumi, Brian. 2005. "The future birth of an affective fact". Conference Proceedings: Genealogies of Biopolitics. Available at browse.reticular.info/text/collected/massumi.pdf. Accessed 23 May 2014.

— 2009. "National enterprise emergency: steps toward an ecology of powers". *Theory, Culture & Society* 26: 153–186.

MCC. 2003. Manchester City Centre Strategic Plan 2004–2007. Manchester: MCC. Available at www.manchester.gov.uk/download/downloads/id/2754/manchester_city_centre_strategic_plan_2004-2007. Accessed 23 May 2014.

MCC. 2009. *A Strategic Plan for Manchester City Centre 2009–2012*. Available at http://cityco.com/city-centre-strategic-plan-2009-2012/. Accessed 23 May 2014.

MCC and NHS Manchester. 2011. City Centre Ward Profile. Version 2011/02a. Manchester. Available at www.manchester.gov.uk/download/downloads/id/17987/a26k_city_centre_2011_02a. Accessed 23 May 2014.

NOMA. 2011. *A Pioneering Development*. Video Available at www.youtube.com/watch?v=IlpwWPh4Z3k. Accessed 19 December 2015.

Office for National Statistics 2011a. *2011 Census: Usual Resident Population By Five Year Age Group*. London: Crown.

— 2011b. *Manchester Ward Population Age Structure, Census 2011 – total*. London: Crown. Available at www.manchester.gov.uk/download/downloads/id/17519/a03a_2011_census_wards_by_age-total. Accessed 28 July 2013.

— 2011c. *2011 Census: City Centre Dashboard*. London: Crown. Available at www.manchester.gov.uk/download/downloads/id/19845/q04k_2011_census_city_centre_dashboard. Accessed 23 May 2014.

Parnell, Susan. 2012. "Learning about the world of cities: a geographer's reflections from the bottom of Africa". Paper presented at 'A World Of Cities? Comparison Across The Disciplines'. Manchester, 17–18 May 2012. Paper Available at www.cities.manchester.ac.uk/resources/audio/. Accessed 23 May 2014.

Peck, Jamie and Kevin Ward, eds. 2002. *City of Revolution: Restructuring Manchester*. Manchester: Manchester University Press.

Pieri, Elisa. 2009. "Sociology of expectation and the e-social science agenda". *Information, Communication & Society* 12 (7): 1103–1118.

— 2010. "Predictive genetic testing and the promise of personalised medicine". In *Assessing Life: On The Organisation Of Genetic Testing. Science and Technology Studies*. Vol. 59. B. Wieser and W. Berger, eds. pp. 175–202. München/Wien: Profil.

— 2014. "Emergent policing practices: operation Shop a Looter and urban space securitisation in the aftermath of the Manchester 2011 riots". *Surveillance & Society* 12 (1): 38–54.

Quilley, Stephen. 2002. "Entepreneurial turns: municipal socialism and after". In *City of Revolution: Restructuring Manchester*. J. Peck and K. Ward, eds. pp. 77–94. Manchester: Manchester University Press.

Robson, Brian. 2002. "Mancunian ways: the politics of regeneration". In *City of Revolution: Restructuring Manchester*. J. Peck and K. Ward, eds. pp. 34–49. Manchester: Manchester University Press.

Rose, Nikolas. 1989. *Governing the Soul: The Shaping of the Private Self*. London: Routledge.

Rose, Nikolas, Pat O'Malley, and Mariana Valverde. 2006. "Governmentality". *Annual Review of Law and Social Science* 2: 83–104.

Savage, Michael, Alan Warde, and Kevin Ward. 2003. *Urban Sociology, Capitalism and Modernity*. (2nd ed.) London: Palgrave Macmillan.

Short, John Rennie. 2004. *Global Metropolitan*. London: Routledge.

Smith, Neil. 1996. "After Tompkins Square Park: degentrification and the revanchists city". In *Re-Presenting the City*. D. King, ed. New York: New York University Press.

Stirling, Andy. 2010. "Keep it complex". *Nature* 468 (7327): 1029–1031.

Taylor, Ian, Karen Evans, and Penny Fraser. 1996. *A Tale of Two Cities: Global Change, Local Feeling, and Everyday Life in the North of England: A Study in Manchester and Sheffield.* London: Routledge.

United Nations. 2014. "World Urbanization Prospects: The 2014 Revision: Highlights". UN Department of Economic and Social Affairs. Available at http://esa.un.org/unpd/wup/Highlights/WUP2014-Highlights.pdf. Accessed 14 December 2015.

Watson, Sophie. 2006. *City Publics: The (Dis)Enchantments of Urban Encounters.* New York: Routledge.

Wood, Phil and Charles Laundry. 2008. *The Intercultural City: Planning for Diversity Advantage.* London: Earthscan.

Yaneva, Albena. 2012. *Mapping Controversies in Architecture.* Aldershot: Ashgate.

PART III

REALISING URBAN COMMUNITIES

Figure 7.1 FC United stadium in Moston

7

Urban transformation in football: from Manchester United as a 'global leisure brand' to FC United as a 'community club'

George Poulton

Introduction

Since the 1970s, Manchester's economy has undergone profound change, with the decline of heavy industry and manufacturing and the rise of the service sector and the leisure industries, as well as the inward investment of new global capital. This is part of a broader structural transformation of urban economies across England, and indeed in many cities globally, where a Keynesian system of interventionist economic management at the national level has been replaced by a more de-regulated transnational system. These structural changes have been reflected within English football. The national governance system based on regulations to ensure the financial viability of all clubs and competitive balance within the league was replaced through the 1980s with a de-regulated model which attracted new entrepreneurial and global capital into the sport and unprecedented commercialisation (King 2002, 2003).

At the vanguard of these changes has been Manchester United. Since the 1980s, the club has become a sporting global brand – transnationally owned, marketed and supported all over the world and with an exponentially increased financial worth of $1.5billion (Millward 2011: 22). Given the symmetry between the changes within football and the larger structural changes in the Mancunian and English economy, Manchester United fans provide an excellent site through which to understand how urban economic transformations have been understood and responded to. This chapter explores this process through an investigation of a particular group of Manchester United fans, who in 2005 formed a breakaway club 'FC United of Manchester' (hereafter FC United) in response to a transnational debt-leveraged buy-out of their club. In doing so, it is complementary to chapter 8 in this volume, in building an understanding of the ways in which urban economic transformation has been understood and contested in Manchester.

Ethnographic approach and background to the field site

In 2010, I carried out ethnographic participant observation around FC United games and volunteered on the club's community football programme as part of a PhD research project (Poulton 2013). As part of the ethnography, I also drew on textual sources, analysing the supporters' internet forum, online blogs written by supporters and 'fanzines', fan written and produced magazines sold at low cost around matches or in local shops, which were a key part of the group culture.[1] In this material, supporters often used identifiers such as 'A.H', 'House of Style' and 'Red Heads' rather than real names. In addition, I conducted archival research studying Manchester United fanzines from the late 1980s onwards, which allowed me, alongside supporter interviews, to understand fans' responses to the transformations within football over time and the context which led up to the formation of FC United. This chapter draws on a range of textual forms of data as well as extracts from interviews conducted as part of the ethnographic fieldwork.

In the autumn of 2004, the American multi-billionaire businessmen Malcolm Glazer launched a takeover bid for Manchester United, which was financed through borrowing against the club and then placing the ensuing debt upon them – a practice known as a leveraged buy-out.[2] A notable minority of Manchester United fans launched a vigorous and lengthy protest against the takeover. They were principally motivated by fears that the debt that would be placed upon Manchester United, and also, the loss of the club's independence and the potential for Glazer to either raise ticket prices or asset strip Manchester United to fund the debt interest payments required by a leveraged buy-out.

The opposition to the Glazer takeover came against the backdrop of twenty-five years of rising discontent and protest amongst some Manchester United fans against the mounting commercialisation of the club. However, the protests against the takeover failed, and in response some of these fans launched a supporter-owned club, FC United. The club was set up as an Industrial Provident Society, in which each member (supporter) purchased a single share for a nominal fee and became a co-owner with an equal vote on all major issues within the club, such as the price of tickets. Players were signed on a part-time semi-professional basis. FC United was successfully entered into the North West Counties League for the 2005–2006 season with a ground-share agreed with Bury Football Club to play fixtures at their Gigg Lane ground in the north of the city. Ten years later, the club now has a purpose built stadium in Moston, North Manchester, and through that period has regularly attracted crowds of around 2,000 supporters.

I begin my analysis by looking at how, through the 1990s, as Manchester United commercialised and globalised, notions of place and locality became increasingly charged amongst fans dissatisfied with these changes.

The politics of local exclusion

In the late 1980s, as football took on a more de-regulated form, with a number of cross-club revenue sharing requirements removed, new entrepreneurs moved into the game in search of profit. Ticket prices began to rise rapidly as these owners sought greater commercial value from the sport. At Manchester United between the 1988–1989 season and the 1994–1995 season the cost of season tickets rose by 240.9 per cent. While season ticket prices were increasing rapidly across top-level football in England these were comfortably the biggest price rises at any club (King 2002: 135). During this time Manchester United experienced playing success, and demand for tickets rose rapidly. Meanwhile the club's Old Trafford stadium capacity was reduced while rebuilding work was carried out to remove standing spaces in terraces and make the stadium all-seater. This meant that many supporters were excluded on the grounds of cost and lack of availability of tickets. Amongst some local Mancunian Manchester United fans this issue came to be understood in terms of locality. It was argued that 'local' fans were being excluded in favour of 'out of town' supporters. For example, 'A.H' wrote in *United We Stand* (hereafter *UWS*) fanzine:

> As has been said a million times, going to the match ain't what it used to be. I can no longer attend with my mates, have a laugh and a joke with the lads. They can't afford to come anymore and they can't get tickets. Yet goofballs from Devon to Skegness always seem to have little problem getting tickets (A.H. 1995).

As King (2002) has noted there were widespread complaints – likely true – about the supposedly random draw for tickets being manipulated to award more tickets to non-Mancunian fans (specifically Irish supporters clubs) that were likely to have a higher second spend on club merchandise than local Mancunian supporters.

This criticism of non-Mancunian supporters being preferred for tickets as part of the club's pursuit of profit, was also placed alongside criticism of the perceived inappropriate way in which these 'new' 'out of town' supporters conducted themselves:

> As [Manchester] United become a phenomenal success again, so all the hangers-on return. New fans are attracted, out of towners especially ... And they come. Wide-eyed and camera wielding. No knowledge of any of the songs

and with no desire or even ability to contribute to the atmosphere … Yet they will go home having spent a month's wages in the souvenir shop so naturally the club greets them with open arms. We, the true supporters, who will be there long after the success is gone, do not. (House of Style 1994)

Some supporters, such as 'House of Style', perceived that Manchester United, as a commercial entity, exploited the economic disparity between local and 'out of town' supporters – who were seen as behaving in ways that undermined the match-day experience in terms of atmosphere – to favour the latter group in the pursuit of financial gain. Clearly many 'out of town' supporters would also have been excluded by rising ticket prices and falling availability of tickets (and richer local support would have been favoured by these changes) but what is interesting is that this issue was framed in terms of locality by many Mancunian Manchester United fans. Further to this, in my interviews with supporters, they recalled how historically there had been a positive reaction to out of town support but this had been undermined in the 1990s. Dean, a Manchester United and FC United fan who grew up in London but now lived in Manchester, told me:

We think now of the term Cockney Red as an insult, a Cockney Red means you're a sad fucker who should be supporting your local team who just jumped on the Sky Sports Premiership bandwagon and supported the Beckham and glory show, but of course in the seventies Cockney Red was a term that had a largely positive [connotation], it had a grudging respect to it.[3] … and there was a sense from the people who I've talked to who were around back then that local [Manchester] United fans would give those Cockney Reds more respect than locals, because locals had to come two miles down the road, these were people who cared enough about the club to get the train up from London or Surrey at six in the morning to come to a game, they were kind of given a bit of credit for it and so that whole out of towner thing only becomes an insult when it becomes associated with a certain type of fan, when out of towner gets associated with day trippers, glory seekers. (Dean, interview: 10 December 2010)

As such, it was only when non-Mancunians came to be associated in the 1990s with the process of commercialisation, which threatened 'local' supporters' access to watching Manchester United and active modes of support for the team, that the perceived inauthenticity of 'out of town' support came to be highlighted.

Even though the locality of Manchester United supporters was increasingly highlighted during the 1990s by some Mancunian supporters in defining authentic support, these distinctions were not absolute. Where non-Mancunian Manchester United supporters adopted modes of support that were perceived as appropriate they could still be considered authentic supporters. 'House of Style' (cited earlier) may have criticised 'out of town' support as inappropriate but he also argued later in the article:

> The attitude of wanting only [Mancunian Manchester] United fans gets us nowhere. Some of these non-Mancunian United fans have been there week in, week out for years; and it ain't just a hop, skip and a jump on the Metrolink for them either. Accept these people for what they are; TRUE [Manchester] United fans. (House of Style 1994)

Furthermore, alongside concerns about the exclusions of Mancunian based Manchester United fans, and the effects non-Mancunian fans had on the atmosphere, were counter narratives that 'imagined' (Anderson 1983) Manchester as a tolerant city of immigrants, welcoming of outsiders and therefore 'out of town' supporters. For example, one fanzine contributor described the 'ideal' of Manchester United thus:

> The ideal of a football club born in a city built by immigrants, the sons and daughters of those same immigrants that would later form the bedrock of Manchester United's early support and shape the outlook of a city where the outsider is immediately the insider ... The ideals that shaped a worldwide support of a football club that transcended locality and birthplace just as the immigrants who built its city of birth had done. (Red Heads 1998)

This construction of Manchester as a diverse, cosmopolitan and tolerant city is one that I heard frequently during my research, particularly as part of discussions of supporters' locality. Indeed, as chapter 4 (this volume) discusses in relation to Manchester's Gay Village, this construction of Manchester as a diverse, tolerant and cosmopolitan city has also formed part of local marketing and administrative strategies.

This section has shown how the economic transformation occurring at Manchester United was made sense of by many supporters through a conceptual framework that was intimately tied to notions of locality and the city of Manchester. However, it has also shown that it was not rendered into a straightforwardly exclusionary framework but rather fans also articulated histories and imaginations of Manchester's diversity and cosmopolitanism.

Building the global brand

I now set these discussions of locality and 'Mancunianness' within a wider context of Manchester United's attempts to position itself as a global leisure brand since the 1990s. As Millward (2011: 26) has described, the transnational power of football clubs as 'brands' has grown exponentially over the last twenty years and Manchester United has been at the forefront of this. A 2005

Mori Poll found that Manchester United had 75 million supporters world-wide; research by Sportspro found that Manchester United were the eighth most valuable sports brand in the world and the single most valuable sports team in the world with a worth of $1.495 billion (Millward 2011: 78, 31, 22). Millward posits that this development within English football has mirrored structural changes within the UK (and world) economic system, following free-market de-regulating policies in the 1970s and 1980s, towards 'disorgan-ised capitalism' (Lash and Urry 1987), in which there was 'the quest to find larger markets – or spaces for material profit – which tend to be located at the transnational level and trade upon mobilities of images, information, money, commodities and labour' (Millward 2011: 4). David Harvey's notion of 'time-space compression' (Harvey 1990, 1993) is also useful here, as it points to how the present era of globalisation is marked by the ever-greater frequency of market transactions across transnational geographical space, where football clubs' global branding is but one example of this.

Several scholars have noted that the appointment of Edward Freedman as merchandising manager in 1992 was key in turning Manchester United's global commercial potential into material profits from transnational markets, as he persuaded the club to market and sell merchandise on a global scale (Bose 2007; King 2003; Millward 2011). This attempt to turn a transnational fan-base into monetary profit, known as 'leveraging the global brand' or 'monetising the global fan-base' amongst the Manchester United hierarchy, continued apace from 1992 onwards and dominated the club's commercial strategy (Andrews 2004: 2; Brown 2004: 180). It seems that for many locally based fans the increased attempts by Manchester United to penetrate inter-national markets were perceived both as altering the club's relationship to its locality and also altering the way in which these fans understood the nature of the club itself:

> Manchester United is a football club that happens to be a business, it is not a business that happens to be a football club. Such a distinction is seemingly lost in the global branding world ... The more you hear about activities of 'Manchester United International', the more your red heart blackens at the con-tinued erosion of any sense of local identity and any sense of what the football club actually represents. (Redologist 1998)
>
> The irony is that as the club is being shaped into an all inclusive, all embrac-ing, though ultimately meaningless, brand name that represents no distinct culture or tradition, it continues to exclude and alienate the very supporters, a very localised fan base, that gave it its defining culture and tradition and upheld it for years. Why not ditch 'Manchester' all together, simply call the club 'United', build an 80,000 all seater mega-fuckin-leisure-village-hotel stadium complex in Milton Keynes and have done with it. (Red Heads 1998)

Manchester United's attempts to 'leverage the global brand' under the conditions of 'disorganised capitalism' raised some fans' consciousness both about being a Mancunian Manchester United fan and about the precariousness of the club's relationship to Manchester as its locality. That is, with the ability to trade in many different markets and with a fan-base across the country and internationally, Manchester United no longer necessarily needed a financial relationship with its local fan-base. This is neatly illuminated by this comment by an FC United fan writing in the *Under the Boardwalk* FC United fanzine:

> There are 7 million Manchester United fans in Thailand. I don't get it. I often meet people who tell me they 'support Man U' and I wanna say 'No you don't'. They've never stood on a grass verge watching Billy Garton play and nor would they or should they want to. They deffo wouldn't stand on a grass verge to watch Rory Patterson play. They wouldn't even stand on a grass verge to watch Wayne Rooney play coz if he played for a team that played in front of grass verges they wouldn't wanna know. And why should they. I know it's all down to success (and the timing of [Manchester] United's success being post-Sky and that) and I wouldn't wanna change that, but y'know … 'Manchester' is half the club's name. Be nice if it still counted. (Suede Shoes 2008)

I now show how these concerns about location and Manchester – due to the club becoming a 'global brand' and the exclusion of local supporters through increased price and scarcity of tickets – were channelled by many of these supporters through a moral claim on how a football club should be run and the relationship it should have with the locality in which it is situated.

Community claims

King (2002) described the movement of entrepreneurial capital into football in the 1980s through the emergence of the 'new directors', including Martin Edwards at Old Trafford. He argued that these entrepreneurs, attracted by the de-regulation of English football, saw football club ownership as a potentially profitable business. They looked to maximise their potential financial return from investment in football clubs and in so doing changed the nature of football clubs into profit-seeking capitalist structures. King's argument is particularly insightful on how the creation of the 'customer' played a role in football club owners' profit seeking in this era. King suggests that from the 1980s owners began to see fans as individual 'customers' willing to pay a higher price for a better product within a free market. In particular, they aimed to sell tickets to richer consumers at as high a price as demand would allow. Following from this, he argues that 'the free market argument reduces the relationship of the fans to the club to a purely economic one, given by the market' King (2002: 140). However, a significant group of Manchester United

fans sought to challenge the economic reductionism of those in control of
Manchester United, by arguing that the club was in a position of broader
moral responsibility to the community in which it was located rather than
involved in a series of individual economic transactions with consumers of
the Manchester United brand.

This challenge involves a particular mobilisation of the idea of the 'community' of Manchester which is borne out of, and intrinsically related to, the
issues I have discussed earlier in this chapter as heightening the importance of
issues of locality and 'Mancunianness' amongst local fans. Such a moral claim
about Manchester United's reciprocal duties to the 'community' in which it
is based can be usefully analysed in relation to anthropological debates about
gifts and commodities.

Anthropological interest in gift exchange is often traced to the work of
Malinowski (1978 [1922]), with his famous description of Kula exchange in the
Tobriand Islands of Papua New Guinea, and also to the work of Mauss (1954
[1925]). These accounts focused on how gift exchange was characterised by
the creation of enduring obligation between transactors and of relationships
of reciprocal interdependence. Gregory's (1982) work built on these ideas to
develop a contrasting theoretical analysis between commodity exchange and
gift exchange. Gregory characterises gift exchange as an exchange between
transactors in a state of reciprocal dependence and as establishing personal
qualitative relations between those transacting. In contrast he characterised
commodity exchange as an exchange between transactors in a state of reciprocal *independence* and as acting to establish quantitative relationships between
objects transacted. Such a contrast was critiqued as being over-drawn (see
Appadurai 1986; Parry and Bloch 1989). However, Gregory argued that he
was not attempting to draw a pure distinction between gift economies and
commodity economies but rather utilised such a distinction to understand
how modern Papuans moved back and forwards between these modes of
exchange.

Of particular importance for my own argument is Martin's (2015) work on
the Tolai people of Papua New Guinea. He proposes that, regardless of such
critiques of the extent to which gift and commodity exchanges can be seen
as in binary opposition to one another, 'people the world over … often seem
to be stubbornly attached to drawing stark distinctions between different
types of exchange and to disputing how to characterise particular moments
of exchange or particular ongoing exchange relationship' (2015: 11). Further
to this, he suggests such distinctions and disputes often hinge on 'different
rhetorically opposed perspectives on the honouring of obligations and the
extent of reciprocal interdependence' (2015: 11). Martin's work shifts attention away from attempts by anthropologists to objectively classify particular
exchanges and exchange relationships and instead focuses on how informants

themselves classify and dispute classifications of particular exchanges and exchange relationships. In the conclusion to his book on the Tolai, Martin (2015) suggests that one context in which such disputes over the characterisation of exchange and exchange relationships and the appropriate extent of reciprocal interdependence can also be seen is English football fandom. To this end, Martin cites a passage from Nick Hornby's famous account of football fandom, *Fever Pitch*, in which the author argues:

> Football clubs are not hospitals or schools, with a duty to admit us regardless of our financial wherewithal. It is interesting and revealing that opposition to ... bond schemes has taken on the tone of a crusade, as if the clubs had a moral obligation to their supporters. (Hornby 1998: 222)

Martin contrasts Hornby's view that football clubs have no enduring moral reciprocal obligation to supporters, with his own and others' view that 'the allegiance and loyalty built up over years of exchanges can demand reciprocal recognition [from the football club of enduring obligations to supporters]' (2015: 386)

Martin's provocation about the presence of differing views on how to characterise the exchange involved between fan and football club, and to what extent the football club needs to recognise enduring moral reciprocal obligations, can be usefully applied to the context under discussion here. King's (2002) discussion of the creation of the customer, set out above, can be read as an explicit attempt by the new directors to characterise the operation of the football club as a stand-alone commodity exchange in which the club has no on-going reciprocal responsibility to those who are no longer able to attend due to rising prices. In opposition to this is the quote cited earlier from 'Redologist', arguing 'Manchester United is a football club that happens to be a business, it is not a business that happens to be a football club. Such a distinction is seemingly lost in the global branding world'. This view can be understood as directly disputing the type of exchange they believed Manchester United should be engaged in – as something other than the solely commoditised exchange of 'business' and 'global branding'. Further to this, many Manchester United fans argued that the morally appropriate exchange relationship the club should engage in is one in which they recognised an enduring reciprocal obligation to the 'community' in which it was situated. For example, one fanzine commentator argued:

> In this country, football's commitment to its immediate community is little more than token gesturing that amounts to nothing ... where is the genuine commitment to the community and besides creating more possible sources of income, where is the community's genuine stake in the club? If the city's community commitment is little more than tokenism, [Manchester] United's

is all but non-existent. We've got the disgusting situation that Brian Hughes's Tommy Taylor biog[raphy] isn't available at OT [Old Trafford] because it does not carry the official [Manchester] United seal of naffness.[4] All money raised from the book goes to Collyhurst and Moston lads club, but couldn't somebody at Old Trafford give something back to an area of Manchester that has not only served us well in terms of players but it is traditionally a heartland of red support?[5] That's your community [Manchester] United give something back? Where is the club's presence in Manchester, Salford and Trafford? In comparison to European clubs, [Manchester] United's involvement in the local community is pitiful and urgently needs a new outlook. Such is the current nature of the club that thousands of local kids have no chance of getting anywhere near Old Trafford. (Irwelian Thoughts 1996)

Here the commentator argued that Manchester United should be showing a 'genuine commitment to the community' and supported this moral claim by referencing the economic reductionism of the club's relationship to its fans and the community – 'besides creating more possible sources of income'. This was then related back to the exclusion of local supporters by arguing that 'thousands of local kids have no chance of getting anywhere near Old Trafford'. 'Irwelian Thoughts' argues that it is precisely because areas such as Collyhurst and Moston have given to Manchester United in terms of players and support that the club has a reciprocal duty to 'give something back' to those areas. Linden Burgess, an FC United fan writing within a fan diary, also makes a similar claim about Manchester United's responsibility to its local communities:

> The worst thing though was the social breakdown that was happening in our communities leading to some of the worst poverty and deprivation in the country. Next door to the richest football club in the world. They should have cared. (Brady 2006: 89)

Linden Burgess uses the economic wealth that Manchester United as a global brand has generated to argue that Manchester United has a reciprocal moral obligation to the social collective in which it is situated. This moral claim was also related to the way many fans understood the club's ownership structure and formed a critique of the model of private ownership, a critique that was actively mobilised around the Glazer takeover in 2005. So a Shareholders United advert argued that by virtue of local people having contributed to the club's continued existence, Manchester United was not a privately owned entity but rather belonged to local people collectively:

> This club belongs to the people of Manchester, who have sustained it for over 125 years. Think about what would happen if someone came along, without any knowledge of [Manchester] United, without any interest in our history, and

without any regard whatsoever for us and for our heritage, and simply because he had the money was able to own OUR club. (Shareholders United 2004)

The FC United fan blog, 'It'll Be Off', spoke of a 'strong and staunch belief that Manchester United didn't belong to any one person, but to the people of Manchester' (It'll Be Off 2009), motivating protests against the Glazer takeover. The FC United website meanwhile describes the Glazer takeover thus 'the material theft of a Manchester institution, forcibly taken from the people of Manchester, was the tip of a pyramid of destruction' (FC United of Manchester Undated-a).

It is interesting that Manchester United was conceptualised as rightfully belonging not to the fans per se but rather the locality in which it was situated – 'the club belongs to the people of Manchester' and 'forcibly taken from the people of Manchester' – and as such 'Manchester' was mobilised in opposition to the free-market form of capitalism that allowed the Glazer family's leveraged buy-out. Manchester United has never been collectively owned by local people, but this emphasis upon local people's rightful ownership of Manchester United emerged out of a particular history, described throughout this chapter, which made the relationship between Manchester United, the city of Manchester and Mancunian Manchester United fans precarious. It is out of this sense of precariousness that these fans fashioned a claim for rightful ownership of Manchester United. I now look at how this moral critique of the relationship Manchester United had with the 'community' of Manchester, and the claim that the club had a reciprocal duty to this 'community', shaped how those fans setting up FC United looked to structure their club's relationship to the locality of Manchester.

FC United as a 'community club'

At the formation of FC United, fans voted for the club's formal documents, which included a 'Manifesto' and 'Constitution'. These contained an explicitly localist agenda about the club's obligations to the 'communities of Manchester':

FC United of Manchester is a new football club founded by disaffected and disenfranchised Manchester United supporters. Our aim is to create a sustainable club for the long term which is owned and democratically run by its members, which is accessible to all the communities of Manchester and one in which they can participate fully. (FC United Founding Manifesto Manchester Undated-b)

The Club's objects are, either itself or through a subsidiary company or club trading for the benefit of the community and acting under its control:

    i. to strengthen the bonds between the Club and the community which it serves and to represent the interests of the community in the running of the Club;

ii. to benefit present and future members of the community served by the Club by promoting, encouraging and furthering the game of football as a recreational facility, sporting activity and focus for community involvement;

iii. to ensure the Club takes proper account of the interests of its supporters and of the community it serves in its decisions. (FC United Founding Manifesto Manchester Undated-b)

Such an agenda was conceived in opposition to the perception of Manchester United's free market economically reductionist relationship to supporters and the community at large which has been set out above. When I asked Adam Brown, an FC United board member, and Andy Walsh, the club's then general manager, why the membership had been keen for community responsibilities to be written into the constitution and manifesto they told me:

I think there was a fairly widely shared belief that Manchester United had become removed from its locality, there were long standing complaints about ticket allocations, referencing those who didn't live in Manchester, the out of towners as they were known ... there was that sense that [Manchester] United weren't that engaged in the city and they wanted FC United to be much more so. (Adam Brown, interview: 10 November 2010)

I think that they [members/supporters] recognised that what we were doing wasn't just about the members of the club or the supporters of the club, it was the club's wider impact on the community within which it's based and the opposition to the existing model of ownership. Within football and in particular Manchester United, community was very much of an add-on and we wanted to make sure it was central to everything we did. (Andy Walsh, interview: 3 December 2010)

Both Adam and Andy reference a widespread sense that Manchester United's relationship to Manchester and its locality had become more remote– 'there was a fairly widely shared belief that Manchester United had become removed from its locality' and 'community was very much an add-on'. Andy makes clear how claims as to what FC United's responsibility to the community should be – 'the club's wider impact' – were related to a critique of the free-market 'existing model of ownership' at Manchester United which was seen as creating a more precarious relationship between Manchester United and its locality.

Adam locates the desire for FC United to have a wider responsibility to the local community directly to the sense of exclusion Mancunian Manchester United fans felt over issues of ticket pricing, scarcity and distribution, discussed at the beginning of the chapter. The point is that the issues of exclusion raised the consciousness amongst these fans of issues of location and 'Mancunianness' but by the time of FC United's formation these issues had come to be framed as a moral claim about a football club's reciprocal responsibility to its locality. This claim stood in opposition to the economic reductionism of the commodity-exchange relationship Manchester United was seen as having created with its 'customers'. This comment from Pete Crowther, in his FC United fan diary, further elucidates this argument:

> Some of us want to see a club that stands proudly at the heart of its community. Some of us want to see a club that gives back to its community – not because of some cynical calculation that this will attract more punters through the turnstiles, but because it sincerely believes that a club that loses its connection with its community loses its soul. (Crowther 2007: 42)

Here Crowther demonstrates how the importance placed by FC United fans on an enduring reciprocal relationship between club and community – 'a club that gives back to its community' in order for the club to continue to have a 'soul' – was framed in opposition to the instrumental and economically reductionist relationship other clubs, implicitly Manchester United, were perceived as having with their locality: 'some cynical calculation that this will attract more punters through the turnstiles'.

In an interview, another FC United fan, Steven, also voiced a similar conception of how FC United stood in opposition to Manchester United in terms of the relationship it had to the communities of Manchester:

> It is about us as Mancunians, and everyone else that wants to come. It's not exclusively for Mancunians – Salfordians as well – but it is about doing something for your community and not being diluted by people who are just coming to spend a bit of money. That doesn't benefit the community, it benefits Manchester United quite handsomely but it doesn't do anything for the Greater Manchester community. (Steven, interview: 13 August 2009)

Steven frames supporting FC United as part of an on-going reciprocal relationship with the 'community' in which it is situated, in contrast with those who support Manchester United in what he perceives as a purely monetised commoditised manner. Such a distinction between Manchester United's and FC United's modes of exchange were most straightforwardly articulated by Paul who told me 'FC United is a community club whereas Manchester United is a business' (Field notes 2009).

Conclusion

This chapter has focused on the ways in which the economic transformation which has occurred at Manchester United has been understood and contested by a section of the club's fans. To begin, I outlined the synergies between the economic changes which occurred at Manchester United and in football more broadly, and the structural changes within the economy of Manchester and England at large. Given these connections, I argue the discussion provides insight into the way in which locality and community are conceptualised by people to understand and contest the changing urban economic realities of recent decades. In doing so, two wider points can be made.

Firstly, there has been a long-standing argument within the social sciences that the concept of 'community' is now redundant, as it harks back to an earlier era which has been superseded by processes of modernity and capitalist transformation (Rapport and Overing 2000: 4; Rogaly and Taylor 2009: 15). More recently analysts have argued that 'community' provides a conceptual resource through which social transformation can be understood and contested, and new and continuing forms of belonging can be expressed (Amit 2002; Dawson 2002; Delanty 2010). This chapter gives clear empirical support to the second proposition but does so in a particular way. As Manchester United was transformed by the adoption of commercial practices in line with the wider free-market reality of English football and English society in the 1990s, the language of community became a means to contest this transformation by demanding the recognition of a moral obligation to a social collective – the 'community' of Manchester. Indeed, it is a means of contesting the 'dislocation' that Lewis (ch 8, this volume) describes as arising from these socio-economic changes. 'Community' then becomes a political language but one that was not only used to contest a process of capitalist transformation but also to bring a new reality into being – that of a football club owned collectively by its members, which was explicitly committed to being of benefit to its local 'community'.

This chapter also raises important points in relation to debates on economic exchange. Mauss (1990 [1925]) in the conclusion to his famous essay on 'The Gift' proposed that the morally charged notions of reciprocity and obligation found in gift economies could also be found within Western societies:

> much of our everyday morality is concerned with the question of obligation and spontaneity of the gift. It is our good fortune that all is not yet couched in terms of purchase and sale. Things have values which are emotional as well as material … Our morality is not solely commercial. (Mauss 1990 [1925]: 63)

This chapter provides evidence that such a morality of obligation, that goes beyond purely commercial values, persists in this particular contemporary context, explicitly in the drawing of a distinction between the values of 'community' and those of 'business'. Furthermore, we have seen in this context how claims over the appropriate forms of exchange and the recognition of reciprocal obligation can become politically charged – playing a part in the formation of FC United as a 'community' football club.

Notes

1 Further details about fanzines in general, and those at Manchester United and FC United in particular, can be found in Poulton (2013: 39–47)
2 Millward (2011: 40–41) provides a useful wider overview of the practice of leveraged buy-outs.
3 'Cockney Red' refers to a Manchester United fan from London or the south-east of England. 'Beckham' refers to David Beckham who played for Manchester United between 1993 and 2003.
4 Tommy Taylor was a Manchester United player in the 1950s who died in the 1958 Munich airdisaster.
5 Collyhurst and Moston are areas of North Manchester.

References

A.H. 1995. "There is a dream…". *United We Stand* (43).
Amit, Vared (ed). 2002. *Realizing Community: Concepts, Social Relationships and Sentiments*. London: Routledge.
Anderson, Benedict. 1983. *Imagined Communities: Reflections on the Growth and Spread of Nationalism*. New York and London: Verso.
Andrews, David L. 2004. "Introduction: situating Manchester United PLC". In *Manchester United: A Thematic Study*. D.L. Andrews, ed. pp. 1–11. London: Routledge.
Appadurai, Arjun. 1986. *The Social Life of Things: Commodities in Cultural Perspective*. Cambridge: Cambridge University Press.
Bose, Mihir. 2007. *Manchester DisUnited: Trouble and Takeover at the World's Richest Football Club*. (2nd ed.) London: Aurum Press Ltd.
Brady, Robert. 2006. *An Undividable Glow: The First Ever Book on the Formation and First Season of FC United of Manchester*. Manchester: Rubberybubberyboy.
Brown, Adam. 2004. "'Manchester is red?' Manchester United, fan identity and the 'Sport City'". In *Manchester United: A Thematic Study*. D.L. Andrews, ed. pp. 175–190. London: Routledge.
Crowther, Peter. 2007. "Our club our rules". Lulu.com.
Dawson, Andrew. 2002. "The mining community and the ageing body: towards a phenemonology of community?" In *Realizing Community: Concepts, Social Relationships and Sentiments* V. Amit, ed. pp. 21–38. London: Routledge.
Delanty, Gerard. 2010. *Community*. (2nd ed.) London: Routledge.
FC United of Manchester. Undated-a. "A history of FC United". Available at www.fc-utd.co.uk/m_history.php.
— Undated-b. "FC United manifesto: who we are and what we mean". Available at www.fc-utd.co.uk/manifesto.php.
Gregory, Chris. 1982. *Gifts and Commodities*. London: Academic Press Inc.

Harvey, David. 1990. "Between space and time: reflections on the geographical imagination". *Annals of the Association of American Geographers* 80 (3): 418–434.

— 1993. *From Space To Place and Back Again: Reflections on the Condition of Postmodernity.* London: Routledge.

Hornby, Nick. 1998. *Fever Pitch.* New York: Riverhead Books.

House of Style. 1994. "Old Trafford's House of Style". *United We Stand* (36).

Irwelian Thoughts. 1996. Substance. *United We Stand* (58).

It'll Be Off. 2009. "Welcome to Manchester". It'll Be Off. 8 August 2011. Available at http://itllbeoff.wordpress.com/2009/11/25/welcome-to-manchester/.

King, Anthony. 2002. *End of the Terraces: The Transformation of English Football.* London: Bloomsbury Publishing.

— 2003. *The European Ritual: Football in the New Europe.* Aldershot: Ashgate.

Lash, Scott and John Urry. 1987. *The End of Organized Capitalism.* Madison, WI: University of Wisconsin Press.

Malinowski, Bronislaw. 1978 [1922]. *Argonauts of the Western Pacific: An Account of Native Enterprise and Adventure in the Archipelagoes of Melanesian New Guinea.* London: Routledge.

Martin, Keir. 2015. *Big Men and Big Shots.* New York; Oxford: Berghahn Books.

Mauss, Marcel. 1954 [1925]. *The Gift: Forms and Functions of Exchange in Archaic Societies.* London: Cohen & West.

— 1990 [1925]. *The Gift: The Form and Reason of Exchange in Primitive and Archaic societies.* London and New York: Routledge.

Millward, Peter. 2011. *The Global Football League: Transnational Networks, Social Movements and Sport in the New Media Age.* Palgrave Macmillan.

Parry, Jonathan and Maurice Bloch. 1989. *Money and the Morality of Exchange.* Cambridge: Cambridge University Press.

Poulton, George. 2013. "FC United of Manchester: community and politics amongst English football fans". Unpublished Thesis, University of Manchester.

Rapport, Nigel and Joana Overing. 2000. *Social and Cultural Anthropology: The Key Concepts.* London: Routledge.

Red Heads. 1998. "Red Headed". *United We Stand* (75).

Redologist. 1998. "Love will tear us apart". *United We Stand* (75).

Rogaly, Ben and Becky Taylor. 2009. *Moving Histories of Class and Community: Identity, Place and Belonging in Contemporary England.* London: Palgrave Macmillian.

Shoes, Suede. 2008. "First aspect of the same thing". *Under the Boardwalk* (12).

Thoughts, Irwelian. 1996. "Substance". *United We Stand* (58).

United, Shareholders. 2004. "Where's your voice?" *Red Issue* (73).

Figure 8.1 Billboard advertising East Manchester's future urban regeneration

8

'PEOPLE WANT JOBS, THEY WANT A LIFE!'
DEINDUSTRIALISATION AND LOSS IN EAST MANCHESTER

Camilla Lewis

During fieldwork in East Manchester, I spent one morning every week with Colin, a man in his early sixties, who worked on a fruit and vegetable van. The van was set up by a local healthy-eating initiative and was supported by public funding from the NHS and the local Council. Their aim was to supply reasonably priced fruit and vegetables to areas of East Manchester where there was limited access to fresh food. Since the Asda supermarket was built in Beswick in 2002, many local grocery shops had closed down in the residential areas. Colin said the area had become a 'food desert'.

As we drove around East Manchester, Colin explained how the landscape was unrecognisable compared to when he was growing up. While the built environment had changed dramatically, he still referred to old landmarks as he navigated around the area. He told me that when he travelled on the number 219 bus from Manchester city centre back to his home in the neighbourhood of Clayton, without thinking he would ask for a single to 'the Don', the name of a cinema which was demolished thirty years ago.

In order to show me local places of interest, Colin made detours from his usual route on the fruit and vegetable van. In Clayton, he pulled up outside what looked like a boarded up house (Figure 8.2) and pointed upwards to an impressive brick façade, alerting me to the impressive *Droylsden Industrial Co-operative Society* banner on the smoke covered brickwork, which was adorned with a crowned chimney.

To an outsider, the former purpose of the run-down, boarded up building was unclear. Amidst the boarded up houses the building was easy to miss. But for long-standing residents like Colin, whose personal and working life was deeply connected to the history of the locality, such buildings remain poignant reminders of the area's industrial past, and continue to play a significant role in shaping his connection to the area.

Figure 8.2 Droylsden Industrial Co-operative Society Building in Clayton

Introduction

This chapter argues that the devastating effects of deindustrialisation in East Manchester have resulted in a strong sense of loss among local residents. Despite millions of pounds of urban regeneration funding and numerous waves of redevelopment, high levels of unemployment and welfare dependency continue to characterise this locality. Even though significant deindustrialisation has occurred, the industrial past continues to shape older residents' sense of place, both through physical reminders in the material environment and also discursively, through sharing memories of previous places of employment.

Historical accounts of deindustrialisation in East Manchester depict a narrative of decline; from the area being a productive hub in the Industrial Revolution to a redundant wasteland in post-industrial Britain (see Introduction). In such accounts, critical urban scholars have drawn attention to enduring social inequalities that continue to shape the city (see, for example, Binnie and Skeggs 2004; Ward 2003; Young, et al. 2006). These analyses depict how post-industrial neighbourhoods in Manchester have been marked by exclusion from the wealth, employment and social life of the regenerated inner-city. They sometimes give the sense that a 'dual city' has developed where inner city inhabitants can only find employment in 'downgraded' low wage, part-time, casualised sections of the labour market (Mellor 2002: 12). And yet, these accounts overlook the profound social effects which economic changes have produced, and which continue to characterise some neighbourhoods. While they make reference to employment loss and widening inequalities, they fall short of exploring the wider implications of economic shifts on working people's everyday experiences and sense of identity.

A general trend is evident more broadly within the literature on gentrification, in which working-class experiences are absent, or treated as homogenous and undifferentiated (Paton 2014). Moreover, critical accounts of urban regeneration tend to focus on displacement, thus ignoring populations who remain living in areas of redevelopment (Doucet 2009). As Mah (2010) suggests, the stories of working-class people tend to be overlooked in the interest of a progress-orientated view of moving forward, focusing on growth and innovation rather than dwelling on the 'necessary' waste left behind. There is, therefore, a gap in the literature of research which examines the views of residents who remain living in sites of urban change. In response, this chapter examines the consequences of deindustrialisation and urban regeneration for residents, who have lived through numerous waves of urban regeneration in East Manchester. It argues that despite substantial redevelopment, progress has been limited, as unemployment is still widespread, and the identity of the newly redeveloped area remains unclear.

Ethnographic approach

This chapter draws on research from a twelve-month period of fieldwork in East Manchester in 2010, in which I spent time in local sites. These included a market, allotments, a number of cafes, local shops, community centre sessions including a weekly coffee morning, the Sure Start centre, Mothers' Union meetings and, after some time, people's homes. The main group of informants I engaged with were mainly older local residents whose ages ranged from 50 to 80 and who had lived in the area for their entire lives. Even though their ages varied considerably, they described themselves as 'older', stressing commonality through their shared sense of 'local', 'Mancunian' and 'working-class' identity. During fieldwork, I explored the effects of urban regeneration, from the perspective of these residents, who remained living in East Manchester through deindustrialisation and numerous waves of urban redevelopment.

This chapter offers a selection of ethnographic vignettes which reveal some of the complexities of my informants' experiences. The accounts presented have been chosen as they illustrate some of the specific issues at hand in East Manchester. They are not representative of all residents, as the 'public' are 'multiple and differentiated' and have different demands on spaces and give it a variety of meanings (Massey 2001). My intention is to discuss a selection of fieldwork encounters, which all indicate the strong sense of loss that was evident among older residents living in East Manchester.

Analysing post-industrial change

A growing body of ethnographic work on post-industrial life in Britain has drawn attention to the diverse social changes occurring across neighbour-hoods, due to dramatic shifts in employment and population change (see, for example, Degnen 2015; Edwards, et al. 2012; Evans 2006; McKenzie 2015; Smith 2012). This chapter draws on and develops some of the themes presented in this body of work. I briefly mention a few studies which have influenced my approach.

In his research with older people in Ashington, in the north-east, Dawson (2002) describes how older people 'work out' change through leisure activities. The population was once fairly stable but, since the closure of the coal mining pits, there has been a large outmigration and feelings of uncertainty about the future. Dawson explains how leisure pursuits in familiar localities, such as keeping an allotment, provided a 'cultural resource' through which to negotiate the practicalities of change (2002: 116). In a similar vein, this chapter explores the cultural resources which were used by older residents in order to work out change in East Manchester. In contrast though, the ethnography describes how the key sites of leisure have disappeared, and absences in the landscape have become poignant reminders of the past as they are deeply symbolic for people coming to terms with significant economic and social change (see also ch 5, this volume, on public parks).

Examining the negative social implications of deindustrialisation in an ex-steel town in south Wales, Walkderine's (2010) work describes how the community experienced a sense of 'collective trauma'. Former shared spaces and activities which had once held the community members together and provided 'a sense of being' disappeared (2010: 92). Walkerdine explains how a strong sense of loss was also directly related to the shifts in the rhythms of life associated with the closure of the steelworks. Similarly, in her work on Walker, in Newcastle-upon-Tyne, Mah (2010) describes how industrial decline has been protracted, traces of old industrial activity remain, and regeneration has yet to transform the landscape of industrial ruination. In this context, local people focused on imminent regeneration rather than mourning or celebrating the industrial past. This chapter picks up the question of how residents living in post-industrial spaces make sense of extended periods of change. Extending these discussions further, it argues that even though the remains of the industrial buildings have been largely erased from the regenerated landscape, narratives about the former industrial identity underpin older residents' connection with the area and with each other (see also Lewis 2016). This chapter also argues that we must explore how place attachment is constructed in specific localities as deindustrialisation and regeneration always have specific social effects.

Historical narrative: industrial leader to post-industrial loser

In the nineteenth century, Manchester was a leading force in the Industrial Revolution, with an abundance of cotton mills and manufacturing activity. The city gained an international reputation for its export of cotton products. In 1853 it had over one hundred mills and was referred to as 'Cottonopolis' (McNeil and Nevell 2000). With further industrial growth, Manchester gained new status as an engineering hub and sustained its position as the financial centre of the region. In 1907, five out of twenty of the largest manufacturing companies in Britain had their headquarters in Manchester (Davenport-Hines 1990 in Dicken 1993). A number of foundries and engineering firms were set up in outlying areas to the east of the city centre. In addition, light engineering industries, such as chemical and textile firms were also established (Tye and Williams 1994). East Manchester contained a number of key industrial sites and was dubbed the 'metal bashing heart of the city', from which a large proportion of the city's wealth emerged (Robson 2002: 40).

From its position at the centre of industrial prominence and wealth, Manchester suffered greatly from the effects of deindustrialisation brought about by global and national competition (Peck and Ward 2002). According to Dicken (1993), despite exerting a powerful influence over global markets, few industries in Manchester had much 'natural protection'. This was because Manchester was heavily dependent on large employers compared to the rest of Britain. The effects of deindustrialisation were particularly prominent in East Manchester as major firms closed down. These included Bradford Colliery (1968), the locomotive manufacturing industry based in Gorton (1965, 1968), English Steel (1973), Bradford Glassworks and Stuart Street Power Station (1975) (Tye and Williams 1994: 45), and caused endemic levels of unemployment. Since the landscape was dominated by industry, the closure of these sites left over 250 hectares of vacant industrial land in addition to widespread dereliction (Tye and Williams 1994).

As Britain moved away from industrial production, ex-industrial neighbourhoods such as those in East Manchester suffered from dramatic economic decline between the 1960s and 1980s. As global competition and trading between nations intensified, and with the introduction of new technologies, advanced capitalist economies like Britain moved away from industrial production to the creation of 'service' economies (Beynon, et al. 1993). Peck and Emmerich liken the scale of deindustrialisation in Manchester to the city losing its 'industrial heart' rather than its 'unwanted industrial blubber'. They describe how the shift to the service economy was characterised by profound economic and social 'dislocations' which emerged due to the scale of deindustrialisation and 'structural' unemployment (Peck and Emmerich 1993: 22). The closure of heavy industrial plants caused the landscape in East Manchester to 'shrink' and become 'perforated' (Mace, et al. 2007: 52).

The second half of the twentieth century saw fundamental shifts in employment, from work in manufacturing and heavy industry to the service sector, which brought about widespread job losses in the city. It is estimated that between 1971 and 1997 employment in Manchester fell by 26 per cent (Mace, et al. 2007: 54). By the 1990s, with mass unemployment and depopulation, Beswick and Openshaw were two of the poorest neighbourhoods in the country. Rapid deindustrialisation created a 'fragile' economic base in East Manchester in which 12 per cent of working people were unemployed and 52 per cent of households were receiving benefits (Parkinson, et al. 2006: 2). The types of jobs available in the service economy and the workers they employed were radically different compared the employment patterns of former industrial times. Jobs in the service sector were often in roles associated with female labour, such as retail work, which has a relatively low income.

The loss of skilled manual jobs was not compensated for 'quantitatively or qualitatively' by the emergence of the service economy (Peck and Emmerich 1993: 22). During this period, the housing market collapsed; 20 per cent of dwellings were vacant and the few residents who did not live in social housing found themselves facing negative equity (Parkinson, et al. 2006: 3). By the 1990s, in accounts written by the City Council, East Manchester was described as having high levels of 'deprivation' – a shorthand for high levels of crime, inferior housing, low educational attainment, widespread unemployment, poor health and poverty.

Industrial ruins

Returning to the fruit and vegetable van, Colin was very knowledgeable about local history and politics. He had lived in Clayton for his entire life, making a living by following his 'old Fella' into the newspaper printing industry where he worked for twenty-seven years. During this time, he became a trade-union activist and campaigned at a number of national demos and strikes. Colin had worked on the fruit and vegetable van for two years, after a period of unemployment. Even though he had been a highly skilled worker in the printing industry, he found it difficult to get a new job when he was made redundant.

Colin felt extremely lucky to find work with the fruit and vegetable van, as many of his ex-colleagues were forced to retire early.

As we crossed a dual carriageway crossroads between Ashton New Road and Alan Turing Way, Colin gestured out of the window, and said with a sigh and a tone of resignation; 'You'd never guess it but there were 20,000 jobs on the Asda site. It was heavy engineering, the steel works, it was a hive of activity. Like Bradford Colliery, there were loads of people employed there'. In our discussions it was clear that even though the built environment had changed a great deal, the industrial past continued to influence the way in which Colin related to East Manchester.

Writing about former industrial landscapes, Edensor (2005) describes how ruins offer spaces in which the interpretation and practice of the city becomes liberated from the everyday constraints which determine what should be done and where, and which encode the city with meanings. As manufacturing moved from one area to another, buildings became disposed of function and rendered temporarily useless. Nevertheless, Edensor argues that ruins continue to possess rich histories, where the 'contingent, ineffable, unrepresented, uncoded, sensual, heterogeneous possibilities of contemporary cities are particularly evident' (2005: 19). While derelict buildings were deeply meaningful for Colin, it was also striking how the absences in the landscape evoked rich historical resonances, such as the memory of the colliery which once dominated the site where the Asda supermarket now stands.

Pointing out the radical change which had occurred in the space of two generations, Colin told me that if he were to bring his 'old Fella', who died fifteen years ago, back to life and place him somewhere in East Manchester, he would not know where he was. These conversations on the fruit and vegetable van revealed the deep sense of alienation which many older residents felt, in light of the deindustrialisation and rapid waves of redevelopments which had taken place. In East Manchester, place attachment had become ruptured for people like Colin, who were highly conscious of the discontinuities between their own experiences and those of previous generations.

'People want jobs, they want a life!'

In a community centre adjoining his church in Openshaw, East Manchester, I talked to Patrick, a United Reformed minister about the area to which he had dedicated over twenty years. The centre provided drop-in sessions offering advice on housing and employment, plus a lunch club and free hot meals to all visitors. The funding for the centre was supported by a Christian charity and staffed by a small team of volunteers and social workers. They also gave out destitution food parcels for asylum seekers, who by law were not allowed to work, and for people who were unemployed and struggling to feed their families on unemployment benefits.

As we were talking, a long queue of people waited expectantly outside the centre to collect food parcels or for their turn to see social workers for advice on a wide range of issues, including housing, employment and schooling for their children. I asked Patrick whether, in light of the intense urban regeneration which had taken place there, he felt optimistic about the future, to which the Minister responded:

> No. They were making steam engines here. This was an area for working people who were highly skilled. Now, due to globalisation because of Korea, Hong Kong, China there is nothing here. There is massive unemployment. All that New East Manchester [the Urban Regeneration Company] have done is build houses, that's all they've done. People want jobs, they want a life! These areas have been redeveloped but they are dislocated.

Patrick's views resonated with discussion I had with other residents, such as Colin. He said that unless more jobs were created, there was no chance of building a sustainable future. When I asked how East Manchester had changed in recent years, the term 'regeneration' was hardly ever mentioned. Instead, the subject of deindustrialisation and widespread unemployment came up time and again.

The radical pace of deindustrialisation and redevelopment in East Manchester has resulted in a strong sense of loss for Patrick, like Colin. Both felt a sense of confusion about the future of the area and a feeling of 'dislocation', geographical and temporal. A deep sense of discontinuity with the material environment was evident as the physical and social landscape had changed dramatically. Even though my informants continued to articulate a strong sense of belonging to the area at the same time, they stressed how the area had changed beyond all recognition and the future was felt to be uncertain.

Manchester's post-industrial re-imagining

During the New Labour period (1997–2010) cities were placed at the heart of plans designed to foster a more inclusive, mutually supportive society (Mace, et al. 2007). Consumption-based, property-led forms of economic regeneration were seen as a 'panacea for urban problems' in localities coming to terms with severe deindustrialisation and the loss of manufacturing employment (Raco 2003: 1869). Under the 'New Deal for Communities' a diverse array of political strategies were introduced in order to encourage private developers to invest in run-down and derelict urban areas (Jones and Evans 2008: 4). In East Manchester urban regeneration was introduced after the 2002 Commonwealth Games. The local government promised it would, 'guarantee economic, social and environmental sustainability; achieve highest standards of physical redevelopment; retain its existing population; and improve its social and economic prospects' (Parkinson, et al. 2006: 3).

East Manchester has been reshaped by a number of different stages of redevelopment. In 2000, New East Manchester (NEM, hereafter) was established. It was one of three Urban Regeneration Companies created by the central New Labour government to deliver physical improvements to the built environment through partnership with existing agencies (Parkinson, et al. 2006). NEM were awarded £51.7million, with the funding drawn from two main sources, the Beacons for a Brighter Future and the New Deal for Communities programme under the Single Regeneration Budget. The company's vision was outlined in its original Regeneration Framework in 2000 with a number of key aims defined. These included increasing the population of East Manchester by 30,000, building 12,500 new homes and improving 7,000 existing properties (Parkinson, et al. 2006: 4). NEM established a masterplan for the area, which public partners used to prioritise the redevelopment of key infrastructure and to look for private funding (Jones and Evans 2008: 18).

Across the area, NEM delivered a wide range of regeneration programmes, including building mixed housing and green spaces, creating greater access to employment, and providing community resources. A variety of new facilities, institutions and commercial sites were built, including, to name a few: the City of Manchester Stadium, an Academy school, new shops, such as the Morrison's shopping complex in Openshaw, Asda supermarket in Beswick and a number of community centres. As a result of this intense period of urban redevelopment, East Manchester has been described as one of the most 'policy thick' areas in the UK (Ward 2003: 123) because of the multiple regeneration projects which were established there.

The Manchester City Council Corporate Research and Intelligence Chief Executive's Department Ward Profile (2011) describes the 'Bradford Ward' (which incorporates Beswick and Openshaw) with continuously high rates of welfare claimants compared to other areas of the city and the national average. The Bradford Ward Profile (2011) presents statistics calculated following government guidelines called the Index of Multiple Deprivation. They measure income, employment, health and disability, education skills and training, barriers to housing and services, living and environment and lastly, crime. The profile is the principle document of reference for regeneration policies and the local authority schemes. It describes the Bradford Ward as 'relatively more deprived' than other parts of Manchester and states that there is a pattern of 'higher deprivation, lower household income and higher benefit claims' across the ward (2011: 13). The profile also states that 43.9 per cent of the population rent their properties from registered social landlords (2011: 18). The 'dominant type' in Bradford are described as 'single parents and pensioners, living in Council terraces', with a high percentage of 'burdened singles' (meaning single pensioners, young singles and lone parents) from the 'hard pressed' category (2011: 11). Also, the profile describes that there are relatively more residents in Beswick and Openshaw who depend on the State for welfare support than in any other ward in Manchester.

'We were self-sufficient around here'

At a coffee morning which I attended twice a week at a community centre, the subject of unemployment came up time and again. At the sessions a group of women in their fifties to eighties would drink cups of tea and discuss their former lives. In particular, they would talk in an animated fashion about the variety of jobs they had in their formative years. They reminisced about their school days, describing how they had to look after themselves when their parents were at work and how as 'latch-key kids' they were trusted with a front door key from a young age as their parents were at work. The women described how they would let themselves into the house and would carry out tasks such as lighting the fire, cleaning or preparing tea. In East Manchester, while a large proportion of work was based in manufacturing and engineering for men, women were also employed in the surrounding industries and leisure spaces. In such discussions, the women engaged in increasingly intensified efforts to shore up what counts as appropriate sociality through sharing narratives which glorified the area as 'self-sufficient' in the past. As I have argued elsewhere, paradoxically, in these settings community was 'regenerated' by drawing a sense of connection to East Manchester through sharing memories of former ways of life and landmarks across the locality (Lewis 2016).

The women at the coffee morning discussed how after they left school aged 14 or 15, they had to 'grow up quickly' and find paid work. They found jobs in factories, as machinists, in local pubs, as cleaners or shop assistants. In such conversations it was said that employment was readily available for hard workers and could be found in various sites in the local area. The women described how vacancies were easy to come by, as news of work was circulated among informal networks. Gail, a woman in her fifties from Beswick told me how when someone was leaving a job, you could go and ask at the factory or workplace whether there was a vacancy. People were never out of a job, as they were in plentiful supply. The older women frequently referred to a dominant set of images about the industrial past which were associated with former ways of living, which Blokland (2001) describes as 'a yardstick' for making sense of the present.

According to these older residents, the industrial period was defined as stable and productive, which was disrupted by the onset of deindustrialisation in the 1970s. Strong social ties connected individuals, since residents commonly worked together in industrial and manufacturing jobs and socialised in the local pubs and terraced streets. My informants stressed that work and community were intrinsically linked and mutually constitutive. There were a variety of jobs available in Beswick and Openshaw and the neighbourhoods close by, which made it a productive and vibrant area of the city. In their view, work was a defining way in which sociality was constructed and differences of status were described.

In her work on the potteries in Stoke-on-Trent in the 1980s, Hart (2005, 2008) reveals how working-class identities were once related to distinctions between different occupational groups inside and outside the industrial work-places, as well as overlapping ties of kinship, friendship and neighbourhood. The nature of working and community life in the potteries permeated the social, moral and spatial distinctions between workers who had been histori-cally classified as those who were seen as 'rough' and those who were seen as 'posh', depending on the type of work they were employed to do (2005: 175). Hart's ethnography demonstrates that the working classes are not a homog-enous group but comprise people occupying a range of positions, both in and outside the workplace.

Revisiting Stoke fifteen years later, Hart (2008) found that nearly three quarters of the pottery industry had disappeared and ex-workers felt as though they were in the 'wilderness'. Many had only ever had experience of working in the potteries and their skills had become obsolete. The ex-workers were 'self-conscious' about their accents and way of life because of negative portrayals of Stoke residents in the media.

I found a similar sense of disenfranchisement evident in East Manchester. But in spaces like the coffee morning, overwhelmingly, conversations tended to focus in a positive tone on work in the industrial past. Older residents found sharing stories of the past cathartic and enjoyable. As an outsider to the area, older people at the coffee morning felt it was important that I should learn about their 'local knowledge', concerned that, amid the dramatic transforma-tions which have taken place in the landscape, their history would disappear.

Memory, nostalgia and post-industrial life

In these discussions, the past was regarded as a period of stability where social ties between neighbours and family were strong. In these accounts, a clear narrative of loss is evident for the intense social relations which were said to characterise the past. In the present day, the women argued that it was impos-sible for people to find sustainable forms of employment in East Manchester. For example, Marie, a woman in her fifties explained how she had been out of work for twenty years and felt that there were fewer opportunities for her children's generation than ever before. Marie told me how everyone living in East Manchester found it extremely difficult to find work. She felt that inner cities were being ignored by the government. Even though a new Morrison's supermarket had been built, she was critical of the relatively small number of jobs which had been created, and very annoyed when she heard that the manager lived outside the area. Marie felt strongly that a local person should have been chosen. I asked her whether or not she felt optimistic about the future, to which she responded:

> Not really, lots of the jobs round here have gone. What's the point of working for five pounds an hour? It's slave labour! We need a decent wage. They've got it all wrong round here. They closed the pits, they closed the textiles. What do they expect? How do the government expect us to live?

Similarly to my discussion with Patrick, the Minister, Marie felt angry about the way that people who were living in what she describes as 'lower class areas' were treated. In her view, politicians were to blame for unemployment in East Manchester and the uncertainty which residents faced. These findings support Skeggs' (2011) work, which suggests that unstable employment is an ever-present, historically haunting reality for the working classes in Britain. Skeggs suggests that we must take into consideration the strong sense of precarity which defines the way in which people like Marie live day to day. It is precarity, rather than futurity that dominates many working-class people's lives.

Similarly, at the coffee morning, Grace, a woman in her seventies living alone in Clayton explained how she felt a bit 'miffed' that everything has been done around where she lived while her street was untouched. She felt that she was left 'just waiting', which made her feel as though she was the last in the 'barrel'. While the physical regeneration which had taken place was often deemed to be positive, local people felt frustrated by the lack of 'progress' made in East Manchester. For the older people at the coffee morning, the changes which had been made had an uneven impact and did not make up for the sense of loss which they felt. In these discussions, my informants described the redevelopments in East Manchester in ambiguous terms, praising some of the changes which had been made to the physical environment and simultaneously raising questions about their impacts for the local community.

Conclusion

From this analysis, it is possible to conclude that the discussions about the industrial past at the coffee morning and among older residents more generally were highly valued as long-standing residents celebrated the former identity of East Manchester. In the face of contemporary processes of change, shared narratives were drawn upon in order to articulate a former sense of collective strength and defiance. As repeated waves of regeneration have taken place, there is a general sense of disillusionment and frustration among local people living in East Manchester who argue that it is impossible for them to build a future without new forms of employment. Further, older people stressed that processes of regeneration must incorporate some sense of the history of the locality in order for older residents to feel a sense of connection and involvement with the redevelopment process.

These findings therefore suggest that there should be recognition of the needs of different generations within cities, and that the notions of place which are meaningful to populations who have lived through periods of accelerated change are taken seriously. They support Phillipson's (2007) argument that understanding older people's nostalgia for former imagined communities is important for policy because it draws attention to the ways in which regeneration processes are only advantageous to certain age groups. The chapter shows the importance of involving older people in developing 'age-friendly urban environments' (Buffel and Phillipson 2014). Buffel, et al. (2012) point to a paradox of neighbourhood participation for older people, who tend to spend a lot time in their neighbourhood but they are often the last to be engaged when it comes to decision-making processes.

The analysis explores some of the tensions which have arisen in this context of rapid urban regeneration. I used the term 'dislocation' analytically, as it offered a useful way of thinking about the temporal and geographical changes in this site of radical urban change (see also May and Muir 2015). The term emerged as a concept in the field when Patrick spoke of the sense of uncertainty about the future, and provided a helpful analytical term through which to tease out some of the tensions and difficulties which have arisen in this project of transformation. My findings reflect how, despite years of de-industrial decline, older residents continue to maintain a strong sense of connection to the area through discussions about the industrial past and absences in the landscape. This chapter demonstrates the need for further attention on how populations remaining on sites of urban regeneration make sense of processes of change. Ethnography, can focus on the specific ways in which people make sense of social and economic changes in their everyday lives.

Acknowledgements

The author wishes to thank the University of Manchester Alumni who funded this research and the residents of East Manchester for their involvement in the research.

References

Beynon, Huw, Diane Elson, David Howell, Jamie Peck, and Linda Shaw. 1993. "The remaking of economy and society: Manchester, Salford and Trafford 1945–1992". *Manchester International Centre for Labour Studies.* Working Paper 1.

Binnie, Jon and Beverley Skeggs. 2004. "Cosmopolitan knowledge and the production and consumption of sexualized space: Manchester's gay village". *The Sociological Review* 52 (1): 39–61.

Blokland, Talja. 2001. "Bricks, mortar, memories: neighbourhood and networks in collective acts of remembering". *International Journal of Urban and Regional Research* 25 (2): 268–283.

Bradford Ward Profile. 2011. Available at www.manchester.gov.uk/downloads/down load/6010/bradford_ward_plan. Accessed 26 May 2017.

Buffel, Tine and Chris Phillipson. 2014. "Negotiating urban space: contested generational and ethnic boundaries". In *Intergenerational Space*. N.W. Robert Vanderbeck, ed. pp. 314–329. London: Routledge.

Buffel, Tine, Chris Phillipson, and Thomas Scharf. 2012. "Ageing in urban environments: developing 'age-friendly' cities". *Critical Social Policy* 32 (4): 597–617.

Dawson, Andrew. 2002. "The mining community and the ageing body: towards a phenemonology of community?" In *Realizing Community: Concepts, Social Relationships and Sentiments*. V. Amit, ed. pp. 21–38. London: Routledge.

Degnen, Cathrine. 2015. "Socialising place attachment: place, social memory and embodied affordances". *Ageing and Society*, 36 (8): 1645–1667.

Department, Corporate Research and Intelligence Chief Executive's. 2011. Available at www.manchester.gov.uk. Accessed 12 December 2012.

Dicken, Peter. 1993. "Manchester's economy in a global context". *Manchester International Centre for Labour Studies*. Working Paper 3.

Doucet, Brian. 2009. "Living through gentrification: subjective experiences of local, non-gentrifying residents in Leith, Edinburgh". *Journal of Housing and the Built Environment* 24 (3): 299–315.

Edensor, Tim. 2005. *Industrial Ruins: Spaces, Aesthetics and Materiality*. Oxford: Berg.

Edwards, Jeanette, Gillian Evans, and Katherine Smith. 2012. "Introduction: the middle class-ification of Britain". *Focaal – Journal of Global and Historical Anthropology* 62: 3–16.

Evans, Gillian. 2006. *Educational Failure and Working Class White Children in Britain*. London: Palgrave Macmillan.

Hart, Elizabeth. 2005. "Anthropology, class and the 'big heads': an ethnography of distinctions between 'rough' and 'posh' amongst women workers in the UK pottery industry". *The Sociological Review* 53 (4): 710–728.

— 2008. "Once made in England: how former pottery workers explain the decline of the UK pottery industry". In ESRC conference: from esrcsocietoday.ac.uk/ ESRCInfoCentre. Accessed 12 April 2015.

Jones, Phil and James Evans. 2008. *Urban Regeneration in the UK: Theory and Practice*. London: Sage.

Lewis, Camilla. 2016. "'Regenerating community'? Urban change and narratives of the past". *The Sociological Review* 64 (4): 912–928.

Mace, Alan, Peter Hall, and Nick Gallent. 2007. "New East Manchester: urban renaissance or urban opportunism?" *European Planning Studies* 15 (1): 51–65.

Mah, Alice. 2010. "Memory, uncertainty and industrial ruination: Walker Riverside, Newcastle upon Tyne". *International Journal of Urban and Regional Research* 34 (2): 398–413.

Massey, Doreen. 2001. "Living in Wythenshawe". In *The Unknown City: Contesting Architecture and Social Space*. I. Borden, J. Kerr, J. Rendell, and A. Pivaro eds. pp. 458–476. Cambridge, MA; London: MIT Press.

May, Vanessa and Stewart Muir. 2015. "Everyday belonging and ageing: place and generational change". *Sociological Research Online* 20 (1): 8.

McKenzie, Lisa. 2015. *Getting By: Estates, Class and Culture in Austerity Britain*. Bristol: Policy Press.

McNeil, Robina and Michael Nevell. 2000. *A Guide to the Industrial Archaeology of Greater Manchester*. Association for Industrial Archaeology.

Mellor, Rosemary. 2002. "Hypocritical city: cycles of urban exclusion". In *City of Revolution: Restructuring Manchester* J. Peck and K. Ward, eds. pp. 214–235. Manchester: Manchester University Press.

Parkinson, Michael, Richard Evans, Richard Meegan, Jay Karecha, and Mary Hutchins. 2006. "New Evaluated Manchester: Interim Evaluation of New East Manchester – Executive Summary". Liverpool John Moores University. European Institute for Urban Affairs.

Paton, Kirsteen. 2014. *Gentrification: A Working-Class Perspective*. Aldershot: Ashgate.

Peck, Jamie and Mike Emmerich. 1993. "Manufacturing Manchester? Industrial and labour market restructuring in Greater Manchester". *Manchester International Centre for Labour Studies*. Working Paper 4.

Peck, Jamie and Kevin Ward. 2002. *City of Revolution: Restructuring Manchester*. Manchester: Manchester University Press.

Phillipson, Chris. 2007. "The 'elected' and the 'excluded': sociological perspectives on the experience of place and community in old age". *Ageing & Society* 27 (3): 321–342.

Raco, Mike. 2003. "Remaking place and securitising space: urban regeneration and the strategies, tactics and practices of policing in the UK". *Urban Studies* 40 (9): 1869–1887.

Robson, Brian. 2002. "Mancunian ways: the politics of regeneration". In *City of Revolution: Restructuring Manchester*. J. Peck and K. Ward, eds. pp. 34–49. Manchester: Manchester University Press.

Skeggs, Beverley. 2011. "Imagining personhood differently: person value and autonomist working-class value practices". *The Sociological Review* 59 (3): 496–513.

Smith, Katherine. 2012. *Fairness, Class and Belonging in Contemporary England*. London; New York: Palgrave Macmillan.

Tye, Rachel and Gwyndaf Williams. 1994. "Urban regeneration and central–local government relations: The case of East Manchester". *Progress in Planning* 42 (Part 1): 1–97.

Walkerdine, Valerie. 2010. "Communal beingness and affect: an exploration of trauma in an ex-industrial community". *Body & Society* 16 (1): 91–116.

Ward, Kevin. 2003. "Entrepreneurial urbanism, state restructuring and civilizing 'New' East Manchester". *Area* 35 (2): 116–127.

Young, Craig, Martina Diep, and Stephanie Drabble. 2006. "Living with difference? The 'cosmopolitan city' and urban reimaging in Manchester, UK". *Urban Studies* 43 (10): 1687–1714.

Figure 9.1 Handprints in chalk, North Manchester

9

'DON'T CALL THE POLICE ON ME, I WON'T CALL THEM ON YOU': SELF-POLICING AS ETHICAL DEVELOPMENT IN NORTH MANCHESTER

Katherine Smith

Introduction

This chapter explores the relationship between experiences of poverty, the penalisation of poverty through state and bureaucratic disciplinary measures, and ethical decision making in everyday life in one of the poorest areas of Britain – Harpurhey, Manchester. It addresses the ethical dimensions of social life by exploring the everyday practice of self-policing in Harpurhey as a practice of evaluation and judgment of situations that present what may be viewed by some as momentous ethical dilemmas or moral breakdowns (Zigon 2007). Rather, as part of everyday lives and decision making, self-policing is a matter of living one's life in Harpurhey where individuals must constantly negotiate and judge changing circumstances and contingencies. The shared experiences of being faced with increasing levels of poverty, reliance on state benefits, having those benefits cut and/or sanctioned (or the threat thereof), and the experiences of feeling the sharp end of punitive actions taken by the State in the name of austerity, inform everyday ethical decision making in the process of self-policing. Expressing the feeling of living under the intense gaze of the State, residents explain that everyday life in Harpurhey consists of negotiating the degree to which individuals draw, or not, on the State to intervene in tensions and conflicts on this social housing estate, thereby raising the fear of potentially putting one's own and others' welfare provisions, wellbeing and livelihoods at risk.

Ethnographic approach

The ethnographic and analytical contributions of this chapter are situated within the broader project of understanding the changing dynamics of household economics in the context of austerity and what is being fought for when calls for social and personal worth are felt to be ignored in British public and political discourse. There is a balancing act of survival and ethical decision making in the everyday lives and experiences of people and families who live in poverty. Here we explore the ways in which ethical decision making is reasoned and explained, and placed outside of discourses of the State. This chapter explores the tensions and ambiguities of ethical development through the ways in which individuals police the behaviours of themselves and each other. Based on two-and-a-half years of ethnographic research with neighbouring families who all live in a small cul-de-sac at the edge of the main social housing estate in Harpurhey, this chapter raises and addresses the questions of, what does self-policing in the city actually look like? How are judgments made when illegal, immoral or unethical actions occur in this part of the city? The act of judgment of the behaviours and actions of others, and the assessment of where, when and whether or not to bring in the arms of the State to fulfil the role of policing of those actions and behaviours suggests that self-policing is not simply an outcome of neoliberal ideologies of self-management, but is in actuality an ethical engagement with the quotidian aspects of everyday life on this Manchester social housing estate. Ethical development in practice involves considering the situations and standpoints of others, thereby maintaining a sense of fairness between residents on the housing estate.

Below I explore the ways in which ethical judgments are made in practice, as a form of self-policing in the everyday. The chapter offers a particular understanding of the everyday in the city by re-examining moral standpoints and taking ethical development out of the sphere of political and moral discourse into everyday life in Manchester. The discussion shows that self-policing as ethical development is as much about the maintenance of a sense of fairness that is distinctive to this area of Manchester (Smith 2012b) as it is a critique of the law-and-order state that frames, in policy and practice, the responsibilised, self-policing individual.

Harpurhey in a law-and-order state

Harpurhey is a small suburban area in Manchester, just three-and-a-half miles north east of the city centre. It is home to a large open-air market, a few locally run shops and a large grocery store, several empty buildings, a police station, a well-established and well-attended food bank based at Harpurhey Community Church, and a small collection of pubs and social clubs scattered around the area, which are all within walking distance. Harpurhey also includes a large social housing estate with visible poverty in localised areas. It is the case that Harpurhey is an area that suffers from ongoing welfare reforms and the ongoing evisceration of public sector services. The resulting landscape reflects this structural disinvestment. The need for regeneration in the area has been reflected most recently in the government's publication on 'Indices of Deprivation' via Oxford University, which named Harpurhey in 2007 and again in 2013 as 'the most deprived neighbourhood in England', where the quality of life is the poorest. While signalling the need for more public funds to be spent in the area, there were no structural adjustment recommendations provided. Rather, identifying deprivation in terms of (lack of) education, (lack of) independent income, disability and mortality rates, housing, crime and environment, can further adjust the goal posts for subsequent welfare reforms and benefits assessments. No tangible structural investment has resulted in Harpurhey. Rather, we have a new benchmark for 'poverty' and 'depravity' for future post-welfare policy making.

The landscape of Harpurhey carries the legacy of Conservative New Right policies since the early 1980s, a period of time frequently recognised for its marked shift from older forms of governance of the State toward the class-based ideological project of neoliberalism (Ferguson 2010: 166; Hyatt 2011; Rose 1993; Tyler 2007). The particular histories of free-market economic policies in the UK, particularly from the 1980s onwards, when rapid deindustrialisation transformed the labour market, urban environments and household economics, tend to be divorced from new frames of poverty and deprivation. What is produced is a picture of 'the person' in poverty as the orchestrator of their own demise, rather than the outcome of a historically specific set of economic and political circumstances (Evans 2012: 14). They also produce an image of a post-welfare landscape and its inhabitants, thus the problem of poverty can be shifted from governmental level to individual self-motivation, or lack thereof.

The idea and the impacts of a government deliberately devolving responsibility onto citizens themselves have opened up spaces of ongoing intellectual discussion and debate within and outside academe. Discussions and debates throughout the social sciences have focused on the significant cultural shifts in notions about the functions of government, the art of governance, ideas of citizenship, framings of individualism and (in)dependence, and constructions and values of personhood in relation to poverty. These are as part of a constellation of shifts in governance and political technologies, which Nikolas Rose (1993) notably outlined as carried out through 'advanced liberal technologies'. 'Advanced liberalism', according to Rose, places an emphasis on particular constructions of values such as independence, freedom and individual choice, and today is couched in the Conservative rhetoric of a 'fairer' and 'smarter Britain' (see Cameron, 2009; Duncan Smith, 2013; Osborne, 2010).

Advanced liberalism simultaneously produces new understandings and discourses of the 'problem' of poverty, and places privilege on local understandings and knowledge of that problem. As Susan Brin Hyatt (1997, 2011) and others have noted, this transforms categories of people from the objects of policy into the practitioners of policy who are responsible for renewing their own communities from the ground up (Hyatt, 1997, 2011; Rose 1993, 2000;

Shore and Wright 1997). The poor, then, empowered to take control over their own advancement, and given the freedom to take control over their own aspirations for a good life through entrepreneurialism, self-management and improvement, may then constitute themselves as particular moral citizens who live up to the social obligation of 'giving back' to society, and aspire to look after, maintain and police their own communities and themselves (Hyatt 2011). Like indexing levels of deprivation, new understandings and discourses of the 'problem' of poverty are produced. However, the value of local knowledge in addressing that problem is now privileged.

A transition from the kinds of policies and programmatic innovations that have characterised advanced liberal policy to what today Hyatt refers to as a 'law-and-order state', has involved an ideological shift towards policing as the primary mechanism for governance (Hyatt 2011: 105–106). This is an idealised shift as it is embedded in policy and law, enshrined in discourses of fiscal austerity and enforced in and through public sector cuts and various disciplinary mechanisms of the State. The responsibilised citizen in the post-welfare landscape is at once a citizen who is self-managing, independent, forward thinking, and/or reformed, and who polices and agrees to be policed in local and familial contexts (Hyatt 1997, 2011: 107).

The struggles to engage with a law-and-order state in Harpurhey involve everyday decision making and strategising as to when and in what vein one might exercise ethical and moral judgment, and where the limits of an individual's capacities to self-police might lie in a given context. Harpurhey is understood by residents themselves to be home to some rather dangerous spaces where unscrupulous acts of illegal behaviour and violence take place. When and where one ought to, or ought not to, call upon the help of the State in the form of the police, Housing Association, local MP or Councillors is a decision heavily laden with the requirement to have a particular knowledge of the area, the people in it, and the local and at times individual experiences of poverty, feelings of abandonment and a sense of fairness. In Harpurhey, self-policing is an ethical practice that occurs in the everyday, not simply in relation to extraordinary events that arise when in contact with the State.

Self-policing of conflicts and tensions is an ordinary practice in everyday life in Harpurhey. If we conceive of self-policing as the act of judgment of the behaviours and actions of others, as well as the assessment of where, when and whether or not to bring in the arms of the State to fulfil the role of policing of those actions and behaviours, the quotidian aspects of everyday life emerge as sites where ethical sensibilities are regularly practiced in the process of policing. Those ethical sensibilities might well be coarsened or heightened with respect to broad social forces, such as policy reform and ideological transitions in governance; however, as will be illustrated below, everyday life consists of negotiating the degree to which individuals draw or not on the State to intervene in tensions and conflicts on this social housing estate.

The legality of actions and behaviours does not always resonate with the particular moralities and ethical decisions that are made by local residents. In Harpurhey, which is known for its high levels of crime and illegal activity, what does self-policing on a local scale actually look like? How are judgments made when illegal, immoral or unethical actions occur in this part of the city? Hyatt explains: 'Crime fighting measures are predicated on the assumption that everyday citizens will be able to assess accurately who belongs in the community and who does not, whose intentions are good and whose are malign' (Hyatt 2011: 115). However, while individuals in Harpurhey continually practice the micro-process of self-policing, the practice of describing a situation, action or behaviour and making a particular judgment about it highlights the discontinuities and disjuncture between State sponsored moral codes and local, and indeed individual, ethical sensibilities in the everyday.

Self-policing tension and conflict

As I walked through the leaves and litter that had accumulated in the gutter along the road leading to the cul-de-sac where I was carrying out fieldwork, I saw two neighbours, Jenny and April, standing on April's front doorstep smoking cigarettes. It was a cool, quiet autumn afternoon and I pulled my hand from my coat to wave hello. When I joined them, I discovered Jenny and April discussing the party Jenny had thrown at her house at the weekend and how Jenny's neighbour had phoned the police to complain about the loud music coming from Jenny's house. As they discussed the complaint, Jenny was annoyed because her neighbour had not complained to her directly. If her neighbour had come to Jenny to explain that the music was disturbing her, since sharing a wall between their attached Council houses meant she could hear the music almost as loud as Jenny was hearing it, Jenny would have turned it down. I listened as April and Jenny expressed their annoyances at the 'unfair' behaviour of Jenny's neighbour. 'It's such an unfair thing to do, that', Jenny explained. 'Fair enough if the music is too loud', April responded, 'but she should have just said to you first – not get the police and housing involved!' At the moment of the conversation Jenny faced the threat of having her stereo removed from her home by a local Community Support Officer.[1]

April and Jenny perseverated on their frustrations with the unfairness of the situation in which Jenny found herself. The violation of fairness occurred when Jenny's neighbour chose to disregard any potential agreement that they could have reached. Refusing to engage in a potentially productive discussion, she chose instead to draw upon the discipline of the bureaucratic arms of the

State to manage what should have otherwise been dealt with between them as neighbours. This was perceived as a profoundly unethical decision and action; a sense of fairness had been breached. Other ethical scenarios were re-rehearsed for what went on for about thirty minutes on April's doorstep. Their ethical insights into fairness were made explicit as they discussed what the neighbour ought to have said and done, and when (cf. Lambek 2010: 1). Something 'unfair' had happened, a particular kind of ethic was breached, which gave rise to a litany of shared contempt for the neighbour and alternative actions and outcomes imagined. The character of Jenny's neighbour was criticised as 'unfair', 'snobbish', 'inconsiderate' and 'ignorant'. Jenny felt denied the opportunity to perform her capacity to 'do the right thing' by turning the music down herself, and felt threatened that she might lose her personal stereo.

As we continued to discuss the limits of their contempt, I noticed a young boy, around ten-years-old, running across the cul-de-sac. The school backpack he was wearing appeared to be slowing his pace, but he continued his strides. Jenny and April's conversation finally fell silent when he reached the crossroad at the edge of the cul-de-sac and was rapidly approached by a car, which stopped abruptly in front of him. A man, who looked in his mid-thirties, emerged from the car and began yelling at the boy, inaudibly from where we were standing. The man pushed the young boy to the ground and kicked him once in the legs as he continued to yell in the boy's face. The boy remained silent, his eyes fixed on the man yelling at him, and he scrambled to his feet and rapidly ran off. The man got back into his car and drove off at quite a speed.

Jenny and April remained silent. I reached for my phone without hesitation. I intended to call the police to report an act of abuse towards a child. Jenny asked what I was doing. I explained to her that I was calling the police. Jenny put her hand over my phone and said, 'No, no. Don't do that'. I looked at her and then to April and back to Jenny again. 'She's right, Katie. No, don't', April replied. The cul-de-sac was quiet again.

I asked if they knew who the boy was, or if they recognised him. They explained that they did not recognise the boy or the man, but they were likely part of a family who live somewhere on the housing estate. I was shocked and concerned for the wellbeing of the young boy. Equally, I was puzzled by what appeared to be a profound lack of expressed concern from Jenny and April. It was in this moment that I felt the ostensible and tacit limits of my own understanding of both the event I had just witnessed and the action that one 'ought' to take in this context. I could feel my eyes blinking rapidly when I asked them why they would not phone the police to report what had happened.

April replied with a contextualisation. She explained, because it was the afternoon in the middle of the week, and because the young boy was wearing a school uniform and backpack, it looked like he was 'playing truant' from school. Both Jenny and April agreed that they were shocked, too, at the level of violence aimed at the boy. April repeated that she thought what had happened was 'disgusting', and that she had never once been violent towards her own son. However, calling the police in response to this situation would likely make matters worse for the boy and his family. With the nodding affirmation of Jenny, April explained that parents receive monetary fines from the local Council if their child is playing truant from school. She added that what may seem minimal or 'reasonable' fines by the government actually amount to a great deal of money for people in Harpurhey:

> A small amount of money makes a huge difference around here, Katie. Sixty quid is a week's food, a bill paid, someone's boiler fixed. It's not insignificant. It's not affordable, no matter what the government says. I was speaking to one of the women who works in the office at my son's school about these fines and penalties once. And I remember her saying, [April pitches her voice higher to mock the woman] 'If my child was playing truant and I got a fine, I'd just pay it! I'd' be more concerned with why my child isn't going to school', she said! And I thought, well isn't that great for you? And that's when I realised, Katie, this is not something people with money will ever understand. This is not a problem they will face. This is a problem for people who haven't got a lot of money, not for people with money. (Fieldwork notes 2010)

April was raising a series of concerns about both the event we had just witnessed and what she (and Jenny) inferred from it – that the boy was playing truant and the man, who was likely his father, was stressed and angry because of the threatening consequences of missing school from the State. By providing this interpretation of situational context, April set up an ethical framework by which one can come to a decision about what one ought to do in response. A decision must be made, so consider the context. Part of this context was the (albeit interpreted) state of mind of 'the father' who did bring about the morally problematic situation that required ethical judgment. He was supposedly stressed and anxious. His family was at risk, threatened; his response was influenced by his state of mind (see Williams 1993).

While the context April provided was detailed and emotive, she went on to explain that there are limits to a particular kind of awareness that someone from outside Harpurhey might have of what happens there. She went on to explain that the poverty people experience weighs heavily on their decisions and actions, especially when faced with the sharp end of ever-increasing punitive disciplinary policies aimed at the poor. There are limits, as April explains, in how much one can 'know' about experiences of poverty and the particular subjective realities of those people who face it in the everyday. April is explaining a caution against assuming that one particular moral outlook may be the same for all people. Reflecting on her son's school administrator, she identified an exclusive and privileged way of thinking about the actions of people in Harpurhey by people who do not know poverty in the same way; a privileged way of thinking about school fines which allows people who do not understand the subjectivities of poverty to contextualise and talk about it whilst never really experiencing it. So when a parent is fined, responses will be different depending on the level of poverty someone (and their family) faces.

Penalising the poor

The precariousness of situations of increasing poverty beyond the control of citizens themselves affects the everyday lives and subjectivities in the most intimate of ways. The 'penalization of poverty' (Wacquant 2009, 2010: 201), designed to manage the efforts of advanced liberal policies as they play out amongst the 'lower end of the social hierarchy', or what Nikolas Rose calls the 'penal-welfare complex' (2000: 335), is a system of disciplinary measures implemented by the 'law-and-order state' whereby citizens who are dependent upon state support can be managed as welfare provisions are rapidly retracted. A dense transfer point for these mechanisms of governance can be found in the particular penalties imposed on parents of truanting schoolchildren.

Working collaboratively with local Councils and courts of law, state schools can impose fines on parents if a child is not in attendance for a day, or more, without a valid doctor's note, without parental interventions with the school directly or without any form of documentation that evidences a child cannot attend school (in the case of illness, for example, a prescription for medication). If a parent calls the school in the morning of the day of their child's absence to inform the school the child is unwell, the school will request evidence of illness. If evidence cannot be provided, say if the child has not visited their doctor, and is unwell with a passing illness, fines are commonly waved, so long as the parent has provided a sufficiently satisfactory explanation to the school. It is often the case that the school administration will require a doctor's note, but this is a grey area in which the school administrator's judgment can be exercised in a phone conversation. If, however, the parent notified the school that the child is staying home for avoidable reasons (such as holidays, family visits or birthdays), the parents will receive a fine of £60 per child, which can rise to £120 per child if the fine is not paid within twenty one working days of the day of absence. Parents can be prosecuted in a court of law by the local Council if the fine remains unpaid, which can result in a £2,500 fine and a three-month prison sentence for the parent(s).

As one of the several disciplinary measures enforced by the State on parents of schoolchildren, parents in Harpurhey experience the financial penalties as serious and as threatening as the subsequent levels of prosecution a parent can face if their child is repeatedly truanting and they cannot afford the fines. Local Councils and schools, working together in prosecution of the parent(s), can use various additional legal powers beyond a fine if the child does not attend school without permission. Regular truancy can lead to a Parenting Order, which requires the parent(s) to attend parenting classes and to undergo extra supervision of the child's school attendance from a Council worker or Community Support Officer; an Education Supervision order, for which the courts assign an Education Officer to the household to 'enforce a child's attendance' and engagement with education; and/or a School Attendance Order, which is a court ordered requirement of the parent(s) to provide documented evidence that the child is enrolled in school and that they are receiving adequate education at home as well. This Order also requires the parent(s) to send their child to a court appointed school – not of the parent or child's choosing.[2]

As schools work with local Councils and courts of law to enforce these disciplinary measures and their mechanisms the threat of financial and legal outcomes amounts to increased pressure and anxieties around the regulations and movements of children in everyday life. The education, learning experience, mental health and the reasons why a child might play truant are perceived locally not to be primary concerns of these institutional arms of the State or in these processes of penalisation. Rather, it is attendance, evidence of consistent attendance, and the invasion of the household and pockets of the parent(s) that are under threat. And, as April explained, people who are dependent on state benefits experience these penalties acutely.

Self-policing as ethical development

April's reflections echo ongoing discussions within the social and political sciences of poverty and advanced liberal policies that appear to decrease dependency on the State, but in actuality generate new forms of inequalities (Davis 2004; Morgen and Maskovsky 2003). However, at the same time as signaling the generation of new forms of inequalities, April provided a detailed description and analysis of a situation in which ethical decision making takes place in a familiar occurrence in Harpurhey. She addresses where contradictions and inconsistencies of what is 'right' and 'wrong' in this situation can be negotiated. Self-policing here is seen as the responsibility to assess the situation involved, taking into account the entire context, as interpreted by April and Jenny. This included what Bernard Williams (1993) has outlined as cause, intention, state and response: that something bad had happened, the boy had been physically assaulted, the 'father' was under a particular kind of strain in poverty, and whether the police should be called or not. As April went on to explain:

Don't get me wrong, Katie. What that guy did to that boy was wrong and I certainly wouldn't do that to my own son. But if you bring in the police, those parents will get fined. They won't be able to sort it out with the school. They'll have social services involved as well. The boy and the family could be unsettled for a long time. It's best to keep out of it and let them sort it out themselves. People don't realise how much the threat of a fine, or even sanction – or losing money – really does cause panic for people around here. So, it's not something we should interfere with, you know? That man shouldn't have pushed and kicked that boy. Yes, that was wrong. It was disgusting. But that boy should have been in school and they're probably facing a fine now, or worse! So, if you call the police, you just make it worse for them. Do you see what I mean? What's worse, Katie? That's what you have to weigh up. Calling the police causes more harm than good. We all know that. And we all know: 'you don't call the police on me, I won't call them on you'. Most things are best sorted out by themselves. (Fieldwork notes 2010)

April and Jenny made a judgment based on their own surface interpretation of an event, or what Webb Keane has discussed as the 'surface of things' (Keane 2010: 66), insofar as their response to the event was based on their own projections and interpretations. April describes her interpretation of the event and the circumstances surrounding it in order to determine that a decision had to be made carefully and with consideration of a series of potentialities. If, as Kwame Appiah writes, 'the act of describing a situation, and thus determining that there's a decision to be made – is itself a moral task' and indeed, 'it's often the moral task' (2008: 196), then April was providing a context with which to engage in ethical decision making, as part of ethical development that is located outside the State and bureaucracy. She was demonstrating particular competencies and capacities in understanding the circumstances of others, a capacity that is referred to locally as 'being fair' (Smith 2012a, 2012b, 2014). In this sense, April is providing an understanding of ethical decision making that was breached when Jenny's neighbour called the police without discussion with Jenny. Indeed, the detailed rehearsing of criteria and circumstances raised in response to the breach of fairness by Jenny's neighbour provided a moral standpoint from which to justify the 'right thing to do' in the event that followed immediately after. Our subsequent reactions in the following event in which a young boy was assaulted was unquestionably informed by both the context April provided and the rehearsing of the ethics of fairness in the conversation between Jenny and April immediately before.

Both conversations were moral tasks that provided the foundations for the exercise of judgment of what we had witnessed and how we 'ought' to respond. April and Jenny spent a great amount of effort to explain that what the 'father' had done was wrong, and the fact that the boy was (potentially) playing truant was also wrong. That the State imposes such harsh penalties on parents for their child's truancy is nevertheless wrong according to those who face the threat and risk. To make a decision on how to react to the physical assault, one must weigh up the greater risk – to the family and all involved. Such weighing up involves the shared experience of living in poverty. To call the police risked the child suffering twice: from the assault and from the reduced family income and privacy.

What April and Jenny are explaining is not a conventional morality. As Lambek has pointed out, 'pervasiveness need not entail agreement with respect to either what constitutes an ethical field or what the ethical thing to do is in any given instance' (2010: 28). Rather, in this instance the 'right thing to do' was to weigh up what was April and Jenny's interpretation of the event. Through our conversation, we saw a conjunction of criteria, circumstances and subjective realities to assess. Neither Jenny nor April agreed with the actions of the 'father'. Yet, they went on to provide a sort of theoretical framework for recognising that something may be seen as ethical for someone and 'to see how it fits into a particular context need not entail advocating it' (see also Keane 2010; Lambek 2010: 13; and and ch 1, this volume). Equally, the differences in our 'reactive attitudes' (Strawson 2008 [1962] cited in Laidlaw 2014: 184–185) also touched on the extraordinariness of this event for me, and the everydayness of the event for Jenny and April. This form of self-policing required a knowledge of how to weigh up the 'greater evil', as it were, the causal contributions to the event, the attribution of responsibility to not call the police or get the State involved, and a series of related considerations for which I became sharply aware.

When a child is physically assaulted, there is, to my mind, no form of reasoning that might justify that behaviour. The outcomes outweigh potential reasoning for it. However, in and through April's contextualisation and description of the circumstances around the event, this clash of moral and ethical outlooks was addressed through providing a different ethical field wherein alternative options for ethical development could be acknowledged. April also points here to a virtuous circle of ethical responsibility to neighbours in and around the cul-de-sac. This is not the relationship of responsibility prescribed by the State or desired by residents in some other recent ethnographic accounts of social life on housing estates in other parts of the UK (e.g. Koch 2014). In Harpurhey, the State is placed outside of the ethical development in self-policing, especially when what are at stake are the threatening consequences of state disciplinary measures. This event and other situations like it are not extraordinary situations in which a particular ethical dilemma comes up and is in tension with the everyday (cf. Zigon 2007). The tacit agreement that, 'if I don't call the police on you, then you don't call the police on me', reflects the ordinary ethics of everyday life. It opens up a space for allowance, and provides a framework for the maintenance of ethical decision making and relations between neighbours. Self-policing as everyday practice draws on a particular kind of ethical sensibility that involves determining to what extent, if any, moralities of the State are relevant, and legal frameworks ought to be drawn upon. To know and express that knowledge as well as knowledge of the complexities, anxieties and stresses of others is a form of self-policing in practice. Knowing when and when not to draw on the arms of the State hinges on the ordinary ethics of everyday life in Harpurhey (cf. Lambek 2010).

Conclusion

In many respects, self-policing of illegal, abusive behaviour presents a moral impasse in more generalisable terms beyond a Manchester suburb. The self-policing of urban violence is not uncharted territory for ethnographers interested in the lived experiences of marginalised groups (Auyero, et al. 2015; Bourgois 2003), particularly as ethnographers search for the internal logics and sensibilities that influence particular life choices, contingencies and chances in various social contexts. This chapter has provided an example of self-policing as ethical development, in that it requires the judgment of the behaviours of others as well as the assessment of where, when and whether or not to draw on state interventions to fulfil the role of policing. It has argued that ethical decision making and development in everyday life in Harpurhey is practiced regularly in the process of policing one's self and others.

We have seen from April and Jenny's interpretations of an event where a child was physically assaulted by an adult, that my assumed shared morality of reporting that assault as 'the right thing to do' was challenged through the interpretation and contextualisation of the incident. Here we see a caution against assuming that one particular moral outlook may be the same for all people and their situations. Coming up against my own convictions, as it were, I was faced with a description of what is 'fair' and what one 'ought to do' that is informed by a particular kind of political and economic subjectivity wherein poverty and the experiences of it affect the everyday lives and decision making of the people in and around this cul-de-sac in Harpurhey. This caution raises important considerations in the process of self-policing, which involve taking into consideration the various potentialities that may occur as a result of one's own behaviour and decision making, such as phoning the police.

In this post-welfare landscape, what we can see emerging is an indirect critique of the moralising rhetoric of the responsibilised citizen of advanced liberal ideology, whereby self-policing plays a multifaceted role: firstly, everyday life consists of negotiating the degree to which individuals draw or not on the State to intervene in tensions and conflict. This negotiation involves taking into consideration both what is 'fair' and what one 'ought to do' in a given circumstance, as ethical development. Secondly, experiences of poverty, threats of the penalisation of individuals and families in poverty and the allowance of others, then, to choose to 'do the right thing' maintains a local sense of fairness, as in what it means to 'be fair'. Finally, what we can see emerging here, through the above ethnographic vignette is a critique of the advanced liberal framing of the responsible, moral, self-policing individual. The potential of the child and his family to suffer twice – both the assault as well as the certain fine and surveillance the family would endure – was weighed up, and the decision to not act as a responsibilised citizen as set out in policy and law is framed in everyday life as the more ethical, more responsible way to be. The potential of the State to become a threat rather than a protector was a common and shared knowledge in Harpurhey, one by which daily actions and ethical decisions were informed.

Notes

1 Two weeks later, a Community Support Officer arrived at Jenny's house and took her stereo. It now sits in the local police station for an indefinite period.
2 For more information about legal action to 'enforce school attendance', see: https://www/gov/uk/school-attendance-absence/legal-action-to-enforce-school-attendance. Accessed 4 January 2016.

References

Appiah, Anthony. 2008. *Experiments in Ethics*. Cambridge, MA: Harvard University Press.

Auyero, Javier, Philippe Bourgois, and Nancy Scheper-Hughes, eds. 2015. *Violence at the Urban Margins*. Oxford: Oxford University Press.

Bourgois, Philippe. 2003. *In Search of Respect: Selling Crack in El Barrio*. Vol. 10. Cambridge: Cambridge University Press.

Cameron, D. 2009. "Making progressive conservativism a reality" Speech to Demos, London, 22 January. Available at www.demos.co.uk/files/File/David_Cameron_Making_progressive_conservatism_a_reality.pdf. Accessed 12 October 2013.

Davis, Dana-Ain. 2004. "Manufacturing mammies: the burdens of service work and welfare reform among battered black women". *Anthropologica*: 273–288.

Duncan Smith, I. 2013 "Restoring fairness to the welfare system", Speech, Conservative Party Conference, Manchester. BBC. Available at www.bbc.co.uk/news/av/uk-politics-11479292/duncan-smith-welfare-reforms-will-restore-fairness. Accessed 12 October 2013.

Evans, Gillian. 2012. "Big man system, short life culture: working-class boys and street violence in Southeast London". In *Young Men in Uncertain Times*. V. Amit and N. Dyck, eds. New York: Berghahn Books.

Ferguson, James. 2010. "The uses of neoliberalism". *Antipode* 41 (s1): 166–184.

Hyatt, Susan Brin. 1997. "Poverty in a 'post-welfare' landscape". In A*nthropology of Policy: Critical Perspectives on Governance and Power*. C. Shore and S. Wright, eds. pp. 217–238. London: Routledge.

— 2011. "What was neoliberalism and what comes next? The transformation of citizenship in the law-and-order state". In *Policy Worlds: Anthropology and the Analysis of Contemporary Power*. C. Shore, S. Wright, and D. Però, eds. pp. 105–123. Oxford: Berghahn Books.

Keane, Webb. 2010. "Minds, surfaces, and reasons in the anthropology of ethics". In *Ordinary Ethics: Anthropology, Language and Action*. M. Lambek, ed. pp. 64–83. New York: Fordham University Press.

Koch, Insa. 2014. "Everyday experiences of state betrayal on an English council estate". *Anthropology of This Century* 9. Available at http://aotcpress.com/articles/every day-experiences-state-betrayal-english-council-estate/. Accessed 26 May 2107.

Laidlaw, James. 2014. *The Subject of Virtue: An Anthropology of Ethics and Freedom*. Cambridge: Cambridge University Press.

Lambek, Michael. 2010. "Introduction". In *Ordinary Ethics: Anthropology, Language and Action*. M. Lambek, ed. pp. 1–38. New York: Fordham University Press.

Morgen, Sandra and Jeff Maskovsky. 2003. "The anthropology of welfare 'reform': new perspectives on US urban poverty in the post-welfare era". *Annual Review of Anthropology*: 315–338.

Osborne, G. 2010. "Emergency budget speech". *Guardian*. Available at www.theguard ian.com/uk/2010/jun/22/emergency-budget full-speech-text. Accessed 13 October, 2013.

Rose, Nikolas. 1993. "Government, authority and expertise in advanced liberalism". *Economy and Society* 22 (3): 283–299.

— 2000. "Government and control". *The British Journal of Criminology* 40 (2): 321–339.

Shore, Chris and Susan Wright. 1997. *Anthropology of Policy: Critical Perspectives on Governance and Power* (European Association of Social Anthropologists). London: Routledge.

Smith, Katherine. 2012a. *Fairness, Class and Belonging in Contemporary England*. London; New York: Palgrave Macmillan.

— 2012b. "Anxieties of Englishness and participation in democracy". *Focaal – Journal of Global and Historical Anthropology* 62: 30–41.

— 2014. "Fairness as rhetorical force and the micro-politics of intentionality in a North Manchester town". In *Rhetoric in British Politics and Society*. A.F.J. Atkins, J. Martin, and N. Turnbull, eds. pp. 160–172. London: Palgrave Macmillan.

Tyler, Katharine. 2007. "Race, genetics and inheritance: reflections upon the birth of 'black' twins to a 'white' IVF mother". In *Race, Ethnicity and Nation: Perspectives From Kinship and Genetics*. P. Wade, ed. pp. 33–51: Oxford: Berghahn Books.

Wacquant, Loïc. 2009. *Punishing the poor: the neoliberal government of social insecurity*. London: Duke University Press.

— 2010. "Crafting the neoliberal state: workfare, prisonfare, and social insecurity". *Sociological Forum* Vol. 25, pp. 197–220. Oxford: Blackwell.

Williams, Bernard. 1993. *Shame and Necessity*. Berkeley: University of California Press.

Zigon, Jarrett. 2007. "Moral breakdown and the ethical demand a theoretical framework for an anthropology of moralities". *Anthropological Theory* 7 (2): 131–150.

AFTERWORD: THE TENSION IN MAKING
AND REALISING A CITY

Jessica Symons

A city is *realised* through the accumulative efforts of everyone who engages with it. It comes into being and is transformed instantly. Following Deleuze on events, cities are the 'becoming of becoming' – forever in their realisation; never realised (Badiou 2007: 38; Deleuze and Guattari 1987).

This edited collection captures the day-to-day practical dynamics of a vibrant and rapidly changing post-industrial city. 'Ethnographic moments' explore the activities of city makers such as politicians, administrators, company leaders, activists and residents. The accounts show how a city may never be produced from a singular vision or set of activities, but how people act as if it will. This conflicted understanding gives a city dynamism but also creates disruptions and spaces of contestation or 'friction' (Tsing 2004). From residential neighbourhoods to cultural events in the City Council, from businesses to the city's airport, people's decisions and actions co-produce the city daily and give it shape.

A city is forever held in tension: both directed and responsive; controlled and open. Making and realising the city act as a spectrum through which urban dynamics oscillate. People may seek to make a city through directed actions and decisions but it is also realised through unpredictable and unexpected activity. In chapter 2, I argue that urban decision makers should reframe their role as 'enabling an emergent city'. Here I build on the ethnographic accounts in this volume to discuss what this approach might look like.

Wittgenstein's 'rule-governing' paradox states that 'no course of action could be determined by a rule because every course of action can be made out to accord with the rule' (Wittgenstein 1958, #201, discussed in Verheggen 2003). His paradox is used by Mouffe (2000) to emphasise that the challenge of democracy lies in the negotiation of pluralism – different individuals and groups have different agendas and their political status determines their ability to realise their aspirations. The ethnographic accounts in this volume provide real on-the-ground insight into how people wrestle daily with these tensions in a democratic context.

At the same time, Wittgenstein's paradox also points out how rules are needed to define rules – you cannot make a rule without first defining your criteria, and this definition of criteria is a rule in itself. In Manchester, urban decision makers are creating new rules to support the development of the city, whilst also working within their responsibilities and obligations as democratic representatives of government. As discussed in the Introduction, when Councillor Sir Richard Leese and Chancellor of the Exchequer, George Osborne MP met to agree devolution of budgetary and decision-making powers from central to local government, they were defining the criteria by which the city, and the country, would be governed. When the government's civil servants and related organisations moved to develop policies and processes to enable this devolution process, they created rules and also wove the landmark decision into an existing set of rules and regulations. This *bricolage* approach to democracy in the UK is both its strength and its weakness.

Urban actors can use this tension productively, working between making the city according to their own aspirations and desires and experiencing the city as being realised – made real – around them through the actions of others. This tension can also be destructive, creating obstacles and challenges, winners and losers – as the politics emerge. The greatest challenge of all is tackling who gets to decide what happens in a city? If everyone wants to have a say, if everyone wants the city to be shaped according to *their* vision, then whose vision comes to be realised? Who decides whose rules should be followed? These questions are particularly pertinent when politically elected representatives and the civil servants that support them, make landmark decisions such as installing a City Mayor in Manchester despite a referendum that opposed it.

The chapters in this volume show how the paradox of rule making and shaping manifests in practice. Working backwards through the volume, in Part III, the chapters reveal how Manchester communities are affected by political and socio-economic change in the city and how people act to articulate their sense of identity and belonging. In Part II, the authors show how public spaces are contested sites where contradictory ambitions for the city are played out. Part I shows how the rule-making process is itself partial and conflicted, developed through ongoing dialogue and negotiation.

Considering these chapters together, we see how Manchester's industrial past and attendant social values hold strong resonance for communities coming to terms with rapid urban change. These endured throughout decades of deindustrialisation, high levels of unemployment or in some cases precarious, low-income, low prospect work. Smith describes how in North Manchester local people find austerity measures crippling, and government interference in their lives oppressive, so they find new ways of articulating values that sit outside the law. Freedom of expression and autonomy is maintained by creating rules of social engagement beyond broader social and legal expectations of what is appropriate for some. The police and school authorities are institutions to be feared rather than sought out for aid and support.

Smith argues that self-policing is not simply an outcome of ideologies of self-management, but an ethical engagement with the quotidian aspects of everyday life on this Manchester social housing estate. This experience is similar in East Manchester where Lewis found a deep sense of loss for industrial times, when employment was readily available and residents felt that their contribution and autonomy in the area actually meant something. In the present day, regeneration of the area may have been well-meant but it was imposed by external parties without proper engagement or understanding of local priorities and preferences. People benefited from improved housing and retail jobs but they lost their sense of ownership and autonomy over their area. Poulton shows how ideas of solidarity and community produced through supporting football clubs was diminished as Manchester United commercialised their operation. Supporting your local football club was a social practice woven into the cultural identity of these communities, whose visceral reaction to the club's change of management and approach produced feelings of anger and loss. When the aggrieved fans set up FC United as a new club with an explicit focus on community, they resisted attempts to make the club commercial.

These findings reveal how people have become economically ostracised from new structural and cultural processes developing in the city. They could not get jobs that were valued, afford tickets to their favourite football club, or pay fines if their children refuse to go to school. The ethnographies reveal how individuals seek ownership over their lives and their communities. They want to feel supported by politicians and civil servants to realise their own ideas and aspirations.

Disputes over self-determination and who gets to decide which rules to follow are also manifest in a spatial context through defining public spaces in the city in Part II. Pieri shows how imagining and designing the city centre is part of a political and administrative strategy, essential for ordered city planning and development, but it alienates even those who have financial means to participate. City residents may be able to afford to buy expensive flats in the city but their own ideas and aspirations about what city spaces should be used for conflicts with broader plans. These differing needs compete with the decision makers as they seek to define the city.

Tension in realising competing visions for city spaces is evident at different scales, as Lang demonstrates in her analysis of shared areas in Cheetham Hill, North Manchester. She shows how people negotiate developing their local green spaces as a shared commons. Change is possible when urban decision makers are local and have discretion. As different interests in a shared space scale up, however, the complexity similarly increases, making the potential for resolution much less likely. Public spaces deteriorate while people wait for action.

Negotiation over land usage is not just about its purpose, as Atkins argues in his exploration of Manchester's Gay Village, it is also about its branding. He shows how the people worked collaboratively over many years to foster awareness and celebration of LGBT communities. The ensuing bars, clubs and parades led to the designation of the Gay Village as a tourist destination and its appropriation by the marketing and branding departments of the City Council and related organisations looking for commercialisation opportunities. This absorption of the area into Council development plans led to some activities being marginalised and pushed out of sight. Vulnerable young men carrying out sexual activities for money along the canal and under bridges became even more marginalised and at risk. Since the original aim of the Gay Village was to bring LGBT into the mainstream and provide a sense of community, the whitewashing effect of tourism led instead to further isolating these young men.

So the control of public spaces produces unintentionally alienating effects. Whose ambitions are realised in such spaces is determined by their ability to influence the levers of power. These ethnographic accounts show how control over areas plays out in the lives of those affected. When the Chief Executive of Manchester City Council tells Pieri that 'we need more social housing in Manchester like we need a hole in our head', he reveals an attitude which produces the sense of loss and uncertainty that local people in the chapters demonstrate. They don't feel welcome.

In Part I, the constitution of Manchester's decision-making networks helps make sense of people who do have power, those who are supposedly 'in control'. The authors demonstrate the distributed nature of organisations and the networks through which priorities are mobilised and decisions made in the city. They show how decisions are negotiated rather than made.

O'Doherty's account of Manchester Airport shows how conceptualisations of leisure activity and impressions of Manchester are woven into the design of an airport lounge. Interpretations are combined and made manifest as a physical entities – a room layout, furnishings, colours, pictures and background music. Decisions have to be made and this analysis of options and possibilities promises to point to where control lies. Yet as O'Doherty pursues lines of authority, even to Manchester's Chief Executive, Sir Howard Bernstein, he finds no centre of power, only the distributed nature of urban dynamics. The decision makers are unsure about who decides.

Symons argues for a more nurturing role from civic leaders by drawing on an analysis of parade makers who 'knit together' different community groups' ideas. She asks if urban decision makers can have the confidence to *allow the city to emerge* rather than dictating its constitution from the outset. This organising principle would facilitate self-determination and self-expression; an attitude the City Council wants to foster anyway. But it also tackles Smith's concern that 'advanced liberalism' leaves people alone and isolated. Rather than putting forward the illusion of control, urban decision makers would do better to acknowledge their lack of direct power and re-emphasise their role as public servants.

Where Symons considers an attitudinal change among decision makers, Knox shows how grassroots groups and motivated individuals productively use political networks and relationships to stimulate structured and organised activity in relation to climate change. Working both within and outside the civic administration and drawing in policies from outside the city, determined groups influenced the development of environmental policies and practices. It was through a sophisticated understanding of the levers of power and the dynamics of decision making in the City Council, that the campaigners were able to mobilise change. They worked productively with measures they were uncomfortable with to achieve their agenda.

These ethnographic accounts have unpacked the relationship between government and citizens, exploring the notion of publics and what happens when a city administration tries to bring a certain kind of vision for a city into being. Attempts by the Council and its partners to create cultural events, city districts, commercial services and even football clubs according to the rubric of commercial appreciation actually blocks out the independent emergence of publics of substance. By taking up civic space and resources with Council-led cultural representations focused largely on generating financial income for the city, the Council inhibit more organic and spontaneous forms of emergent publics. State bodies who excessively control citizen activity, who create rules that must be followed, are generating expensive and stressful strategies that are not necessarily needed. These ethnographies show how people have their own ideas and aspirations for how to 'be' in their cities. What they need is support and enabling services from the city administrators. Meanwhile city administrators struggle with a tautological requirement to both enable and support, to give freedom and to restrict.

This book shows how ethnography can reveal a city constituted of people who are both agents and subjects, workers and residents, architects of a city and experiencers of the decisions that shape it. The network of relations do not necessarily follow lines of authority. People may be connected through their workplace but they also have shared relationships and understandings through their geography, sexuality, community and political alignments. An ethnographic account can trace these overlapping and sometimes conflicting identities and allegiances. Our approach is easily replicable in other cities where urban ethnographies can reveal key actors, moral codes and activities which shape the city.

Manchester is a mature democracy, a city with a long history of innovation and responsiveness to political, social and infrastructural change. These ethnographic explorations of Manchester in the 2000s reveal a city in flow, booming from capital and cultural growth and yet also struggling to tackle serious deprivation and political disengagement. Other cities have similar issues, both those undergoing primary industrialisation in the developing economies such as China, Brazil, Africa and India, and those attempting to remake themselves in the Western post-industrialisation era.

Each ethnographic account provides comparative opportunities to understand how a city such as Manchester, with such a strong record of regeneration and a model to be emulated worldwide still has people within target areas experiencing a sense of dislocation and lack of jobs. The ethnographies complicate the binary them-and-us dualism between state and citizens through accounts that draw out the good intentions of those working at the local Council and unintended impacts leading to feelings of alienation. In particular, the ethnographies show how attempts to engage with modern agendas of growth, capital development, stimulation of tourism and a command-and-control approach from government bodies actually inhibits attempts at self-determination from citizens.

As city administrations worldwide pay increasing attention to this level of detail in civic activity and expression, the impact of such involvement in local lives must be more carefully identified. A better understanding of local processes would further enable mediation between all citizens as they seek to realise their aspirations. Ethnography can find out what is happening 'on the ground' and provide insight. This in turn will enable supporting and nurturing people to allow a more democratic city to emerge and take its shape.

References

Badiou, Alain. 2007. "The event in Deleuze". *Parrhesia* 2: 37–44.

Deleuze, Gilles and Félix Guattari. 1987. *Thousand Plateaus: Capitalism and Schizophrenia.* Vol. 2. Minneapolis: University of Minnesota Press.

Mouffe, Chantal. 2000. *The Democratic Paradox.* London: Verso.

Tsing, Anna. 2004. *Friction: An Ethnography of Global Connection.* Princeton, NJ: Princeton University Press.

Verheggen, C. 2003. www.yorku.ca/cverheg/documents/paradoxandobjectivity.pdf.

Select bibliography

Adey, Peter. 2006. "Airports and air-mindedness: spacing, timing and using the Liverpool Airport, 1929-1939". *Social & Cultural Geography* 7 (3): 343-363.

— 2009. "Facing airport security: affect, biopolitics, and the preemptive securitisation of the mobile body". *Environment and Planning D: Society and Space* 27 (2): 274-295.

Agamben, Giorgio. 2002. "On security and terror". *Theory and Event* 5 (4): Available at http://muse.jhu.edu/journals/theory_and_event/v005/5.4agamben.html. Accessed 12 April 2014.

Alfonso, Ana Isabel. 2004. "New graphics for old stories: representation of local memories through drawings". In *Working Images: Visual Research and Representation in Ethnography*. A.I. Alfonso, L. Kurti, and S. Pink, eds. pp. 72-90. London: Routledge.

Allen, Chris. 2007. "Of urban entrepreneurs or 24-hour party people? City-centre living in Manchester, England". *Environment and Planning A* 39: 666-683.

Amin, Ash. 2002. "Ethnicity and the multicultural city: living with diversity". *Environment and Planning A* 34: 959-980.

— 2008. "Collective culture and urban public space". *City* 12 (1): 5-24.

— 2013. "Telescopic urbanism and the poor". *City* 17 (4): 476-492.

Amin, Ash, Doreen B. Massey, and Nigel J. Thrift. 2000. *Cities for the Many Not the Few*. Bristol: Policy Press.

Amit, Vared (ed). 2002. *Realizing Community: Concepts, Social Relationships and Sentiments*. London: Routledge.

Amoore, Louise. 2011. "Data derivatives: on the emergence of a security risk calculus for our times". *Theory, Culture & Society* 28: 24-43.

Anderson, Ben. 2010. "Preemption, precaution, preparedness: anticipatory action and future geographies". *Progress in Human Geography* 34 (6): 777-798.

Anderson, Benedict. 1983. *Imagined Communities: Reflections on the Growth and Spread of Nationalism*. New York and London: Verso.

Andersson, Jenny. 2006. "Choosing futures: Alva Myrdal and the construction of Swedish Futures Studies, 1967-1972". *Internationaal Instituut voor Sociale Geschiedenis* 51 (2): 277-295.

Andrews, David L. 2004. "Introduction: Situating Manchester United PLC". In *Manchester United: A Thematic Study*. D.L. Andrews, ed. London: Routledge.

Appadurai, Arjun. 1986. *The Social Life of Things: Commodities in Cultural Perspective.* Cambridge: Cambridge University Press.

Appiah, Anthony. 2008. *Experiments in Ethics.* Cambridge, MA: Harvard University Press.

Atkinson, Paul. 2005. "Qualitative research – unity and diversity". Forum: *Qualitative Social Research* 6 (3): Art 26.

Auyero, Javier, Philippe Bourgois, and Nancy Scheper-Hughes, eds. 2015. *Violence at the Urban Margins.* Oxford: Oxford University Press.

Bache, Ian and Matthew Flinders. 2004. "Multi-level governance and British politics". In *Multi-Level Governance.* I. Bache and M. Flinders, eds. pp. 130–136. Buckingham: Open University Press.

Badiou, Alain. 2007. "The event in Deleuze". *Parrhesia* 2: 37–44.

Bain, Peter and Phil Taylor. 2000. "Entrapped by the 'electronic panopticon'? Worker resistance in the call centre". *New Technology, Work and Employment* 15 (1): 2–18.

Ball, Kirstie. 2010. "Workplace surveillance: an overview". *Labor History* 51 (1): 87–106.

Barthes, Roland. 1957. *Mythologies.* Paris: Editions du Seuil.

— 1977. *Image, Music, Text.* London: HarperCollins.

Batty, Michael. 2012. "Smart cities, big data". *Environment and Planning B: Planning and Design* (39): 191–193.

Baudrillard, Jean. 1994. *Simulacra and Simulation.* Ann Arbor: University of Michigan Press.

Beck, Ulrich. 1992. *Risk Society: Towards a New Modernity.* London: Sage.

Bell, David and Jon Binnie. 2004. "Authenticating queer space: citizenship, urbanism and governance". *Urban Studies* 41 (9): 1807–1820.

— 2005. "What's eating Manchester? Gastro-culture and urban regeneration". *Architectural Design* 75 (3): 78–85.

Benjamin, Walter. 1932. "Excavation and memory". In *Selected Writings Volume Two, Part Two: 1931-1934.* H.S. Eiland and M.W. Jennings, eds. London: Belknap Press of Harvard University.

— 1969 [1935]. "Paris, the capital of the nineteenth century". *Perspecta* 12: 165–172.

Bennett, Julia. 2014. "Gifted places: the inalienable nature of belonging in place". *Environment and Planning D: Society and Space* 32 (4): 658–671.

Beynon, Huw, Diane Elson, David Howell, Jamie Peck, and Linda Shaw. 1993. "The remaking of economy and society: Manchester, Salford and Trafford 1945–1992". *Manchester International Centre for Labour Studies.* Working Paper 1.

Bezerra, George C.L. and Carlos F. Gomes. 2015. "The effects of service quality dimensions and passenger characteristics on passenger's overall satisfaction with an airport". *Journal of Air Transport Management* 44: 77–81.

Binnie, Jon and Beverley Skeggs. 2004. "Cosmopolitan knowledge and the production and consumption of sexualized space: Manchester's gay village". *The Sociological Review* 52 (1): 39–61.

Binnie, Jon and Gill Valentine. 1999. "Geographies of sexuality: a review of progress". *Progress in Human Geography* 23 (2): 175–187.

Blakeley, Georgina. 2010. "Governing ourselves: citizen participation and governance in Barcelona and Manchester". *International Journal of Urban and Regional Research* 34 (1): 130–145.

Blok, Anders and Ignacio Farías. 2016. *Urban Cosmopolitics: Agencements, Assemblies, Atmospheres.* London: Routledge.

Blokland, Talja. 2001. "Bricks, mortar, memories: neighbourhood and networks in collective acts of remembering". *International Journal of Urban and Regional Research* 25 (2): 268–283.

Borden, Iain, Joe Kerr, Jane Rendell, and Alicia Pivaro. 2000. *The Unknown City: Contesting Architecture and Social Space:* Cambridge, MA; London: MIT Press.

Born, Georgina. 2005. "On musical mediation: ontology, technology and creativity". *Twentieth-Century Music* 2 (1): 7–36.

Borup, Mads, Nik Brown, Kornelia Konrad, and Harro Van Lente. 2006. "The sociology of expectations in science and technology". *Technology Analysis & Strategic Management* 18 (3/4): 285–298.

Bose, Mihir. 2007. *Manchester DisUnited: Trouble and Takeover at the World's Richest Football Club.* (2nd ed.) Aurum Press Ltd.

Bourdieu, Pierre. 1979. "Symbolic power". *Critique of Anthropology* 77 (4): 77–85.

Bourgois, Philippe. 2003. *In Search of Respect: Selling Crack in El Barrio.* Vol. 10. Cambridge: Cambridge University Press.

Bramley, Warren and Ra Page. 2009. *Manchester Forward.* Manchester: Marketing Manchester.

Brenner, Neil and Christian Schmid. 2015. "Towards a new epistemology of the urban?" *City* 19 (2–3): 151–182.

Brown, Andrew. 2004. "'Manchester is red?', Manchester United, fan identity and the 'Sport City'". In *Manchester United: A Thematic Study.* D.L. Andrews, ed. pp. 175–190. London: Routledge.

Brown, Nik and Mike Michael. 2003. "A sociology of expectations: retrospecting prospects and prospecting retrospects". *Technology Analysis and Strategic Management* 15 (1): 3–18.

Brown, Nik, Brian Rappert, and Andrew Webster, eds. 2000. *Contested Futures: A Sociology of Prospective Techno-Science.* Aldershot: Ashgate.

Buffel, Tine and Chris Phillipson. 2014. "Negotiating urban space: contested generational and ethnic boundaries". In *Intergenerational Space.* N.W. Robert Vanderbeck, ed. pp. 314–329. London: Routledge.

Buffel, Tine, Chris Phillipson, and Thomas Scharf. 2012. "Ageing in urban environments: developing 'age-friendly' cities". *Critical Social Policy* 32 (4): 597–617.

Burgess, Jacquelin, Andy Stirling, Judy Clark, Gail Davies, Malcolm Eames, Kristina Staley, and Suzanne Williamson. 2007. "Deliberative mapping: a novel analytic-deliberative methodology to support contested science-policy decisions". *Public Understanding of Science* 16: 299–322.

Burrows, Roger and Nicholas Gane. 2006. "Geodemographics, software and class". *Sociology* 40 (5): 793–812.

Callon, Michel. 1998. *The Laws of the Markets*. Oxford: Blackwell.

Callon, Michel, Yuval Millo, and Fabian Muniesa. 2007. *Market Devices*. (Sociological Review monographs). Oxford: Blackwell.

Candea, Matei. 2010. "'I fell in love with Carlos the meerkat': engagement and detachment in human–animal relations". *American Ethnologist* 37 (2): 241–258.

Castel, Robert. 1990. "From dangerousness to risk". In *The Foucault Effect: Studies in Governmentality with Two Lectures by and an Interview with Michel Foucault.* G. Burchell, C. Gordon, and P. Miller, eds. pp. 281–298. London: Harvester Wheatsheaf Publishing.

Cefkin, Melissa (ed). 2010. *Ethnography and the Corporate Encounter: Reflections on Research in and of Corporations* (Studies in Public and Applied Anthropology; Vol. 5). New York: Berghahn Books.

Coaffee, Jon, David Murakami Wood, and Peter Rogers. 2009. *The Everyday Resilience of the City*. London: Palgrave Macmillan.

Cochrane, Allan. 1993. *Whatever Happened to Local Government?* Buckingham: Open University Press.

Cochrane, Allan, Jamie Peck, and Adam Tickell. 1996. "Manchester plays games: exploring the local politics of globalisation". *Urban Studies* 33 (8): 1319–1336.

— 2002. "Olympic dreams: visions of partnership". In *City of Revolution: Restructuring Manchester.* J. Peck and K. Ward, eds. pp. 95–115. Manchester: Manchester University Press.

Colomb, Claire and John Tomaney. 2016. "Territorial politics, devolution and spatial planning in the UK: results, prospects, lessons". *Planning Practice & Research* 31 (1): 1–22.

Conquergood, Dwight. 2002. "Performance studies: interventions and radical research". *TDR/The Drama Review* 46 (2): 145–156.

Cooper, Malcolm and Faiza Shaheen. 2008. "Winning the battles but losing the war? Regeneration, renewal and the state of Britain's cities". *Journal of Urban Regeneration and Renewal* 2 (2): 146–151.

Corsín Jiménez, Alberto. 2007. "Introduction: re-institutionalisations". In *The Anthropology of Organisations* (The international library of essays in anthropology), pp. xiii–xxxii. Aldershot: Ashgate.

Corsín Jiménez, Alberto and Adolfo Estalella. 2016. "Ecologies in beta: the city as infrastructure of apprenticeships". In *Infrastructure and Social Complexity*. P Harvey, C.B. Jensen, A. Morita, eds, pp. 141–157. London: Routledge.

Crapanzano, Vincent. 2004. *Imaginative Horizons: An Essay in Literary-Philosophical Anthropology*. Chicago; London: University of Chicago Press.

Davis, Dana-Ain. 2004. "Manufacturing mammies: the burdens of service work and welfare reform among battered black women". *Anthropologica*: 273–288.

Dawson, Andrew. 2002. "The mining community and the ageing body: towards a phenemonology of community?" In *Realizing Community: Concepts, Social Relationships and Sentiments*. V. Amit, ed. pp. 21–38. London: Routledge.

de Certeau, Michel. 1984. *The Practice of Everyday Life*. Berkeley: University of California Press.

De Landa, Manuel. 2006. *A New Philosophy of Society: Assemblage Theory and Social Complexity*. London: Continuum.

Deas, Iain. 2014. "The search for territorial fixes in subnational governance: city-regions and the disputed emergence of post-political consensus in Manchester, England". *Urban Studies* 51 (11): 2285–2314.

Degen, Monica. 2009. *Sensing Cities: Regenerating Public Life in Barcelona and Manchester*. London: Routledge.

Degnen, Cathrine. 2015. "Socialising place attachment: place, social memory and embodied affordances". *Ageing and Society* 36 (8): 1645–1667.

Delanty, Gerard. 2010. *Community: Second Edition*. London: Routledge.

Deleuze, Gilles. 1990. *The Logic of Sense*. Trans. Mark Lester with Charles Stivale. London and New York: Continuum.

— 2001. *Pure Immanence: A Life*. Trans. Anne Boyman. New York: Zone Books.

Deleuze, Gilles and Félix Guattari. 1987. *Thousand Plateaus: Capitalism and Schizophrenia*. Vol. 2. Minneapolis: University of Minnesota Press.

Denny, Rita Mary and Patricia Sunderland, eds. 2016. *Handbook of Anthropology in Business*. Abingdon, Oxon: Routledge.

Dicken, Peter. 1993. "Manchester's economy in a global context". *Manchester International Centre for Labour Studies*. Working Paper 3.

Doucet, Brian. 2009. "Living through gentrification: subjective experiences of local, non-gentrifying residents in Leith, Edinburgh". *Journal of Housing and the Built Environment* 24 (3): 299–315.

Douglas, Mary. 1966. *Purity and Danger: An Analysis of Concepts of Pollution and Taboo*. London: Routledge.

Duneier, Mitchell, Philip Kasinitz, and Alexandra Murphy, eds. 2014. *The Urban Ethnography Reader*. Oxford; New York: Oxford University Press.

Edensor, Tim. 2005. *Industrial Ruins: Spaces, Aesthetics and Materiality*. Oxford: Berg.

Edwards, Elizabeth. 1999. "Beyond the boundary: a consideration of the expressive in photography and anthropology". In *Rethinking Visual Anthropology*. M. Banks and H. Morphy, eds. pp. 53–81. New Haven; London: Yale University Press.

Edwards, Jeanette, Gillian Evans, and Katherine Smith. 2012. "The middle class-ification of Britain". *Focaal – Journal of Global and Historical Anthropology* 62: 3–16.

Eizenberg, Efrat. 2011. "Actually Existing commons: three moments of space of community gardens in New York City". *Antipode* 44 (3): 764–782.

Eller, Jack David. 2016. *Cultural Anthropology: Global Forces, Local Lives.* London; New York: Routledge.

Emerson, Robert M. 2002. *Contemporary Field Research: Perspectives and Formulations.* Wiley Online Library.

Engels, Friedrich. 1993 [1845]. *The Condition of the Working Class in England.* Oxford: Oxford University Press.

Entman, Robert M. 1993. "Framing: toward clarification of a fractured paradigm". *Journal of Communication* 43 (4): 51–8.

Eriksen, Thomas Hylland. 1995. *Small Places, Large Issues: An Introduction to Social and Cultural Anthropology.* London: Pluto.

Evans, Gillian. 2006. *Educational Failure and Working Class White Children in Britain.* London: Palgrave Macmillan

— 2012. "Big man system, short life culture: working-class boys and street violence in Southeast London". In *Young Men in Uncertain Times.* V. Amit and N. Dyck, eds. New York: Berghahn Books.

— 2013. "What documents make possible". In *Objects and Materials: A Routledge Companion.* P. Harvey, H. Knox, G. Evans, N. Thoburn, E. Casella, E. Silva, K. Woodward, and C. Mclean, eds. pp. 309–409. London: Routledge.

Fairclough, Norman. 2010. *Critical Discourse Analysis: The Critical Study of Language.* (2nd ed.) Harlow: Longman.

Farías, Ignacio and Thomas Bender. 2012. *Urban Assemblages: How Actor-Network Theory Changes Urban Studies.* London: Routledge.

Ferguson, James. 2010. "The uses of neoliberalism". *Antipode* 41 (s1): 166–184.

Fielding, Steven and Duncan Tanner. 2006. "The 'rise of the Left' revisited: Labour Party culture in post-war Manchester and Salford". *Labour History Review* 71 (3): 211–233.

Fletcher Jr, Bill and Fernando Gapasin. 2008. *Solidarity Divided: The Crisis in Organized Labor and a New Path Toward Social Justice.* Berkeley and Los Angeles, California: University of California Press.

Florida, Richard. 2003. *Boho Britain.* London. Demos.

— 2005. *Cities and the Creative Class.* New York: Routledge.

Flusty, Steven. 2001. "The banality of interdiction: surveillance, control and the displacement of diversity". *International Journal of Urban and Regional Research* 25 (3): 658–664.

— 2006. "Culturing the world city: an exhibition of the global present". In *The Global City Reader.* N. Brenner and R. Keil, eds. Abington (Oxon): Routledge.

Foot Whyte, William. 1943. *Street Corner Society: The Social Structure of an Italian Slum.* Chicago: University of Chicago Press.

Foucault, Michel. 1980. *Power/Knowledge: Selected Interviews and Other Writings, 1972–1977.* New York: Pantheon

Freedberg, David and Vittorio Gallese. 2007. "Motion, emotion and empathy in esthetic experience". *Trends in Cognitive Sciences* 11 (5): 197–203.

Freud, Sigmund. 2003 [1919]. *The Uncanny*. London: Penguin.

Friedberg, Anne. 1993. *Window Shopping: Cinema and the Postmodern*. Berkeley; London: University of California Press.

Fuller, Gillian and Ross Harley. 2004. *Aviopolis: A Book About Airports*. London: Black Dog Publishing.

Galman, Sally A.C. 2009. "The truthful messenger: visual methods and representation in qualitative research in education". *Qualitative Research* 9 (2): 197–217.

Gell, Alfred. 1998. *Art and Agency: An Anthropological Theory*. Oxford: Clarendon.

Giddens, Anthony. 1999. "Risk and responsibility". *The Modern Law Review* 62 (1): 1–10.

Gidwani, Vinay and Amita Baviskar. 2011. "Urban commons". *Economic & Political Weekly* 46 (50): 42–43.

Graham, Stephen and Simon Marvin. 2001. *Splintering Urbanism: Networked Infrastructures, Technological Mobilities and the Urban Condition*. London: Routledge.

Green, Sarah F. 1997. *Urban Amazons: Lesbian Feminism and Beyond in the Gender, Sexuality, and Identity Battles of London*. Basingstoke: Macmillan.

Green, Sarah, Penny Harvey, and Hannah Knox. 2005. "Scales of place and networks: an ethnography of the imperative to connect through information and communications technologies". *Current Anthropology* 46 (5): 805–826.

Gregory, Chris. 1982. *Gifts and Commodities*. London: Academic Press Inc.

Grey, Christopher. 1994. "Career as a project of the self and labour process discipline". *Sociology* 28 (2): 479–497.

Guy, Simon and Simon Marvin. 2001. "Constructing sustainable urban futures: from models to competing pathways". *Impact Assessment and Project Appraisal* 19 (2): 131–139.

Haider, Donald. 1992. "Place wars: new realities of the 1990s". *Economic Development Quarterly* 6 (2): 127–134.

Hall, Tim and Phil Hubbard. 1998. *The Entrepreneurial City: Geographies of Politics, Regime, and Representation*. Chichester: John Wiley & Sons.

Halpern, Nigel and Anne Graham. 2013. *Airport Marketing*. Abingdon, Oxon: Routledge.

Hammersley, Martyn. 2016. *Reading Ethnographic Research*. London: Routledge.

Hannerz, Ulf. 1969. *Soulside: Inquiries into Ghetto Culture and Community*. New York: Columbia University Press.

— 1980. *Exploring the City: Inquiries Toward an Urban Anthropology*. New York; Guildford: Columbia University Press.

Hardin, Garrett. 1968. "The tragedy of the commons". *Science* 162 (3859): 1243–1248.

Harris, Richard, Peter Sleight, and Richard Webber. 2005. *Geodemographics, GIS and Neighbourhood Targeting*. West Sussex: Wiley.

Hart, Elizabeth. 2005. "Anthropology, class and the 'big heads': an ethnography of distinctions between 'rough' and 'posh' amongst women workers in the UK pottery industry". *The Sociological Review* 53 (4): 710–728.

Harvey, David. 1989a. *The Condition of Postmodernity: An Enquiry into the Origins of Cultural Change*. Oxford: Basil Blackwell.

— 1989b. "From managerialism to entrepreneurialism: the transformation in urban governance in late capitalism". *Geografiska Annaler* 71 (1): 3–17.

— 1990. "Between space and time: reflections on the geographical imagination". *Annals of the Association of American Geographers* 80 (3): 418–434.

— 1993. *From Space to Place and Back Again: Reflections on the Condition of Postmodernity*. London: Routledge.

— 2009. *Social Justice and the City*. Athens: University of Georgia Press.

— 2012. *Rebel Cities: From the Right to the City to the Urban Revolution*. London: Verso Books.

Harvey, Penelope. 2005. "The materiality of state-effects: an ethnography of a road in the Peruvian Andes". In *State Formation: Anthropological Perspectives*. C. Krohn-Hansen and K.G. Nustad, eds. pp. 123–141. London: Pluto Press.

— 2009. "Between narrative and number: the case of ARUP's 3D Digital City Model". *Cultural Sociology* 3 (2): 257–276.

Harvey, Penny, Eleanor Conlin Casella, Gillian Evans, Hannah Knox, Christine McLean, Elizabeth B. Silva, Nicholas Thoburn, and Kath Woodward. 2014. *Objects and Materials: A Routledge Companion*. London: Routledge.

Haslam, Dave. 1999. *Manchester, England: The Story of the Pop Cult City*. London: HarperCollins.

Haslop, Craig, Helene Hill, and Ruth A. Schmidt. 1998. "The gay lifestyle-spaces for a subculture of consumption". *Marketing Intelligence & Planning* 16 (5): 318–326.

Hastrup, Kirsten. 2005. "Performing the world: agency, anticipation and creativity". *Creativity and Cultural Improvisation* 44: 5–19.

Hatherley, Owen. 2011. *A Guide to the New Ruins of Great Britain*. London; New York: Verso Books.

Haughton, Graham, Iain Deas, Stephen Hincks, and Kevin Ward. 2016. "Mythic Manchester: Devo Manc, the Northern Powerhouse and rebalancing the English economy". *Cambridge Journal of Regions, Economy and Society* 9 (2): 355–370.

Headlam, Nicola. 2014. "Liverchester/Manpool? The curious case of the lack of intra-urban leadership in the twin cities of the North-West". In *European Public Leadership in Crisis?* J. Diamond and J. Liddle, eds. pp. 47–61. Emerald Group Publishing Limited. Published online: 20 October 2014 http://dx.doi.org/10.1108/S2045-794420140000003012.

Hebbert, Michael, and John Punter. 2009. "Manchester: making it happen". In *Urban Design and the British Urban Renaissance*. J. Punter, ed. pp. 51–67. London: Routledge.

Hedgecoe, Adam and Paul Martin. 2003. "The drugs don't work: expectations and the shaping of pharmacogenetics". *Social Studies of Science* 33 (3): 327–364.

— 2007. "Genomics, STS and the making of sociotechnical futures". In *The Handbook of Science and Technology Studies*. E. Hackett, O. Amsterdamska, M. Lynch, and J. Wajecman, eds. pp. 817–839. Cambridge, MA: MIT Press.

Hertzfeld, Michael. 1993. *The Social Production of Indifference: Exploring the Symbolic Roots of Western Democracy.* Chicago: University of Chicago Press.

Hindle, Paul. 1994. "Gay communities and gay space in the city". In *The Margins of the City: Gay Men's Urban Lives.* S. Whittle, ed. Vol. 6, pp. 7–25. Aldershot: Ashgate.

Holbraad, Martin, Morten Axel Pedersen, and Eduardo Viveiros de Castro. 2014. "The politics of ontology: anthropological positions". *Cultural Anthropology* 13. https://culanth.org/fieldsights/461-the-politics-of-ontology.

Holcomb, Briavel. 1999. "Marketing cities for tourism". In *The Tourist City.* D.R. Judd and S.S. Fainstein, eds. pp. 54–70. New Haven, CT: Yale University Press.

Holden, Adam. 2002. "Bomb sites: the politics of opportunity". In *City of Revolution: Restructuring Manchester.* J. Peck and K. Ward, eds. pp. 131–155. Manchester: Manchester University Press.

Hornby, Nick. 1998. *Fever Pitch.* New York: Riverhead Books.

Hoskin, Keith W. and Richard Macve. 1986. "Accounting and the examination: a genealogy of disciplinary power". *Accounting, Organizations and Society* 11 (2): 105–136.

Hubbard, Phil. 2008. "Here, there, everywhere: the ubiquitous geographies of heteronormativity". *Geography Compass* 2 (3): 640–658.

Hughes, Howard L. 2003. "Marketing gay tourism in Manchester: new market for urban tourism or destruction of 'gay space'?" *Journal of Vacation Marketing* 9 (2): 152–163.

Hull, Matthew S. 2012. *Government of Paper: The Materiality of Bureaucracy in Urban Pakistan.* Berkeley, California; London: University of California Press.

Hyatt, Susan Brin. 1997. "Poverty in a 'post-welfare' landscape". In *Anthropology of Policy: Critical Perspectives on Governance and Power.* C. Shore and S. Wright, eds. pp. 217–238. London: Routledge.

— 2011. "What was neoliberalism and what comes next? The transformation of citizenship in the law-and-order state". In *Policy Worlds: Anthropology and the Analysis of Contemporary Power.* C. Shore, S. Wright, and D. Però, eds. pp. 105–123. New York: Berghahn Books.

Jackson, Peter. 1985. "Urban ethnography". *Progress in Human Geography* 9 (2): 157–176.

Jivraj, Stephen. 2013. "Local dynamics of diversity: evidence from the 2011 census". University of Manchester/CoDE.

Jonas, Andrew E.G., David Gibbs, and Aidan While. 2011. "The new urban politics as a politics of carbon control". *Urban Studies* 48 (12): 2537–2554.

Jones, Phil and James Evans. 2008. *Urban Regeneration in the UK: Theory and Practice.* Los Angeles, California: Sage.

Keane, Webb. 2010. "Minds, surfaces, and reasons in the anthropology of ethics". In *Ordinary Ethics: Anthropology, Language and Action.* M. Lambek, ed. pp. 64–83 New York: Fordham University Press.

King, Anthony. 2002. *End of the Terraces: The Transformation of English Football.* London: Bloomsbury Publishing.

— 2003. *The European Ritual: Football in the New Europe.* Aldershot: Ashgate.

Kitzinger, Jenny. 2007. "Framing and frame analysis". In *Media Studies: Key Issues and Debates*. E. Devereux, ed. pp. 134–162. London: Sage.

Kleinman, Arthur, Veena Das, and Margaret M. Lock. 1997. *Social Suffering*. Berkeley; London: University of California Press.

Knox, Hannah Catherine. 2003. "'Blocks to convergence' in the new media industries: an anthropological study of small and medium sized enterprises in Manchester". Unpublished PhD thesis, University of Manchester.

Knox, Hannah, Damian O'Doherty, Theo Vurdubakis, and Christopher Westrup. 2015. "Something happened: spectres of organization/disorganization at the airport". *Human Relations*, 68 (6), 1001–1020.

Koch, Insa. 2014. "Everyday experiences of state betrayal on an English council estate". *Anthropology of This Century* 9. http://aotcpress.com/articles/everyday-experi-ences-state-betrayal-english-council-estate/. Accessed 26 May 2017.

Kotler, Philip, Donald Haider, and Iriving Rein. 1993. *Marketing Places: Attracting Investment, Industry And Tourism To Cities, States And Nations*. New York: Free Press.

Laidlaw, James. 2014. *The Subject of Virtue: An Anthropology of Ethics and Freedom*. Cambridge: Cambridge University Press.

Lambek, Michael. 2010. "Introduction". In *Ordinary Ethics: Anthropology, Language and Action*. M. Lambek, ed. pp. 1–38. New York: Fordham University Press.

Lash, Scott and John Urry. 1987. *The End of Organized Capitalism*. Madison, WI: University of Wisconsin Press.

Latour, Bruno. 1993. *We Have Never Been Modern*. Cambridge, MA: Harvard University Press.

Latour, Bruno and Tomás Sánchez-Criado. 2007. "Making the 'res public'". *Ephemera: Theory & Politics in Organization* 7 (2): 364–371.

Lave, Jean and Etienne Wenger. 1991. *Situated Learning: Legitimate Peripheral Participation*. Cambridge: Cambridge University Press.

Lefebvre, Henri. 2003 [1970]. *The Urban Revolution*. Trans. Robert Bononno. Minneapolis: University of Minnesota Press.

Levy, Robert I. 1975. *Tahitians: Mind and Experience in the Society Islands*. Chicago; London: University of Chicago Press.

Lewins, Ann and Christina Silver. 2007. *Using Software in Qualitative Research: A Step-by-Step Guide*. London: Sage.

Lewis, Camilla. 2016. "'Regenerating community'? Urban change and narratives of the past". *The Sociological Review* 64 (4): 912–928.

Linebaugh, Peter. 2009. *The Magna Carta Manifesto: Liberties and Commons for All*. California: University of California Press.

Low, Setha. 1999. *Theorising the City: The Urban Anthropology Reader*. New Brunswick: Rutgers University Press.

Lyon, David. 2001. *Surveillance Society: Monitoring Everyday Life*. Buckingham: Open University Press.

Macdonald, Sharon. 2002. *Behind the Scenes at the Science Museum*. Oxford: Berg.

Mace, Alan, Peter Hall, and Nick Gallent. 2007. "New East Manchester: urban renaissance or urban opportunism?" *European Planning Studies* 15 (1): 51–65.

MacKenzie, Donald. 2006. *An Engine, Not a Camera: How Financial Models Shape Markets*. Cambridge, MA: MIT Press.

MacLeod, Gordon. 2002. "From urban enterpreneurialism to a 'revanchist city'? On the spacial injustices of Glasgow's renaissance". *Antipode* 34: 602–624.

— 2011. "Urban politics reconsidered: growth machine to post-democratic city?" *Urban Studies* 48 (12): 2629–2660.

MacLeod, Gordon and Kevin Ward. 2002. "Spaces of utopia and dystopia: landscaping the contemporary city". *Geografiska Annaler: Series B, Human Geography* 84 (3–4): 153–170.

Mah, Alice. 2010. "Memory, uncertainty and industrial ruination: Walker Riverside, Newcastle upon Tyne". *International Journal of Urban and Regional Research* 34 (2): 398–413.

Malinowski, Bronislaw. 1978 [1922]. *Argonauts of the Western Pacific: An Account of Native Enterprise and Adventure in the Archipelagoes of Melanesian New Guinea*. London Routledge.

Marres, Noortje and Javier Lezaun. 2011. "Materials and devices of the public: an introduction". *Economy and Society* 40 (4): 489–509.

Martin, Keir. 2015. *Big Men and Big Shots*. New York; Oxford: Berghahn Books.

Marx, Karl. 1976 [1867]. *Capital: A Critique of Political Economy*. London: Penguin.

Mason, Jennifer. 2006. "Mixing methods in a qualitatively driven way". *Qualitative Research* 6 (1): 9–25.

Massey, Doreen. 1993. "Power-geometry and a progressive sense of place". In *Mapping the Futures* J. Bird, B. Curtis, T. Putnam, G. Robertson, and L. Tickner, eds. pp. 59–70. London: Routledge.

— 2001. "Living in Wythenshawe". In *The Unknown City: Contesting Architecture and Social Space*. I. Borden, J. Kerr, J. Rendell, and A. Pivaro eds. pp. 458–476. Cambridge, MA; London: MIT Press.

— 2005. *For Space*. London: Sage.

— 2007. *World City*. Cambridge: Polity.

Massumi, Brian. 2009. "National enterprise emergency: steps toward an ecology of powers". *Theory, Culture & Society* 26: 153–186.

Mathur, Nayanika and Laura Bear. 2015. "Remaking the public good: a new anthropology of bureaucracy". *The Cambridge Journal of Anthropology* 33 (1): 18–34.

Mauss, Marcel. 1954 [1925]. *The Gift: Forms and Functions of Exchange in Archaic Societies*. London: Cohen & West.

— 1990 [1925]. *The Gift: The Form and Reason of Exchange in Primitive and Archaic Societies*. London and New York: Routledge.

May, Vanessa and Stewart Muir. 2015. "Everyday belonging and ageing: place and generational change". *Sociological Research Online* 20 (1): 8.

McFall, Liz. 2009. "Devices and desires: how useful is the 'new' new economic sociology for understanding market attachment?" *Sociology Compass* 3 (2): 267–282.

McKenzie, Lisa. 2015. *Getting By: Estates, Class and Culture in auSterity Britain.* Bristol. Policy Press.

McNeil, Robina and Michael Nevell. 2000. *A Guide to the Industrial Archaeology of Greater Manchester.* Association for Industrial Archaeology.

Mellor, Rosemary. 2002. "Hypocritical city: cycles of urban exclusion". In *City of Revolution: Restructuring Manchester* J. Peck and W. Kevin, eds. pp. 214–235. Manchester: Manchester University Press.

— 1997. "Cool times for a changing city". In *Transforming Cities.* N. Jewson and S. MacGregor, eds. pp. 53–69. London: Routledge.

Millward, Peter. 2011. *The Global Football League: Transnational Networks, Social Movements and Sport in the New Media Age.* London: Palgrave Macmillan.

Mitchell, Timothy. 1991. "The limits of the state: beyond statist approaches and their critics". *The American Political Science Review*: 77–96.

— 1998. "Fixing the economy". *Cultural Studies* 12 (1): 82–101.

— 2002. *Rule of Experts: Egypt, Techno-Politics, Modernity.* Berkeley: University of California Press.

— 2006. "Society, economy, and the State effect". In *The Anthropology of the State.* Aradhana Sharma and Akhil Gupta, eds. pp. 169–186. Malden, MA: Oxford: Blackwell.

Mol, Annemarie. 2002. *The Body Multiple: Ontology in Medical Practice.* North Carolina: Duke University Press.

Moran, Leslie, Beverley Skeggs, Paul Tyrer, and Karen Corteen. 2003. "The formation of fear in gay space: the 'straights' story". *Capital & Class* 27 (2): 173–198.

Morgan, Gareth. 1986. *Images of Organization.* Beverly Hills: Sage Publications.

Morgen, Sandra and Jeff Maskovsky. 2003. "The anthropology of welfare 'reform': new perspectives on US urban poverty in the post-welfare era". *Annual Review of Anthropology*: 315–338.

Mouffe, Chantal. 2000. *The Democratic Paradox.* London: Verso.

Myslik, Wayne. 1996. "Renogtiating the 'heterosexual street': lesbian productions of space". In *BodySpace: Destabilizing Geographies of Gender and Sexuality.* N. Duncan, ed. London: Routledge.

Nash, Catherine Jean. 2006. "Toronto's gay village (1969–1982): plotting the politics of gay identity". *The Canadian Geographer/Le Géographe canadien* 50 (1): 1–16.

Navaro-Yashin, Yael. 2002. *Faces of the State: Secularism and Public Life in Turkey.* Princeton, NJ; Oxford: Princeton University Press.

— 2009. "Affective spaces, melancholic objects: ruination and the production of anthropological knowledge". *Journal of the Royal Anthropological Institute* 15 (1): 1–18.

Nietzsche, Friedrich. 1969 [1887]. *On the Genealogy of Morals.* Trans. Walter Kaufmann and R.J. Hollingdale. New York: Random House.

O'Connor, Justin. 2007. "Manchester: the original modern city". *The Yorkshire and Humber Regional Review*: 13–15.

O'Doherty, Damian. 2017. *Reconstructing Organization: The 'Loungification' of Society.* London: Palgrave Macmillan.

Ostrom, Elinor. 1990. *Governing the Commons: The Evolution of Institutions for Collective Action.* Cambridge: Cambridge University Press.

Pardo, Italo and Giuliana B. Prato. 2016. *Anthropology in the City: Methodology and Theory.* Aldershot: Ashgate.

Parry, Jonathan and Maurice Bloch. 1989. *Money and the Morality of Exchange.* Cambridge: Cambridge University Press.

Paton, Kirsteen. 2014. *Gentrification: A Working-Class Perspective.* Aldershot: Ashgate.

Peck, Jamie and Kevin Ward. 2002. *City of Revolution: Restructuring Manchester.* Manchester: Manchester University Press.

Peck, Jamie and Adam Tickell. 1995. "Business goes local: dissecting the business agenda in Manchester". *International Journal of Urban and Regional Research* 19 (1): 55–78.

Peck, Jamie and Mike Emmerich. 1993. "Manufacturing Manchester? Industrial and labour market restructuring in Greater Manchester". *Manchester International Centre for Labour Studies.* Working Paper 4.

Phillipson, Chris. 2007. "The 'elected' and the 'excluded': sociological perspectives on the experience of place and community in old age". *Ageing & Society* 27 (3): 321–342.

Pickering, Andrew. 1995. *The Mangle of Practice: Time, Agency, and Science.* Chicago: University of Chicago Press.

Picri, Elisa. 2009. "Sociology of expectation and the e-social science agenda". *Information, Communication & Society* 12 (7): 1103–1118.

— 2010. "Predictive genetic testing and the promise of personalised medicine". In *Assessing Life: On The Organisation of Genetic Testing: Science and Technology Studies.* B. Wieser and W. Berger, eds. Vol. 59, pp. 175–202. München/Wien: Profil.

— 2014. "Emergent policing practices: Operation Shop a Looter and urban space securitisation in the aftermath of the Manchester 2011 riots". *Surveillance & Society* 12 (1): 38–54.

Pink, Sarah. 2013. *Doing Visual Ethnography* (3rd ed.) London: Sage.

Pole, Christopher and Marlene Morrison. 2003. *Ethnography for Education* (Doing qualitative research in educational settings). Buckingham: Open University Press.

Poulton, George. 2013. "FC United of Manchester: community and politics amongst English football fans". Unpublished Thesis, University of Manchester.

Price, Jane. 2002. *The Mancunian Way.* Manchester: Clinamen Press.

Pritchard, Annette, Nigel Morgan, and Diane Sedgley. 2002. "In search of lesbian space? The experience of Manchester's gay village". *Leisure Studies* 21 (2): 105–123.

Quilley, Stephen. 1997. "Constructing Manchester's 'new urban village': gay space in the entrepreneurial city." In *Queers in Space: Communities/ Public Places/Sites of Resistance.* G.B. Ingram, A.-M. Bouthillette, and Y. Retter, eds. Seattle, WA: Bay Press.

— 1999. "Entrepreneurial Manchester: the genesis of elite consensus". *Antipode* 31 (2): 185–211.

— 2000. "Manchester first: from municipal socialism to the entrepreneurial city". *International Journal of Urban and Regional Research* 24 (3): 601–615.

— 2002. "Entepreneurial turns: municipal socialism and after". In *City of Revolution: Restructuring Manchester.* J. Peck and K. Ward, eds. pp. 77–94. Manchester: Manchester University Press.

Raco, Mike. 2003. "Remaking place and securitising space: urban regeneration and the strategies, tactics and practices of policing in the UK". *Urban Studies* 40 (9): 1869–1887.

Rapport, Nigel, and Joana Overing. 2000. *Social and Cultural Anthropology: The Key Concepts.* London: Routledge.

Redhead, Steve. 1997. *Subculture to Clubcultures: An Introduction to Popular Cultural Studies.* Oxford: Blackwell.

Riles, Annelise. 2013. "Market collaboration: finance, culture, and ethnography after neoliberalism". *American Anthropologist* 115 (4): 555–569.

Robson, Brian. 2002. "Mancunian ways: the politics of regeneration". In *City of Revolution: Restructuring Manchester,* J. Peck and K. Ward, eds. pp. 34–49. Manchester: Manchester University Press.

Robson, Keith. 1992. "Accounting numbers as 'inscription': action at a distance and the development of accounting". *Accounting, Organizations and Society* 17 (7): 685–708.

Rogaly, Ben and Becky Taylor 2009. *Moving Histories of Class and Community: Identity, Place and Belonging in Contemporary England.* London: Palgrave Macmillian.

Rose, Nikolas. 1989. *Governing the Soul: The Shaping of the Private Self.* London: Routledge.

— 1993. "Government, authority and expertise in advanced liberalism". *Economy and Society* 22 (3): 283–299.

— 2000. "Government and control". *The British Journal of Criminology* 40 (2): 321–339.

Rose, Nikolas, Pat O'Malley, and Mariana Valverde. 2006. "Governmentality". *Annual Review of Law and Social Science* 2: 83–104.

Ruby, Jay. 1995. "The moral burden of authorship in ethnographic film". *Visual Anthropology Review* 11 (2): 77–82.

Rushbrook, Dereka. 2002. "Cities, queer space, and the cosmopolitan tourist". *GLQ: A Journal of Lesbian and Gay Studies* 8 (1): 183–206.

Sanjek, Roger. 2000. "Urban history, culture and urban ethnography". *City & Society* 12 (2): 105–113.

Savage, Michael, Alan Warde, and Kevin Ward. 2003. *Urban Sociology, Capitalism and Modernity.* (2nd ed.) London: Palgrave Macmillan.

Savage, Mike and Roger Burrows. 2007. "The Coming Crisis of Empirical Sociology". *Sociology* 41 (5): 885–899.

Schaberg, Christopher. 2012. *The Textual Life of Airports: Reading the Culture of Flight.* London: Continuum.

Schatzki, Theodore R. 2006. "On organizations as they happen". *Organization Studies*, 27 (12), 1863–1873.

Scheper-Hughes, Nancy. 1992. *Death Without Weeping: The Violence of Everyday Life in Brazil.* London; Berkeley: University of California Press.

Scott, James C. 1998. *Seeing Like a State: How Certain Schemes to Improve the Human Condition have Failed.* New Haven: Yale University Press.

Shore, Chris and Susan Wright. 1997. *Anthropology of Policy: Critical Perspectives on Governance and Power* (European Association of Social Anthropologists). London: Routledge.

Shore, Cris, Susan Wright, and Davide Però. 2011. *Policy Worlds: Anthropology and the Analysis of Contemporary Power.* New York: Berghahn Books.

Short, John Rennie. 2004. *Global Metropolitan.* London: Routledge.

Simone, AbdouMaliq. 2004. "People as infrastructure: intersecting fragments in Johannesburg". *Public Culture* 16 (3): 407–429.

Skeggs, Beverley. 1999. "Matter out of place: visibility and sexualities in leisure spaces". *Leisure Studies* 18 (3): 213–232.

— 2011. "Imagining personhood differently: person value and autonomist working-class value practices". *The Sociological Review* 59 (3): 496–513.

Sloterdijk, Peter. 2014. *In the World Interior of Capital: For a Philosophical Theory of Globalization.* Cambridge: Polity Press.

Smith, Katherine. 2012a. *Fairness, Class and Belonging in Contemporary England.* London: Palgrave Macmillan.

— 2012b. "Anxieties of Englishness and participation in democracy". *Focaal – Journal of Global and Historical Anthropology* 62: 30–41.

— 2014. "Fairness as rhetorical force and the micro-politics of intentionality in a North Manchester town". In *Rhetoric in British Politics and Society.* A.F.J. Atkins, J. Martin, and N. Turnbull, eds. pp. 160–172. London: Palgrave Macmillan.

Smith, Martin John and David Richards. 2016. "Devolution in England, the British political tradition and the absence of consultation, consensus and consideration". *Representations*: 1–18.

Smith, Neil. 1996. "After Tompkins Square Park: degentrification and the revanchists city". In *Re-Presenting the City.* D. King, ed. New York: New York University Press.

Smith, Robin James and Kevin Hetherington. 2013. "Urban rhythms: mobilities, space and interaction in the contemporary city". *The Sociological Review* 61 (S1): 4–16.

Stirling, Andy. 2010. "Keep it complex". *Nature* 468 (7327): 1029–1031.

Strathern, Marilyn. 1996. "Cutting the network". *Journal of the Royal Anthropological Institute* 2 (3): 517–535.

Swyngedouw, Erik. 2009. "The antinomies of the postpolitical city: in search of a democratic politics of environmental production". *International Journal of Urban and Regional Research* 33 (3): 601–620.

Symons, Jessica. 2015. "Shaping the flow: ethnographic analysis of a Manchester parade event". *Ethnos* "Anthropology and Festivals": 1–15.

— 2016. "Untangling creativity and art for policy purposes: ethnographic insights on Manchester International Festival and Manchester Day Parade". *International Journal of Cultural Policy*: 1–15.

Taussig, Micheal T. 1997. *The Magic of the State.* New York: Routledge.

Taylor, Ian, Karen Evans, and Penny Fraser. 1996. *A Tale of Two Cities: Global Change, Local Feeling and Everyday Life and the North of England: A Study in Manchester and Sheffield* London: Routledge.

Teunis, Niels. 2001. "Same-sex sexuality in Africa: a case study from Senegal". *AIDS and Behavior* 5 (2): 173–182.

Thompson, Edward P. 1971. "The moral economy of the English crowd in the eighteenth century". *Past & Present* 50: 76–136.

— 1993. *Customs in Common: Studies in Traditional Popular Culture.* New York: The New Press.

Throop, C. Jason. 2005. "Hypocognition, a 'sense of the uncanny', and the anthropology of ambiguity: reflections on Robert I. Levy's contribution to theories of experience in anthropology". *Ethos* 33 (4): 499–511.

Tickell, Adam and Jamie Peck. 1996. "The return of the Manchester men: men's words and men's deeds in the remaking of the local state". *Transactions of the Institute of British Geographers* 21 (4): 595–616.

Tilly, Louise A. 1978. "The social sciences and the study of women: a review article". *Comparative Studies in Society and History* 20 (1): 163–173.

Townley, Babara. 1994. *Reframing Human Resource Management: Power, Ethics and the Subject at Work.* London: Sage.

Tsing, Anna. 2004. *Friction: An Ethnography of Global Connection.* Princeton, NJ: Princeton University Press.

Turner, Mark W. 2003. *Backward Glances: Cruising the Queer Streets of New York and London.* London: Reaktion.

Tye, Rachel and Gwyndaf Williams. 1994. "Urban regeneration and central–local government relations: the case of East Manchester". *Progress in Planning* 42 (Part 1): 1–97.

Tyler, Katharine. 2007. "Race, genetics and inheritance: reflections upon the birth of 'black' twins to a 'white' IVF mother". In *Race, Ethnicity and Nation: Perspectives From Kinship and Genetics.* P. Wade, ed. pp. 33–51: Oxford: Berghahn Books.

Valocchi, Steve 1999. "The class-inflected nature of gay identity". *Social Problems* 46 (2): 207–224.

Visser, Gustav. 2003. "Gay men, tourism and urban space: reflections on Africa's gay capital". *Tourism Geographies* 5 (2): 168–189.

Wacquant, Loïc. 2009. *Punishing the Poor: The Neoliberal Government of Social Insecurity.* London: Duke University Press.

— 2010. "Crafting the neoliberal state: workfare, prisonfare, and social insecurity". *Sociological Forum* Vol. 25, pp. 197–220. Oxford: Blackwell.

Walker, Richard. 2015. "Building a better theory of the urban: a response to 'Towards a new epistemology of the urban?'" *City* 19 (2–3): 183–191.

Walkerdine, Valerie. 2010. "Communal beingness and affect: an exploration of trauma in an ex-industrial community". *Body & Society* 16 (1): 91–116.

Wall, Derek. 2014. *The Commons in History: Culture, Conflict and Ecology.* Cambridge, MA: MIT Press.

Walshe, Kieran, Anna Coleman, Ruth McDonald, Colin Lorne, and Luke Munford. 2016. "Health and social care devolution: the Greater Manchester experiment". *British Medical Journal*: 1–5. https://manchester.idm.oclc.org/login?url=http://search.proquest.com/docview/1777837174?accountid=12253. Accessed 26 May 2017.

Ward, Kevin. 2000. "Front rentiers to rantiers: 'active entrepreneurs', 'structural speculators' and the politics of marketing the city". *Urban Studies* 37 (7): 1093–1107.

— 2003a. "Entrepreneurial urbanism, state restructuring and civilizing 'New' East Manchester". *Area* 35 (2): 116–127.

— 2003b. "The limits to contemporary urban redevelopment: 'doing' entrepreneurial urbanism in Birmingham, Leeds and Manchester". *City* 7 (2): 199–211.

Watson, Sophie. 2006. *City Publics: The (Dis)Enchantments of Urban Encounters.* New York: Routledge.

Webber, Richard. 2009. "Response to 'The coming crisis of empirical sociology': an outline of the research potential of administrative and transactional data". *Sociology* 43 (1): 169–178.

Wedel, Janine R. 2011. 'Shadow Governing: What the Neocon Core Reveals About Power and Influence in America'. In *Policy Worlds: Anthropology and the Analysis of Contemporary Power.* C. Shore, S. Wright, and D. Però, eds. pp. 151–168. New York: Berghahn Books.

While, Aidan, Andrew E.G. Jonas, and David Gibbs. 2004. "The environment and the entrepreneurial city: searching for the urban 'sustainability; fix' in Manchester and Leeds". *International Journal of Urban and Regional Research* 28 (3): 549–569.

Williams, Bernard. 1993. *Shame and Necessity.* Berkeley: University of California Press.

Wood, Phil and Charles Laundry. 2008. *The Intercultural City: Planning for Diversity Advantage.* London: Earthscan.

Wright, Susan. 2006. "Anthropology of policy". *Anthropology News* 47 (8): 22.

Yaneva, Albena. 2012. *Mapping Controversies in Architecture.* Aldershot: Ashgate.

— 2016. "Politics of architectural imaging: elements of architecture". *Assembling Archaeology, Atmosphere and the Performance of Building Spaces*: 238.

Young, Craig, Martina Diep, and Stephanie Drabble. 2006. "Living with difference? The 'cosmopolitan city' and urban reimaging in Manchester, UK". *Urban Studies* 43 (10): 1687–1714.

Young, Michael and Peter Willmott. 1957. *Family and Kinship in East London.* London: Routledge.

Zigon, Jarrett. 2007. "Moral breakdown and the ethical demand: a theoretical framework for an anthropology of moralities". *Anthropological Theory* 7 (2): 131–150.

INDEX

EU authorised representative for GPSR:
Easy Access System Europe, Mustamäe tee 50,
10621 Tallinn, Estonia
gpsr.requests@easproject.com